SERIES
IN
HUMAN
RESOURCE
DEVELOPMENT

THE
1987 ANNUAL:
DEVELOPING
HUMAN RESOURCES

(The Sixteenth Annual)

Edited by
J. WILLIAM PFEIFFER, Ph.D., J.D.

UNIVERSITY ASSOCIATES, INC.
8517 Production Avenue
San Diego, California 92121

Printed in the United States of America

Published by
University Associates, Inc.
8517 Production Avenue
San Diego, California 92121
619-578-5900

University Associates of Canada
4190 Fairview Street
Burlington, Ontario L7L 4Y8
Canada

University Associates International
Challenge House
45-47 Victoria Street
Mansfield, Notts NG18 5SU
England

PREFACE

The contents of this sixteenth volume of the *Annual* series are evidence of the incredibly rapid expansion and integration of the field of human resource development (HRD), which incorporates training, career development, personnel, management development, and organization development functions. The changes in the title of the *Annual* over the last fifteen years reflect the changing nature of HRD and are an indication of our intention to remain at the cutting edge of this field.

From the outset, the central purpose of the *Annual* has been to keep our readers aware of and involved in the current developments in the field. Each year, to achieve this purpose, the contents of the *Annual* are selected and edited to reflect our best understanding of these developments. In the last few years, we have observed a fuller integration of the HRD function in most organizations and a heightened awareness of the importance of human resources in implementing the long-range strategies of organizations. The articles selected for this *Annual* serve as further evidence of the progress and richness of the field today. They provide ample evidence for optimism for the future and also, we believe, provide some food for thought about the needs and requirements of that future.

In this year's *Annual,* the Lecturette, Theory and Practice, and Resources sections again are integrated into a single Professional Development section. This format, initiated in 1984, allows us greater flexibility in selection and permits us to maintain a more coherent overview of what is occurring in the HRD field.

In the Instrumentation section, we intend to continue to publish practical measurement devices that are useful for trainers, consultants, and managers. Moreover, we now include both the theoretical background for each instrument and practical suggestions for its administration and application. This should increase the ease of use as well as the value of the Instrumentation section to our readers. Those persons who intend to submit instruments and other materials to the *Annual* are advised to take these standards into account.

There are several aspects of the *Annual* series that have not changed, nor do we intend for them to change. One is our continuing bias that the *Annual* be strongly user oriented, that everything in the *Annual* be potentially useful to our readers. We believe that our readers are the professional cadre of the HRD field—trainers, consultants, facilitators, and managers. This year's volume is especially strong with how-to-do-it material; and the content of the *Annual* will continue to focus on increasing the professional competence of our readers and, therefore, their impact on the world of work. To further this objective, we continue to allow users to duplicate and modify materials from the *Annuals* for *educational and training* purposes, so long as the credit statement found on the copyright page of the particular volume is included on all copies. However, if University Associates materials are to be reproduced in publications for sale or are intended for large-scale distribution (more than one hundred copies in twelve months), *prior written permission* is required. Also, if a footnote indicates that the material is copyrighted by some source other than University Associates, no reproduction is allowed without the written permission of the actual copyright holder.

We continue to solicit materials from our readers, especially materials with a clear organizational focus and those that reflect the changing nature of the HRD field. The success of the *Annual* as a clearing house for HRD professionals depends on the continual flow of materials from our readers. We encourage the submission of structured experiences, instruments, and articles, including both innovative methods and tried-and-true procedures. The continued sharing of these materials is one of the most important aspects of our professional development. We have compiled new guidelines for contributors to UA publications. These guidelines are published at the end of the Professional Development section of the *Annual*.

We want to express our heartfelt appreciation to the people who have made this year's *Annual* a reality: Mary Kitzmiller, the UA managing editor, who served as the copy and production editor on this volume; Arlette C. Ballew and Carol Nolde, UA senior editors, who provided valuable assistance; Ann Beaulieu, production artist; and Beverly Byrum, Ph.D., who for several years has reviewed the structured experiences from a facilitator's perspective and added to their usefulness. As always, we also express our deep appreciation to our authors—our peers and colleagues—for sharing with all of us their professional ideas, materials, and techniques.

J. William Pfeiffer

San Diego, California
November, 1986

About University Associates

University Associates is engaged in publishing, training, and consulting in the broad field of human resource development (HRD). UA has earned an international reputation as the source of practical publications that are immediately useful to today's facilitators, trainers, consultants, and managers. A distinct advantage of these publications is that they are designed by practicing professionals who are continually experimenting with new techniques. Thus, UA readers benefit from the fresh but thoughtful approach that underlies UA's experientially based materials, resources, books, workbooks, instruments, and tape-assisted learning programs. These materials are designed for the HRD practitioner who wants access to a broad range of training and intervention technologies as well as background in the field.

UA's practical, applied, theory-based approach is evident in its training and consulting activities as well. Its experienced trainers and consultants conduct training programs in both the public and private sectors, train trainers, and consult with organizations and communities to solve human and organizational problems. Activities include workshops on fundamental and current topics in human resource development and organization development, as well as workshops that are customized to meet specific client needs. In addition, professional certification is offered by the UA Graduate School through its intern program in laboratory education and its master's degree in human resource development.

The wide audience that UA serves includes training and development professionals, internal and external consultants, managers and supervisors, and those in the helping professions. For its clients and customers, University Associates offers a practical approach aimed at increasing people's effectiveness on an individual, group, and organizational basis.

TABLE OF CONTENTS

---

*See Structured Experience Categories, p. 7, for an explanation of numbering.

GENERAL INTRODUCTION TO THE 1987 ANNUAL

The 1987 Annual: Developing Human Resources is the sixteenth volume in the *Annual* series. The series is, and will continue to be, a collection of practical and useful materials for human resource professionals, materials written by professionals for their colleagues. As such, the series continues to provide a publication outlet for human resource professionals to share their experiences, their viewpoints, and their procedures with their professional colleagues on a world-wide basis.

Following the changes made in the *Annual* format in 1984, there are now three rather than five sections: Structured Experiences, Instrumentation, and Professional Development. The Professional Development section combines the Lecturettes, Theory and Practice, and Resources sections that appeared in the first twelve volumes of the series. Over the years, some of the distinctions among those three categories had become blurred; it also seemed that some of the materials in those sections would be more useful if placed elsewhere in the volume. Therefore, if a lecturette is required for a structured experience or instrument, or if a lecturette we are publishing is suitable to be used with a structured experience or instrument, then the lecturette will be incorporated *within* the structured experience or instrument. This new arrangement will relate the published pieces more logically and conveniently and will also allow us more flexibility in meeting the needs and interests of practitioners in the growing field of human resource development. The initial response to these changes has been positive, and we await further reactions from our readers.

There is, however, one aspect of the series that has not changed in this volume of the *Annual:* the quality of content. As has been the case from the inception of the series, the materials for the 1987 *Annual* have been selected for their quality of conceptualization, applicability to the real-world concerns of HRD practitioners, relevance to today's HRD issues, clarity of presentation, and ability to provide readers with assistance in their own professional development. We were especially fortunate this year, however, in receiving a wealth of outstanding material from which to choose.

For example, in addition to using the aforementioned criteria for selecting valuable tools, we were also able to choose structured experiences that will create an unusual amount of enthusiasm among the participants and add a great deal of enjoyment to the learning process. As in the past few years, readers will notice a greater focus on organizational issues, which reflects the fact that more and more of our readers are organizationally based or are consultants and trainers for organizations. Thus, there is a need for more structured experiences that have organizational relevance or that can be used with intact groups, especially work groups. A description of the structured experiences that we selected for this volume is given in the "Introduction to the Structured Experiences Section."

The order of the structured experiences in the 1987 *Annual* is dictated by the categorization scheme of our *Structured Experience Kit* and the *Reference Guide to Handbooks and Annuals*. We believe that this order will prove to be more logical and easier to use for our readers, particularly those who regularly use structured experiences in their work and who select them from the *Reference Guide* or the *Structured Experience Kit*.

The Instrumentation section of this *Annual* contains, as usual, four new paper-and-pencil instrumented-feedback scales, questionnaires, or inventories. This year's assortment is both fascinating and useful. The instruments, which are adaptable to many types of situations, are described in the "Introduction to the Instrumentation Section."

The Professional Development section is intended to assist readers of the *Annual* in their own professional development. As usual, the articles in the 1987 *Annual* cover a broad range of issues that confront HRD professionals today. These articles are described in the "Introduction to the Professional Development Section."

This issue of the *Annual* is especially strong in how-to material. We kept the user in mind as we selected the articles, worked with the authors to revise some of the material to make it even more helpful to HRD practitioners, and edited the final versions.

The editor and the editorial staff continue to be surprised and pleased with the high quality of the materials submitted. Nevertheless, just as we cannot publish every manuscript that is submitted, readers may find that not every article published is equally useful to them. We actively solicit feedback from our readers in order that we may continue to select manuscripts that meet their needs.

We follow the stylistic guidelines established by the American Psychological Association, particularly in regard to the use and format of references. Potential contributors to University Associates' publications may wish to purchase copies of the APA's *Publication Manual* from: Order Department, American Psychological Association, 1200 Seventeenth Street, N.W., Washington, DC 20036. University Associates also publishes guidelines for potential UA authors. These were revised in 1986 and appear at the end of the Professional Development section.

Biographies of *Annual* authors are published at the end of each structured experience, instrument, and professional development article; and at the end of each *Annual* is a list of contributors' names, affiliations, addresses, and telephone numbers. This information is intended to contribute to the "networking" function that is so valuable in our field.

INTRODUCTION TO THE
STRUCTURED EXPERIENCES SECTION

Experiential learning continues to gain wider support in the training and development community. There is a greater understanding that adult learning processes are different from those of younger learners and that vehicles for learning other than the traditional lecture need to be utilized in order to promote adult learning. The use of structured experiences, probably the most frequently used of the experiential learning strategies, has grown accordingly.

The 1987 *Annual* continues to provide a balance of materials. The material in this section can be used for a variety of purposes in different settings; however, in selecting structured experiences for publication in this volume, we gave precedence to those that could also be used in organizational settings.

In the past we have attempted to cross-reference the materials in the *Annuals* and the series of *Handbooks* and to publish (at the end of each structured experience) suggestions for "similar structured experiences," "suggested instruments," and "lecturette sources." For several reasons we are discontinuing this practice. In response to a questionnaire, our sample of readers indicated that the cross-references are not being used as frequently as we had anticipated. Because older volumes do not reflect material in later volumes, the cross-referencing in any particular volume is incomplete as soon as a later volume is published. The *Reference Guide to Handbooks and Annuals,* which is revised periodically, is apparently much more beneficial. It provides our readers with the type of help that the cross-referencing was originally intended to give. With each revision, the *Reference Guide* is completely updated and provides an easy way to select appropriate material from *all* the *Annuals* and *Handbooks.*

The twelve structured experiences in the 1987 *Annual* represent a variety of categories and cover interesting topics. The first one, "Performance Appraisal," helps participants to experience the performance appraisal process all the way from creating an agenda through role playing to giving and receiving feedback. The next structured experience, "Seeing Ourselves as Others See Us," gives participants an opportunity to be videotaped and to receive feedback in a nonthreatening way. "Doctor, Lawyer, Indian Chief" increases awareness of occupational stereotypes.

Under the major classification of *communication,* "Poor Listening Habits" helps to identify poor listening habits and allows participants to practice effective listening skills. The next structured experience, "Ranking Characteristics," will be described later in connection with a discussion on decision making by consensus.

"There's Never Time To Do It Right," which focuses on a balance between quality and quantity, involves a competition between teams that are trying to "do it right" and those that are trying to "do it fast." "Unscrambling the Bank Accounts" requires sharing information to solve a group problem. "Society of Taos" entails both competition and collaboration.

"Quantity Versus Quality" allows participants to compare their perceptions with those of peers regarding the way each of them views the relative importance of quantity and quality in productivity. "Instant Survey" provides practice in creating agenda items for team-building sessions. "Winterset High School" is an intergroup-conflict simulation; and the final structured experience, "I Represent," is a getting-acquainted activity.

All structured experiences in this *Annual* contain a description of the goals of the activity, the size of the group(s) that can be accommodated, the time required to do and *process*[1] the activity, the materials and handouts required, the physical setting, and step-by-step directions for facilitating the experiential task and discussion phases of the activity.

Readers of past *Annuals,* and those familiar with other University Associates publications, will note that the structured experiences are presented in an order that reflects their classification into categories, according to their focus and intent. A list of these classifications can be found immediately following this introduction, and an explanation of the categorization scheme can be found in the "User's Guide" to the *Structured Experience Kit,* in the discussion beginning on page 37 of the *Reference Guide to Handbooks and Annuals* (1985 Edition), and in the "Introduction to the Structured Experiences Section" of the 1981 *Annual.*

One of the structured experiences, "Ranking Characteristics," in the 1987 *Annual* deals with three types of decision-making approaches: autocratic, democratic, and consensual. Team members are first asked for opinions, but the leader then makes an autocratic decision. The next phase of the activity allows the team members to vote, and the opinion that receives a majority of the votes is offered as the team's decision. The last phase asks the team to reach consensus. Because decision making by consensus is so important, yet so poorly understood, we have asked Mark Alexander to share some of his perspectives on the subject in the following paragraphs.

CHARACTERISTICS OF DECISION MAKING BY CONSENSUS

Mark Alexander

One of the most important and relevant concepts that has emerged through the increased understanding of groups and group processes is the concept of consensus decision making. Behavioral scientists generally recognize that the ability of a group to make consensus decisions is a sign of its maturity and effectiveness. In a similar sense, teamwork and team development are built on a model of behavior that includes consensus decision making as a key indicator of effective team action.

From another perspective, consensus decision making is seen as an important technique for reducing conflict, because it is built on the notion of a win-win outcome and, in effect, represents the essence of win-win decisions.

In its simplest form, consensus decision making is the process by which a group reaches a decision with which every member of the group can agree. Beyond that basic definition, decision making by consensus includes the *process* of reaching the decision, as well as the *assumptions* or *prerequisites* that must exist for consensus decisions to be made.

Prerequisites for Consensus Decision Making

In order for decision making by consensus to be effective, the parties must believe that a win-win outcome is preferable to a win-lose or lose-lose outcome. There should also be a fundamental belief that solutions can be found and that collaboration and cooperation are important to reaching decisions. Parties must be prepared to trust one another, and they must under-

---

[1]It would be redundant to print here a caveat for the use of structured experiences, but HRD professionals who are not experienced in the use of this training technology are strongly urged to read the "Introduction to the Structured Experiences Section" of the 1980 *Annual* or the "Introduction" to the *Reference Guide to Handbooks and Annuals* (1985 Edition). Both of these articles present the theory behind the experiential-learning cycle and explain the necessity of adequately completing each phase of the cycle in order to allow effective learning to occur.

stand that joint participation is legitimate and should be sought. Finally, the parties must believe in the process of consensus decision making, and they must believe that—in the particular situation—it can produce results that are superior to other kinds of decision making.

Elements of Consensus Decision Making

Consensus decision making works well if the parties attempt to follow certain guidelines while trying to reach a decision:

1. *Focus on the problem (or opportunity).* In many instances, the process of reaching a consensus decision breaks down because the parties do not focus on the problem (or the opportunity). In these cases, the breakdown usually occurs because there is an obsessive concern for protecting power or guarding certain rights. In other instances, the breakdown occurs because the parties have different information and, therefore, cannot agree on what the problem is. An essential step in consensus decision making is an agreement on the definition of the problem (or opportunity) and an agreement to focus attention, effort, and analysis on that problem or opportunity as a paramount concern for the group.

2. *Avoid suboptimal decision-making processes.* In the majority of decision-making situations, nonconsensus decision-making processes are used. Examples include the democratic process of voting, the exercise of authority, and negotiations, bargaining, or trade-offs. Each of those processes has its place, and in many circumstances it is the only way an appropriate decision can be reached. In these nonconsensus decisions, however, there is a loser (the minority in the democratic process), there is no involvement (by the subordinate in an autocratic decision), or something has to be given up (as in the case of bargaining). In order for consensus decision making to work and produce a win-win outcome, the parties must avoid suboptimal methods such as voting, negotiating, and exercising power.

3. *Seek the facts.* The identification of clear, irrefutable information upon which can be built a common understanding of the problem is a powerful incentive to arriving at agreement. Time, energy, and resources devoted to data collection and analysis are well invested if the parties hope to achieve consensus.

4. *Use an agreed-on problem-solving process.* When decision-making groups move too rapidly toward solutions, positions can become hardened and perceptions narrowed. Decision making is improved by adopting an acceptable problem-solving process and following it in a disciplined manner. This requirement for discipline in adhering to the process is particularly important in consensus decision making because it helps to prevent the hardening of positions; allows for more involvement in the problem-definition, data-gathering, and data-analysis stages; and provides a rational basis on which all parties can focus attention. Furthermore, using an agreed-on process directs the parties toward making the process work effectively and away from defending their own positions.

5. *Accept others' viewpoints.* Crucial to reaching a consensus decision is the acceptance of the viewpoints of the other parties and using those viewpoints as legitimate input in the decision-making process. Not only does the acceptance of others' points of view improve the probability of reaching a consensus decision, but it also improves the chances of reaching a quality decision.

6. *Avoid self-oriented behavior.* In many decision-making situations, the parties have their own personal agendas, needs, and wants. The potential for consensus decisions and quality decisions is increased if the participants avoid behavior that suits only their own needs.

7. *Focus on the process.* Decision making tends to be task oriented; for example, information is gathered and analyzed, alternatives are determined, and plans are developed. Because

of this factor, participants too often forget to concentrate on the process they are using. A periodic examination of the group's process—to determine whether all members are satisfied with it and believe it will produce consensus—is important.

Consensus decision making is not easy. As an ideal, it has tremendous appeal; and its benefits in terms of long-term effectiveness, commitment, and conflict resolution are obvious. The elements that lead to consensus are relatively simple; the challenge is to apply the elements effectively.

Mark Alexander is vice president, human resources, for Shirmax Fashions, Ltd., in Quebec, Canada. He formerly was manager, management and organization development, for Air Canada.

STRUCTURED EXPERIENCE CATEGORIES

The 1987 Annual: Developing Human Resources　　　　9

425. PERFORMANCE APPRAISAL: A PRACTICE SESSION

Goals

I. To give participants an opportunity to create agenda for performance appraisals.

II. To allow participants to experience the roles of supervisor, subordinate, and observer in a performance appraisal.

III. To provide participants with an opportunity to give and receive feedback on performance-appraisal techniques.

Group Size

Any number of triads.

Time Required

Approximately two and one-half hours.

Materials

I. One copy of the Performance Appraisal Supervisor's Role Sheet for every participant.

II. One copy of the Performanance Appraisal Subordinate's Role Sheet for every participant.

III. One copy of the Performance Appraisal Observer's Role Sheet for every participant.

IV. Blank paper and a pencil for each participant.

V. A portable writing surface for each participant.

VI. A newsprint flip chart and a felt-tipped marker.

VII. Masking tape for posting newsprint.

Physical Setting

A room that is large enough for triads to work without disturbing one another.

Process

I. The facilitator explains the goals of the activity. (Five minutes.)

II. The participants are assembled into triads. One member of each triad is given a copy of the supervisor's role sheet; another member is given a copy of the subordinate's role sheet; and the third member is given a copy of the observer's role sheet. Blank paper, a pencil, and a portable writing surface are given to every participant.

III. The participants are instructed to read their sheets and ask for clarification on any point they do not understand. (Five minutes.)

IV. The facilitator asks the participants who have the supervisor's role sheets to interview the person playing the role of subordinate according to the instructions on their role sheets. The observer takes notes about the nature of the subordinate's job. (Five minutes.)

V. The facilitator interrupts the interviews and asks each supervisor and subordinate to create and prioritize agenda for the performance appraisal as instructed on the role sheets. The observers take notes on the agreed-upon agenda. (Ten minutes.)

VI. The facilitator instructs the triads to begin the performance-appraisal process. At the end of ten minutes, the facilitator stops the appraisal. (Ten minutes.)

VII. The facilitator instructs each supervisor and his or her subordinate to continue the conversation just long enough to summarize what they have already discussed. The subordinate is instructed to make notes that could be used later to write a summary.

VIII. Each observer is instructed to give feedback to the other two members of the triad and to allow them to ask for clarification and suggestions at the end of the feedback. (Five minutes.)

IX. Each subordinate is given a copy of the supervisor's role sheet; each observer is given a copy of the subordinate's role sheet; and each supervisor is given a copy of the observer's role sheet. The facilitator announces that each participant will play the role that corresponds to the new sheet.

X. Steps III through IX are repeated. Then steps III through VIII are repeated. (Seventy-five minutes.)

XI. The total group is reassembled, and the facilitator leads a discussion on the following questions:

1. How did you feel when you played the role of supervisor? Subordinate? Observer?
2. What did you like/dislike about each role?
3. Which role was most helpful to you in understanding the performance-appraisal process? How?
4. In what ways were the agenda helpful? In what ways were they a hindrance?
5. In what ways were the summaries helpful?
6. What types of statements or topics caused problems during the appraisal? How?
7. What topics, phrases, statements, or behaviors enhanced the process? How?
8. What discoveries have you made about the performance-appraisal process?
9. How can this experience benefit you and your organization in the future?

(Twenty minutes.)

Variations

I. Each participant could be asked to play only one of the roles, and the time for the appraisal could be extended to twenty minutes.

II. A few participants could be asked to interview their partners in depth and prepare agenda in advance of the activity, thus preparing them to give a more realistic demonstration of the performance appraisal. All the other participants would observe and critique the role play.

III. When playing the role of subordinate, the participant could be asked to write a summary of the performance appraisal and to discuss it with the person who played the role of supervisor.

Submitted by John E. Oliver.

John E. Oliver, Ph.D., is an associate professor of management at Valdosta State College in Valdosta, Georgia. His managerial and consulting experience includes work with financial institutions, manufacturing plants, professional firms, and government organizations. Dr. Oliver is a member of the Academy of Management, the American Psychological Association, and the Southern Management Association. His articles have appeared in four textbooks and several management journals.

PERFORMANCE APPRAISAL SUPERVISOR'S ROLE SHEET

You will play the role of the supervisor during a performance appraisal. Before the appraisal process begins, you will interview the person who is playing the role of your subordinate in order to find out what type of organization he or she works for, what kind of work he or she does, and other details that would help you appraise the subordinate's performance.

The facilitator will interrupt your interview and ask you and your subordinate to create agenda for the performance appraisal. You will write down topics that you want to discuss while your subordinate is writing down topics that he or she wants to discuss. When you finish, you and your subordinate will exchange agenda and discuss them and come to an agreement about which items will remain on the final agenda.

Because time is limited for this activity, you will not be able to cover every agendum. Therefore, you and your subordinate will prioritize the items on the final agenda.

Some items that you may want to include on the agenda are listed below:

1. Things that subordinate has done well.

2. Things that the subordinate needs to improve.

3. Progress on previously set goals.

4. Goals toward which the subordinate might work.

5. Things that the supervisor does that help or hinder the subordinate's work.

After you have completed the agenda, the facilitator will tell you to begin the performance appraisal.

When giving feedback to your subordinate, cite specific behavior. For example, say, "Your weekly reports were late twice last month," or "Your errors dropped from six in January to only two in February," not "Your work is always lagging behind," or "Your accuracy seems to be improving."

Resist the temptation to sandwich negative criticism in between compliments. For example, do not say, "Your computer work is excellent, you make too many mistakes on the typewriter, and I think you are a very good organizer." Instead, remind the subordinate that you had to return six letters for corrections last week and that one of his or her goals should be to proofread typed material carefully before giving it to you. Make sure the subordinate understands your complaint before proceeding further.

The facilitator will interrupt the performance appraisal and instruct you and your subordinate to jointly summarize what you discussed during the appraisal. Your subordinate will be instructed to take notes. (In a real situation, the subordinate is sometimes asked to write a summary of the appraisal and to present it the following day to the supervisor for discussion.)

PERFORMANCE APPRAISAL SUBORDINATE'S ROLE SHEET

You will play the role of the subordinate during a performance appraisal. Before the appraisal process begins, you will be interviewed by the person who is playing the role of your supervisor. Expect that person to ask you about where you work, what kind of work you do, and other details that would help in giving a performance appraisal.

The facilitator will interrupt the interview and ask you and your supervisor to create agenda for the performance appraisal. While your supervisor is writing down topics that he or she wants to discuss with you, you should also write down topics that you want discussed. When you finish you will exchange agenda with your supervisor and will discuss them and come to an agreement about which items will remain on the final agenda.

Because time is limited for this activity, you will not be able to cover every agendum. Therefore, you and your supervisor will prioritize the items on the final agenda.

Some items you may want to include on your agenda are listed below:

1. Things that I do well.
2. Things that I need to improve.
3. Progress on previously set goals.
4. Goals for the future.

After you have completed the agenda, wait for the facilitator to tell you to begin the performance appraisal.

If your supervisor asks you for feedback on his or her performance, cite specific behavior. For example, say, "You missed a meeting we scheduled for last Thursday," not "You're never around," or say "The note you wrote me about my report inspired me to try to finish on time every month," not "You are always giving me encouragement."

The performance appraisal will be interrupted by the facilitator, who will instruct you and your supervisor to jointly summarize what you discussed. At this point, you will be asked to make notes so that you would be able to write a summary later. (In a real situation, the subordinate is sometimes required to write a summary of the performance appraisal and to present it to the supervisor the following day for discussion.)

PERFORMANCE APPRAISAL OBSERVER'S ROLE SHEET

You will play the role of the observer during a performance appraisal. When real performance appraisals are conducted, the supervisor's supervisor sometimes observes the process and gives feedback to the person performing the appraisal. Your task will be to give feedback to *both* parties.

Before the performance appraisal, the person playing the role of supervisor will interview the person playing the role of subordinate to obtain information about the person's job. The supervisor and subordinate will also plan the agenda.

During the interview, agenda setting, and performance appraisal, take notes but do not interrupt or join the conversation. The other two members of your triad will probably become so involved in their conversation that they will not even be aware of your presence.

You should not give feedback on the performance appraisal until the facilitator instructs you to do so. When you have finished giving feedback, you should allow the other members of your triad to ask you for clarification and suggestions.

If you play another role after being an observer, try to benefit from the feedback you gave the other members of your triad.

The following items provide a checklist that may be helpful as you observe the supervisor and subordinate:

1. The supervisor and subordinate created the agenda jointly.
2. The supervisor and subordinate followed the agenda they created.
3. The supervisor was in control of the process.
4. The supervisor used concrete examples to describe performance.
5. The subordinate reacted to the supervisor's feedback nondefensively.
6. The supervisor and subordinate set goals jointly.
7. The supervisor solicited feedback about his or her performance.
8. The subordinate used concrete examples to describe the supervisor's performance.
9. The supervisor reacted to the subordinate's feedback nondefensively.
10. The supervisor and subordinate shared the discussion.
11. The supervisor and subordinate summarized the discussion jointly.
12. The subordinate took notes on the summary.

426. SEEING OURSELVES AS OTHERS SEE US: USING VIDEO EQUIPMENT FOR FEEDBACK

Goals

I. To enable participants to compare the images they have of themselves with the images they project.

II. To increase feedback skills.

III. To help participants understand how the differences in self-image and projected image influence interaction.

Group Size

From two to eight dyads plus a person to operate the video equipment.

Time Required

Approximately one hour plus an additional ten minutes for each speaker.

Materials

I. A copy of the Seeing Ourselves as Others See Us: Video Feedback Sheet for each participant and the camera operator.

II. A few sheets of paper and a pencil for each participant.

III. A portable writing surface for each participant.

IV. A video camera with a wide-angle lens.

V. A video monitor for instant replay.

Physical Setting

A room large enough for a video-camera operator to move around and photograph a good portion of the entire group and the speaker.

Process

I. The facilitator explains the advantages of using video equipment for giving feedback and attempts to alleviate fears of being videotaped. (Five minutes.)

II. The goals of the activity are explained as well as the procedure that will be used. The facilitator assures the participants that no one will be coerced into speaking in front of the camera.

III. A copy of the video feedback sheet, several sheets of blank paper, a pencil, and a portable writing surface are given to each participant. Participants are asked to read the video feedback sheet. (Five minutes.)

IV. Participants are assembled into dyads and asked to interview their partners so that they can introduce their partners to the group. The facilitator specifies that each videotaped introduction should last no longer than two minutes. (Five minutes.)

V. The facilitator volunteers to be videotaped first and introduces an imaginary guest.

VI. After the facilitator's introduction has been videotaped, it is shown on the monitor. Participants are asked to focus on the facilitator on the screen and to write brief notes as they watch.

VII. After the participants finish watching the facilitator on the monitor, the facilitator points out something he or she did that could be improved and gives an example of how feedback, based on what was seen on the screen, could be given without being a threat to the person receiving it. (Five minutes.)

VIII. The facilitator's introduction is replayed, but the participants are asked to watch themselves or (if the camera did not include them) other members of the audience on the screen and to take brief notes as they watch.

IX. The facilitator leads a discussion on the following questions:

1. Did you immediately recognize yourself on the screen?
2. What were you doing during the introduction?
3. What was different about what you saw in yourself and your previous perception of yourself?
4. If you were not on the screen, what observations did you make about other members of the audience?
5. What types of things were obvious on the screen that you generally do not observe offscreen?

(Ten minutes.)

X. The facilitator asks for volunteers to make their introductions, and the process is repeated until every participant has had an opportunity to speak before the camera and to be on camera as part of the audience. When the focus is on the speaker, the facilitator asks the speaker to point out something that could be improved and to request feedback from the other participants. When the focus is on the audience, the facilitator leads a discussion on the following questions:

1. What specifically (about yourself or others) did you observe this time?
2. What are you learning from those observations?

(Approximately ten minutes per volunteer.)

XI. After all the introductions are replayed and discussed, the facilitator leads a discussion on the following questions:

1. What conclusions can you draw about the difference between your self-image and your projected image? What can you say about that difference for people in general?
2. How does the difference between the way we see ourselves and the way we come across to others affect our interactions with them?
3. What did you learn from this look at yourself? What changes might you want to make because of this experience?

(Fifteen minutes.)

Variations

  I. Participants could tell a story, give an impromptu speech, or introduce themselves.

 II. The feedback session could have a single focus: either on the speaker or on the listener.

III. Two cameras could be used, thereby providing views of the speaker and the audience throughout the entire presentation.

Submitted by Gilles L. Talbot

Gilles L. Talbot *is a professor of psychology at Champlain Regional College, St. Lawrence Campus, in Quebec, Canada. He is currently involved with life-skills training in motivation, interpersonal relations, and communications for students who are prone to fail or abandon their studies. Professor Talbot has published a number of articles in the areas of motivation and human relations training as they relate to student-teacher relationships.*

SEEING OURSELVES AS OTHERS SEE US:
VIDEO FEEDBACK SHEET

Perhaps you have seen a photograph of yourself that you did not immediately recognize. If your face was blurred or turned away from the camera, you might have even argued that the picture was not of you. Many things that we do can project images that do not coincide with the images we think we are projecting. Sometimes the images we project are more negative than we hope; but in many cases, they are more positive than our own self-images.

The activity planned for your group provides each of you with an opportunity to take part in a nonthreatening situation in which you can see yourself as others see you. The way you walk, the way you stand, and the way you talk are, collectively, as distinct as fingerprints.

In this activity you will interview someone long enough to gather enough facts (or fantasies) to introduce that person to the audience. You will introduce the person as though he or she were going to make a speech, but time will not permit the speech to actually be made.

The facilitator will volunteer to be the first person to speak in front of the camera. You will hear the facilitator's introduction live and then watch it twice on the video monitor. The first time you see it on the screen you will focus on the facilitator's presentation, and the next time you will focus on yourself or another member of the audience. After the first showing, the facilitator will draw your attention to something in his or her presentation and will talk about how it could be used in giving feedback. When the focus is on the audience, you will be asked some specific questions. In answering the questions, try to use examples of behavior you observed while viewing the videotape.

If you volunteer to speak in front of the camera, you should make the introduction in the following manner:

> Enter the room from a doorway, walk to the front of the audience, face the audience, and begin speaking. Finish the introduction by indicating that the speaker is coming on stage. Then take a seat with the audience. The camera will then be turned off, and the person you introduced will remain seated.

You should not deliberately face the camera. The camera operator will obtain the proper shots of you and the audience. If you keep your mind on what you are saying and how you are presenting the information, you may discover that you are unaware of the camera.

Attempt to use your ordinary style. This is not a contest to see who can perform like a movie star. This is an opportunity for you to see yourself as others usually see you.

After you have made the introduction, you will see yourself on the video monitor. The first time your video is played, everyone will be concentrating on you. After you have watched it, you should tell the group one thing you saw that you think could be improved. After viewing this segment the second time, the discussion will center around people in the audience.

427. DOCTOR, LAWYER, INDIAN CHIEF: OCCUPATIONAL STEREOTYPES

Goals

I. To increase awareness of occupational stereotypes and of how they impact interpersonal relationships.

II. To allow participants to discuss their feelings about occupational stereotyping.

Group Size

Five to ten dyads.

Time Required

Approximately two hours. (More than seven dyads require more time.)

Materials

I. One occupational name tag for each participant. Each tag should show a different occupational name. Names on the tags might include, for example, librarian, plumber, secretary, or taxi driver.

II. For each participant, a set of 3" x 5" cards, each of which contains a different occupational name. The number of cards in each set equals the number of participants, and the names on the cards correspond to the names on the occupational name tags.

III. For each participant, an envelope large enough to hold a complete set of cards.

IV. Several sheets of blank paper and a pencil for each participant.

V. A portable writing surface for each participant.

VI. A newsprint flip chart and a felt-tipped marker.

VII. Masking tape for posting newsprint.

Physical Setting

A room that is large enough to allow participants to move around freely. Movable chairs should be provided for the participants. After participants have interviewed one another, the chairs should be arranged in a circle.

Process

I. The facilitator introduces the activity by saying that the participants will be investigating various occupations during the course of the activity.

II. Each participant is given a set of cards, an envelope, several sheets of writing paper, a pencil, and a portable writing surface.

III. The participants are asked to write on each card two words or phrases that they would use to describe a person in the occupation appearing on the card. (Five minutes.)

IV. After all the participants have completed their task, the facilitator instructs each of them to choose the five occupations that represent the most interesting people. Each participant is then instructed to rank order these five cards to indicate an interest in meeting a person from each occupation and to write "1" on the card that represents the greatest interest and to appropriately assign "2," "3," "4," and "5" to the other four cards. (Five minutes.)

V. The facilitator distributes the occupational name tags to the participants but is careful not to assign a tag that designates the participant's real occupation. (If the facilitator does not know the participants' occupations, the participants are instructed not to accept a tag that shows his or her real occupation.) Each participant is instructed to wear the name tag throughout the remainder of the process and to "assume" the occupation listed on the tag.

VI. The participants are instructed to form dyads and to introduce themselves to their partners with their real names and their assumed occupations. (If there is an odd number of participants, one triad should be formed.)

VII. After the introductions have been completed, participants are given the following instructions:

1. Locate the card that shows your partner's assumed occupation and place it in your partner's envelope without allowing him or her to see the handwritten description on the card.

2. Ask your partner two questions about his or her assumed occupation and take notes on the responses. Answer the two questions that your partner asks you.

3. Form a dyad with another participant and continue the process until you have interviewed all the other participants.

(Five minutes per dyad interview.)

VIII. When the interviews have been completed, the participants are asked to arrange their chairs in a circle. They are asked to take a seat and review the cards they have collected. (Five minutes.)

IX. The facilitator leads a discussion and makes notes on newsprint regarding the participants' responses to the following questions. (As the sheets of newsprint are filled, they are posted so that the information will be in view during the entire discussion.)

1. How many of you hold cards that indicate a person in your assumed occupation was among the five that generated the most interest?

2. What words or phrases were used to describe those occupations?

3. What words or phrases were used to describe the occupations that were not among the top five?

4. What conclusions can be drawn about these choices?

5. In what ways was your assumed occupation the object of occupational stereotyping (either positively or negatively)? How do you feel about this?

(Twenty minutes.)

X. After the discussion on stereotyping of the assumed occupations, the facilitator leads a discussion by asking the following questions regarding stereotyping of real occupations:

1. When you have been stereotyped because of your real occupation, how have you felt? How were you treated?
2. How have you ever engaged in occupational stereotyping? How did you relate to people in occupations that you stereotyped? What might be the reasons that people first began to engage in occupational stereotyping?
3. If you could have chosen any occupation you desired, how would your stereotypical views have influenced your decision? How does your stereotyping of your own occupation affect your feelings about working?
4. What do you conclude from these answers about the strength of occupational stereotyping?
5. How might we overcome tendencies to stereotype occupations or the people in those occupations? What might we do differently in relating to people whose occupations we tend to stereotype?

(Thirty minutes.)

Variations

I. If a group is large, it can be subdivided into smaller groups, with each group being assigned the same occupations.
II. The participants can be asked to submit suggestions for occupations in advance, or they can choose their own assumed occupations and create occupational cards during the structured experience.
III. A discussion can be added on stereotyping occupations in relation to gender.

Submitted by Mary Kirkpatrick Craig.

Mary Kirkpatrick Craig is a training manager with Foodmaker, Inc., San Diego, California, where she is responsible for the design of management training and development programs. Her areas of interest include human resource development, group process, and facilitation skills. She is currently involved in the development of video training programs focusing on management skills.

428. POOR LISTENING HABITS: IDENTIFYING AND IMPROVING THEM

Goals

   I. To help participants to identify their poor listening habits.

  II. To allow participants to practice effective listening skills.

Group Size

      Any number of dyads.

Time Required

      Approximately one and one-half hours.

Materials

   I. Enough copies of the Poor Listening Habits: ABC Listening Sheet for half the participants.

  II. Enough copies of the Poor Listening Habits: NL Sheet for half the participants.

 III. One copy of the Poor Listening Habits: Theory Sheet for each participant.

 IV. One copy of the Poor Listening Habits: Effective Listening Sheet for each participant.

  V. A pencil for each participant.

 VI. A writing surface for each participant.

 VII. A newsprint flip chart and a felt-tipped marker.

VIII. Masking tape for posting newsprint.

Physical Setting

      A room that is large enough to allow dyads to converse without disturbing one another.

Process

   I. The facilitator explains the goals of the activity and tells the participants they will be involved in several activities that will require them to exaggerate poor listening habits.

  II. The group is divided into dyads.

 III. A copy of the ABC listening sheet and a pencil are distributed to one person in each dyad. The participants who do not have the ABC listening sheet are designated "speaker number one" and are instructed to start talking to their partners about any subject they wish. (Five minutes.)

IV. The facilitator stops the conversations and asks how it felt to be the speaker. The facilitator explains that the listeners were asked to count the speakers' words that began with "a," "b," and "c." The listeners are asked, "How did this scorekeeping affect your ability to listen?" (Five minutes.)

V. A copy of the NL sheet and a pencil are distributed to each number-one speaker, and the other participants are designated "speaker number two." Each speaker number two is instructed to start talking to his or her partner about any subject that is different from the subject his or her partner chose. (Five minutes.)

VI. The facilitator interrupts the conversation and asks the number two speakers how it felt to be the speaker. The facilitator explains that the listeners were instructed *not* to listen. The number-one speakers are asked what methods they used to keep from listening. They are also asked to recall some of the things the number-two speakers said. The facilitator leads a discussion on which methods seemed to interfere most with listening and how a habit of using such methods can be broken. (Ten minutes.)

VII. The facilitator gives the following instructions:

The number-one speakers will try to talk to their partners about the topics they previously chose, and the number-two speakers will respond by talking about the topics they previously chose. Continue the conversation until you are told to stop.

VIII. After a couple of minutes, the facilitator interrupts the conversations and asks, "What was the biggest listening problem with these conversations?"

IX. The facilitator announces that the number-one speakers should select new topics and that as they talk, the number-two speakers should interrupt repeatedly by asking "why" questions (e.g., "Why did he do that?" or "Why is that important?"). The number-one speakers must begin their responses with the word "because."

X. After a couple of minutes, the facilitator interrupts the conversations and asks, "What were the listening problems in this why-because conversation?"

XI. The facilitator asks the number-two speakers to choose topics about which they feel positively and strongly. The facilitator then announces that each number-one speaker will attempt to argue forcefully against the number-two speaker's position.

XII. After a couple of minutes, the facilitator asks participants how this conversation felt and what the listening problems were.

XIII. The total group is reassembled. Each participant is given a copy of the theory sheet and a copy of the effective listening sheet and is asked to read both handouts and to identify his or her own poor listening habits.

XIV. The facilitator elicits comparisons between the items listed on the theory sheet with the listening methods that were used in each of the activities. The participants' responses are recorded on newsprint. (Ten minutes.)

XV. The facilitator leads a discussion on how to break each habit listed on the theory sheet and how to acquire the skills listed on the effective listening sheet. (Ten minutes.)

XVI. The participants are instructed to resume conversations with their partners. This time one member of each dyad relates a personal experience while his or her partner attempts to use effective listening skills; then the roles are reversed. (Five minutes.)

XVII. The facilitator leads a discussion on the following questions:

1. How did it feel to be a speaker this time? A listener?

2. How was this last experience similar to and different from the previous experiences in this activity? What poor listening skills did you continue to use?
3. How can you improve your listening skills? With whom do you need to practice more effective listening?
4. What can you conclude about effective listening and its benefits?
(Fifteen minutes.)

Variations

I. The activity can be used as an icebreaker by rotating partners for each conversation.

II. Subgroups can be formed for identifying and discussing poor listening habits.

III. The activity can be shortened by eliminating some of the conversations.

Submitted by Joseph Seltzer and Leland Howe.

Joseph Seltzer, Ph.D., is an associate professor and chairman of the management department at LaSalle University. He teaches courses in organizational behavior and analysis and also in managerial and communications skills. Dr. Seltzer's current research interests include leadership, stress, and nonprofit management. He is on the editorial board of the Organizational Behavior Teaching Review *and is treasurer of the Eastern Academy of Management.*

Leland W. Howe, Ph.D., is president of Howe Associates in Vermontville, Michigan. His specialties are consultation skills, organization development, communication skills, and team development. He has authored or co-authored several books. Dr. Howe is a former professor of psychological education at Temple University and is currently a psychotherapist and consultant to a number of schools and other organizations.

POOR LISTENING HABITS: ABC LISTENING SHEET

Do not allow your partner to read this sheet.

As your partner is talking, keep track of the total number of words he or she uses that begin with "a," "b," and "c." Do not count the articles "a" and "an" and do not count the conjunction "and." Do not tell your partner what you are doing.

You can take part in the conversation, but be sure to keep an accurate score while your partner is talking.

A   B   C

- -

POOR LISTENING HABITS: NL SHEET

Do not allow your partner to read this sheet.

The "NL" in the title stands for "Not Listening." While your partner is talking, your task is to *not listen*. You may attempt to not listen in any way you like, as long as you stay in your seat. You may occasionally say something, but it need not relate to what your partner has been saying. Although your partner may realize you are not being attentive, do not tell him or her that you are deliberately not listening.

POOR LISTENING HABITS THEORY SHEET

Most people spend more time listening than they spend on any other communication activity, yet a large percentage of people never learn to listen well. One reason is that they develop *poor* listening habits that continue with them throughout life. The following list contains some of the most common poor listening habits.

1. *Not Paying Attention.* Listeners may allow themselves to be distracted or to think of something else. Also, not wanting to listen often contributes to lack of attention.

2. *"Pseudolistening."* Often people who are thinking about something else deliberately try to look as though they were listening. Such pretense may leave the speaker with the impression that the listener has heard some important information or instructions offered by the speaker.

3. *Listening but Not Hearing.* Sometimes a person listens only to facts or details or to the way they were presented and misses the real meaning.

4. *Rehearsing.* Some people listen until they want to say something; then they quit listening, start rehearsing what they will say, and wait for an opportunity to respond.

5. *Interrupting.* The listener does not wait until the complete meaning can be determined, but interrupts so forcefully that the speaker stops in mid-sentence.

6. *Hearing What Is Expected.* People frequently think they heard speakers say what they expected them to say. Alternatively, they refuse to hear what they do not want to hear.

7. *Feeling Defensive.* The listeners assume that they know the speaker's intention or why something was said, or for various other reasons, they expect to be attacked.

8. *Listening for a Point of Disagreement.* Some listeners seem to wait for the chance to attack someone. They listen intently for points on which they can disagree.

POOR LISTENING HABITS: EFFECTIVE LISTENING SHEET

One way people can improve their listening is to identify their own poor listening habits and make an effort to change them. The list on the Poor Listening Habits Theory Sheet will help people to identify some of their own listening patterns. If the listeners will then pay special attention to the circumstances that seem to invite such behavior, they can consciously attempt to change their habits. For example, if a woman realizes that she is "pseudo-listening" to her husband, she can stop him and ask him to repeat his last idea. She can even say, "I'm sorry; my mind was wandering." The more she becomes conscious of poor listening behavior, the more likely she is to change her poor listening habits.

Besides ridding themselves of *bad* listening habits, people can acquire *positive* listening habits. Listed below are a few descriptions of behavior that can lead to effective listening:

1. *Paying Attention.* If people really want to be good listeners, they must, on occasion, force themselves to pay attention to the speakers. When speakers are dull conversationalists, a listener must sometimes use effort to keep from being distracted by other things. It is important not only to focus on the speakers, but to use nonverbal cues (such as eye contact, head nods, and smiles) to let them know they are being heard.

2. *Listening for the Whole Message.* This includes looking for meaning and consistency or congruence in both the verbal and nonverbal messages and listening for ideas, feelings, and intentions as well as facts. It also includes hearing things that are unpleasant or unwelcome.

3. *Hearing Before Evaluating.* Listening to what someone says without drawing premature conclusions is a valuable aid to listening. By questioning the speaker in a nonaccusing manner, rather than giving advice or judging, a listener can often discover exactly what the speaker has in mind—which many times is quite different from what the listener had assumed.

4. *Paraphrasing What Was Heard.* If the listener nonjudgmentally paraphrases the words of the speaker and asks if that is what was meant, many misunderstandings and misinterpretations can be avoided.

 University Associates

429. RANKING CHARACTERISTICS: A COMPARISON OF DECISION-MAKING APPROACHES

Goals

I. To allow participants to experience three types of decision-making processes: autocratic, democratic, and consensual.

II. To demonstrate and compare the relative time required for each of these processes.

III. To explore the impacts of each of these approaches on the quality of the decisions, the participants' degree of involvement in the processes, and their preferences for a particular approach.

Group Size

Any number of groups of five to nine members each.

Time Required

One to one and one-half hours.

Materials

I. One copy of the Ranking Characteristics of a Good Parent Work Sheet for each participant.

II. One copy of the Ranking Characteristics of a Good Trainer Work Sheet for each participant.

III. One copy of the Ranking Characteristics of a Good Group Leader Work Sheet for each participant.

IV. One copy of the Ranking Characteristics Phase-I Leader's Instruction Sheet for each phase-I leader.

V. One copy of the Ranking Characteristics Phase-II Leader's Instruction Sheet for each phase-II leader.

VI. One copy of the Ranking Characteristics Phase-III Leader's Instruction Sheet for each phase-III leader.

VII. A pencil for each participant.

VIII. A writing surface for each participant.

IX. One newsprint copy of each of the three Ranking Characteristics Tally Forms prepared in advance of the activity.

X. A large clock situated so that all participants can see it.

XI. A newsprint flip chart and a felt-tipped marker.

XII. Masking tape for posting newsprint.

Physical Setting

A room that is large enough for groups to work without disturbing one another.

Process

I. The participants are assembled into groups of five to nine members each, and a writing surface is provided for each participant. Each group selects a phase-I leader, a phase-II leader, and a phase-III leader. (Five minutes.)

II. The facilitator meets in a separate area with the phase-I leaders, distributes the phase-I leader's instruction sheets, asks the leaders to read the sheets, and offers clarification if needed. The facilitator then gives them enough pencils and copies of the good parent work sheet to accommodate all members of their groups and sends them back to their groups. (Five minutes.)

III. While the facilitator is meeting with the leaders, each group discusses important characteristics of a good parent.

IV. The phase-I leaders explain the task to their groups and distribute a pencil and a copy of the good parent work sheet to every group member, including themselves. At this point, the leader notices the time and records it and instructs the group to start the task.

V. When all members of a group have rated their work sheets, the leader asks each of them to share with the group the top five characteristics selected. Then the leader tells them which five he or she selected and announces that his or her own work sheet will be turned in as the group's decision. The leader again records the time and computes how long it took to make the decision.

VI. Each phase-I leader writes the number of minutes it took for the decision to be made at the top of his or her own work sheet and gives the work sheet to the facilitator.

VII. The facilitator meets with the group of phase-II leaders, distributes the phase-II leader's instruction sheets, asks the leaders to read the sheets, and offers clarification if needed. The facilitator then gives them enough copies of the good trainer work sheet to accommodate all members of their groups and sends them back to their groups. (Five minutes.)

VIII. While the facilitator is meeting with the leaders, each group discusses how it felt about the way the decision was made.

IX. The phase-II leaders explain the task to their groups and distribute a copy of the good trainer work sheet to every group member, including themselves. At this point, each leader notices the time and records it and instructs his or her group to start the task.

X. While the groups are working on the second task, the facilitator tallies the results of the first task and writes them on the newsprint copy of the phase-I tally form. The results are not shown to the participants at this point.

XI. When all members of a group have rated their work sheets, the leader asks each of them to share with the group the top five characteristics selected. Then the leader tells them that one work sheet from the group will be turned in as the group's decision. The leader solicits nominations and takes a vote. When one person's work sheet has a majority of votes, the leader again records the time and computes how long it took to make the decision.

XII. The owner of the winning work sheet writes the number of minutes required to make the decision at the top of the work sheet and gives the work sheet to the facilitator.

XIII. The facilitator meets with the group of phase-III leaders, distributes the phase-III leader's instruction sheets, asks the leaders to read the sheets, and offers clarification if needed. The facilitator then gives them enough copies of the good group leader work sheet to accommodate all members of their groups and sends them back to their groups. (Five minutes.)

XIV. While the facilitator meets with the leaders, each group discusses important characteristics of a group leader.

XV. The phase-III leaders explain the task to their groups and distribute a copy of the good group leader work sheet to every group member, including themselves. At this point, the leader notices the time and records it and instructs the group to start the task.

XVI. While the groups are working on the third task, the facilitator tallies the results of the second task and writes them on the newsprint copy of the phase-II tally form.

XVII. When all members of a group have rated their work sheets, the leader asks each of them to share with the group the top five characteristics selected. Then the leader tells them that they must reach consensus on the rankings and gives them suggestions on how to arrive at a consensus. When the group reaches consensus, the leader changes his or her own work sheet to conform with the consensus. Then the leader again records the time and computes how long it took to make the decision.

XVIII. The leader writes the number of minutes required to make the decision at the top of the work sheet and gives the work sheet to the facilitator.

XIX. Within each group the members are asked to discuss how they felt about the three methods of decision making. While these discussions are taking place, the facilitator tallies the results of the third task and writes them on the newsprint copy of the phase-III tally form. (Five minutes.)

XX. The total group is reassembled. The facilitator explains the three methods of decision making that were used, shows the results of each method, and leads a discussion on the following questions:

1. Which process did you prefer? Why?
2. Which process produced the best results? How?
3. In which process were you most involved? In what ways were you involved to a greater degree in that process?
4. Under what circumstances might an autocratic decision be best? A democratic approach? A consensus approach? What might the drawbacks be of each approach?
5. What do the tally sheets suggest about the differences in the three approaches?
6. Which decision-making process seems to be used most frequently in your work group? What changes would you like to see in that process? How could you help to promote those changes?

(Twenty minutes.)

Variations

I. If time is limited, a third of the participants can use the autocratic process; a third, the democratic method; and a third, the consensus method.

II. Post-decision rating forms can be distributed to all participants to determine the satisfaction with, enjoyment of, and involvement in each type of decision-making process.

Submitted by Charles A. LaJeunesse.

Charles A. LaJeunesse, Ph.D., *is an assistant professor of psychology at College Misericordia in Dallas, Pennsylvania. He teaches a variety of undergraduate and graduate courses, including research methodology and industrial and organizational psychology, and serves as an associate of the Center for Professional Development. His specialties include organizational consultation, evaluative research, and classroom innovation.*

RANKING CHARACTERISTICS OF A GOOD PARENT WORK SHEET

Name _____

Instructions: Write your name at the top of this sheet. Below are listed some characteristics of a good parent. Your task is to select the five most important characteristics of a good parent and to rank these five from 1 (most important) to 5 (least important of the five you have selected).

_____ Uses praise as well as punishment.

_____ Sets good examples.

_____ Spends time with child.

_____ Listens willingly to child.

_____ Uses discipline fairly and consistently.

_____ Provides a stimulating environment.

_____ Demonstrates affection.

_____ Provides material necessities.

_____ Allows child to take risks.

_____ Considers child a person with rights.

_____ Prevents child from watching violence on television.

RANKING CHARACTERISTICS OF A GOOD TRAINER WORK SHEET

Name _____

Instructions: Write your name at the top of this sheet. Below are listed some characteristics of a good trainer. Your task is to select the five most important characteristics of a good trainer and to rank these five from 1 (most important) to 5 (least important of the five you have selected).

_____ Is well prepared.

_____ Uses a variety of approaches.

_____ Tries to make sure each participant benefits from the experience.

_____ Knows his or her own limitations.

_____ Knows the material well.

_____ Is well organized.

_____ Recognizes and utilizes the expertise of participants.

_____ Has a good sense of humor.

_____ Presents a balance between theory and practical material.

_____ Seeks feedback from participants.

_____ Socializes with participants during breaks.

University Associates

RANKING CHARACTERISTICS OF A GOOD GROUP LEADER WORK SHEET

Name _____

Instructions: Write your name at the top of this sheet. Below are listed some characteristics of a good group leader. Your task is to select the five most important characteristics of a good group leader and to rank these five from 1 (most important) to 5 (least important of the five you have selected).

_____ Is energetic.

_____ Is skilled at resolving conflict.

_____ Is well organized.

_____ Has experience as group leader.

_____ Is respected by group members.

_____ Is reliable.

_____ Is charismatic.

_____ Is intelligent.

_____ Is creative.

_____ Possesses a sense of humor.

_____ Is effective in achieving results.

RANKING CHARACTERISTICS PHASE-I LEADER'S INSTRUCTION SHEET

Give the members of your group the following instructions:

1. Work independently and rank order the top five characteristics of a good parent.
2. Be conscientious about your rankings, because our group has to give our decision to the facilitator.

Look at the clock and record the time and tell your group to begin the task.

When the members of your group complete the task, ask each one to share his or her top five characteristics along with the assigned numbers.

When all the other members have finished reading their lists, share your top five and announce that you will use your list as the group's decision. You may give the group any of the reasons listed below or you may make up your own reason or give no reason at all.

Reasons for Using Your Rankings

1. "We are running out of time, so I'll just submit my list as our decision."
2. "I've been a parent for x years, so I'm sure my list is as accurate as any of yours."
3. "Next time we can use someone else's list, but this time we're going to use mine."

As soon as your group understands that your list will be used, note the time and compute how many minutes elapsed between the time your group started the task and the time the decision was announced. Write the number of minutes on your copy of the work sheet and give it to the facilitator.

If members of your group object to your decision, reply by saying, "Well, I'm the leader, and that is what I have decided" and stand up and take your work sheet to the facilitator. After you return to the group, you may tell them that later there will be a general discussion on how the decision was made.

University Associates

RANKING CHARACTERISTICS PHASE-II LEADER'S INSTRUCTION SHEET

Give the members of your group the following instructions:

1. Work independently and rank order the top five characteristics of a good trainer.
2. Be conscientious about your rankings, because our group has to give our decision to the facilitator.
3. One of our work sheets will be used as our group's decision, but it will not necessarily be mine.

Look at the clock and record the time and tell your group to begin the task.

When the members of your group complete the task, ask each one to share his or her top five characteristics along with the assigned numbers.

When all the other members have finished reading their lists, share your list and announce that the work sheet of one of the members will be used as your group's decision. Solicit nominations, and when one member's work sheet has received a majority of votes, record the time and compute the number of minutes that were required to make the decision.

Tell the person who holds the winning work sheet to write the number of minutes required for the decision in the upper-right corner of his or her work sheet and to give the work sheet to the facilitator.

RANKING CHARACTERISTICS PHASE-III LEADER'S INSTRUCTION SHEET

Give the members of your group the following instructions:

1. Work independently and rank order the top five characteristics of a good group leader.
2. Be conscientious about your rankings, because our group has to give our decision to the facilitator.

Look at the clock and record the time and tell your group to begin the task.

When the members of your group complete the task, ask each one to share his or her top five characteristics along with the assigned numbers.

When all the other members have finished reading their lists, share your list and announce that the group must arrive at a consensus decision, that is, a decision that everyone is willing to accept. Give the group the following suggestions about how to arrive at a consensus:

1. Discuss the characteristics and try to produce rank orders that everyone in the group can accept.
2. Do not use averaging, majority rule, or "horse trading" to arrive at a decision.
3. Do not attempt to win as an individual.
4. View differences of opinion as a help rather than a hindrance in arriving at a consensus.
5. Listen and contribute, because both of these elements are important in making this type of decision.

When a consensus is reached, change your own work sheet to reflect the group's decision. Note the time, calculate how long your group took to make the decision, write the number of minutes in the upper-right corner of your work sheet, and give your work sheet to the facilitator.

University Associates

RANKING CHARACTERISTICS TALLY FORM

Phase I (Autocratic Process)

Number of Times Ranked

Characteristic	No. 1	No. 2	No. 3	No. 4	No. 5
Praise					
Good Example					
Time					
Listens					
Discipline					
Environment					
Affection					
Necessities					
Risks					
Rights					
TV					

Average time for arriving at decision: _____ minutes

RANKING CHARACTERISTICS TALLY FORM

Phase II (Democratic Process)

Number of Times Ranked

Characteristic	No. 1	No. 2	No. 3	No. 4	No. 5
Prepared	___	___		___	___
Variety	___	___	___	___	___
Benefits	___	___	___	___	___
Limitations	___	___	___	___	___
Knowledge	___	___	___	___	___
Organized	___	___	___	___	___
Recognizes	___	___	___	___	___
Humor	___	___	___	___	___
Balance	___	___	___	___	___
Feedback	___	___	___	___	___
Socializes	___	___	___	___	___

Average time for arriving at decision: _____ minutes

University Associates

RANKING CHARACTERISTICS TALLY FORM

Phase III (Consensus Process)

Number of Times Ranked

Characteristic	No. 1	No. 2	No. 3	No. 4	No. 5
Energetic	_____	_____	_____	_____	_____
Resolver	_____	_____	_____	_____	_____
Organized	_____	_____	_____	_____	_____
Experienced	_____	_____	_____	_____	_____
Respected	_____	_____	_____	_____	_____
Reliable	_____	_____	_____	_____	_____
Charismatic	_____	_____	_____	_____	_____
Intelligent	_____	_____	_____	_____	_____
Creative	_____	_____	_____	_____	_____
Humor	_____	_____	_____	_____	_____
Effective	_____	_____	_____	_____	_____

Average time for arriving at decision: _____ minutes

430. THERE'S NEVER TIME TO DO IT RIGHT: A RELAY TASK

Goals

I. To help participants understand the dilemma of quality versus quantity in terms of productivity.

II. To help participants explore the consequences of focusing primarily on quality or quantity in teamwork.

Group Size

Four or more groups of four or five members each.

Time Required

Approximately one hour.

Materials

I. A copy of the Relay Task A-Team Leader's Instruction Sheet for each leader of the A Teams.

II. A copy of the Relay Task B-Team Leader's Instruction Sheet for each leader of the B Teams.

III. One copy of the Relay Task Problem Sheet for each team.

IV. A sheet of blank paper for each participant.

V. A pencil with an eraser for each participant.

VI. A writing surface for each participant.

VII. A newsprint flip chart and a felt-tipped marker.

VIII. Masking tape for posting newsprint.

Physical Setting

A room that is large enough for the groups to work without disturbing one another.

Process

I. Without revealing the goals of the activity, the facilitator divides the group into teams of four or five members each. (The ideal number is five members. If some teams have only four members, one of the four will also serve as leader of the team.)

II. The facilitator designates one person from each team as the leader. If the team has five members, the leader plays no other role.

III. Copies of the A-team leader's instruction sheet are distributed to half the leaders, and copies of the B-team leader's instruction sheet are distributed to the other half. The facilitator does not reveal that the leaders have received two types of instruction sheets.

IV. Leaders are instructed to read their sheets without allowing anyone else to see them. If clarification is needed, the leaders are instructed to walk over to the facilitator and ask their questions privately. Each participant is given a pencil and a sheet of blank paper. (Five minutes.)

V. When every leader has indicated that he or she is ready to proceed, each team is given a copy of the problem sheet.

VI. The leaders are asked to explain the task and give instructions to their team members, and the participants are instructed to wait until the facilitator tells them to begin.

VII. When all teams have indicated that they are ready to proceed, the facilitator instructs them to begin and records the time on newsprint. As each team arrives at the correct answer, the leader announces, "Our team has finished," and the facilitator records the time on newsprint. (Ten minutes.)

VIII. When every team has either found the correct answer or conceded defeat, the results of the experiment are tabulated on newsprint. The goals of the activity are explained, the facilitator reveals the differences in the leaders' instructions, and each team is identified as an A team or B team. (Ten minutes.)

IX. The facilitator leads a discussion on the following questions:

1. If your leader pressured you to finish the task, how did you react? How did the pressure affect your morale? How was your productivity affected?
2. If your leader encouraged you to take time, work carefully, and obtain the correct answer, how did you react? How did you feel when you realized that other teams would finish the problem before your team did?
3. If your leader encouraged you to concede defeat, how did you react?
4. What results did the two methods produce? What differences are evident from the tabulations?
5. What might you have done differently if you had known what the goals of the activity were?
6. In what ways can members of work teams cooperate in order to enhance both quality and quantity?

(Twenty minutes.)

Variations

I. Three-member teams can be used. In this case, one member would be the leader, another member would do the work outlined for the "first person" and "third person," and the third member would do the work outlined for the "second person" and "fourth person."

II. A problem that does not involve mathematics could be substituted for the given problem.

III. The following question can be added to the discussion between questions 5 and 6: How does your organization view the value of quantity when contrasted with quality? The participants can then be asked to give examples to illustrate their views.

IV. The following additional questions can be discussed: What are your views on focusing on quality? On quantity? What kinds of situations call for giving priority to quality? To quantity?

Submitted by Russell J. Denz.

Russell J. Denz is the director of human resources at Compton Forge, Inc., in Compton, California. He helped to found the Training and Development Club at Grand Canyon College in Phoenix, Arizona, and his primary interest is organizational behavior across wide socioeconomic strata.

RELAY TASK A·TEAM LEADER'S INSTRUCTION SHEET

Do not allow anyone else to read these instructions. Take time to read this sheet thoroughly. If you need clarification on any point, walk over to the facilitator and ask your questions in private.

Your team will be given the following problem but will not be given the answer.

First person, add:

$$
\begin{array}{r}
14 \\
62 \\
28 \\
114 \\
56 \\
921 \\
17 \\
49 \\
\hline
\end{array}
$$

Total =

Second person, multiply the above total by 256. Product = _____

Third person, subtract 384 from the above product. Difference = _____

Fourth person, divide the above difference by 16. Final Answer = 20,152

Important Note to Leader: If your team has only four members, including yourself, you must participate as a problem solver. However, you must *not* assign yourself the role of the "fourth person," because as the leader of the team you are given the solution to the fourth person's task.

Before your team members begin work on the problem, give them the following instructions:

1. You will be competing with all the other teams.

2. You will be given a problem to work on together. The most important thing is to obtain the correct answer.

3. Do not worry about how long it is taking you, because if you do not have the correct answer you will have to do the problem over again.

4. The problem is in four parts. You can decide among yourselves how to assign these parts.

5. You may ask me for suggestions, and you may ask one another for help in solving your part of the problem. If you have a calculator, you may use it. This is a team effort and the most important thing is to get a correct answer. If our team also finishes first, that is even better; but be sure to work carefully and take all the time you need.

After you have read this sheet and have clarified any questions, raise your hand to indicate to the facilitator that you are ready to proceed. When all team leaders are ready, your team will be given a copy of the problem.

You will then give the above instructions to your team and again raise your hand to indicate that your team is ready to proceed. The facilitator will tell your team when to begin.

If your team members have difficulty with the problem, feel free to discuss the task with them. You may not supply the answers, but you may offer suggestions about how to solve the problem. If your team obtains the wrong answer, you may help them discover which part of the problem was worked incorrectly.

When your team arrives at the correct answer, call out loudly enough for everyone to hear, "Our team has finished."

Remember, the correct answer is 20,152.

RELAY TASK B-TEAM LEADER'S INSTRUCTION SHEET

Do not allow anyone else to read these instructions. Take time to read this sheet thoroughly. If you need clarification on any point, walk over to the facilitator and ask your questions in private.

Your team will be given a problem to solve. You may not give the team any help or suggestions. The only instructions you may give your team are the following:

1. You will be given a simple math problem. It is divided into four parts. The person I hand it to will work the first part and hand it to someone else. That person will work the second part and hand it to another person. That person will work the third part and hand it to the last person to finish.

2. This is a very simple task and should be finished quickly. We are competing against the other teams to see who can finish first. So the important part is to work as quickly as you can.

3. You may not receive help from me or from one another. I cannot answer any questions. The object is to work quickly and quietly and get through the problem.

Important Note to Leader: If your team has only four members, including yourself, you will play the role of the "first person" in solving the problem.

After you have read this sheet and have clarified any questions, raise your hand to indicate to the facilitator that you are ready to proceed. When all team leaders are ready, your team will be given a copy of the problem.

You will then give the above instructions to your team and again raise your hand to indicate that your team is ready to proceed. The facilitator will tell your team when to begin.

While your team is working, occasionally make comments like "Now, Jane, hurry up; we want to win, you know"; "Don't spend that much time on it; after all, this is just plain old arithmetic"; or "One team has already finished. Let's try to come in second at least." Also refuse to answer any questions. The object is to put the team under pressure to finish quickly.

The correct final answer is 20,152. If the fourth person does not arrive at that answer, just hand the problem back to the first person and tell the team members they will have to check their work and find out where the error is. Then add, "But do it quickly."

When your team arrives at the correct answer, call out loudly enough for everyone to hear, "Our team has finished." If most of the other teams finish first, encourage your team to concede defeat.

Remember, the correct answer is 20,152.

RELAY TASK PROBLEM SHEET

The following problem has four parts, and four people should work on it. General instructions are given here, but you should also follow your leader's instructions.

First person, add:

```
     14
     62
     28
    114
     56
    921
     17
     49
```

    Total =

Second person, multiply the above total by 256. Product = _____

Third person, subtract 384 from the above product. Difference = _____

Fourth person, divide the above difference by 16. Final answer = _____

University Associates

431. UNSCRAMBLING THE BANK ACCOUNTS: GROUP PROBLEM SOLVING

Goals

   I. To enable participants to experience group problem-solving processes.
  II. To give participants an opportunity to observe and identify behaviors and methods that facilitate or hinder effective teamwork.
 III. To highlight the consequences of conflicts between individual objectives and team objectives.
  IV. To provide a basis for exploring means to make teamwork more effective.

Group Size

Two or more groups of five to eight members each.

Time Required

Approximately one hour.

Materials

   I. A copy of the Unscrambling the Bank Accounts Fact Sheet for each participant.
  II. A set of Unscrambling the Bank Accounts Data Cards for each group.
 III. A pencil and a sheet of blank paper for each participant.
  IV. A writing surface for each participant.
   V. A stop watch.
  VI. A copy of the Unscrambling the Bank Accounts Answer Sheet for the facilitator.
 VII. A newsprint flip chart and a felt-tipped marker.
VIII. Masking tape for posting newsprint.

Physical Setting

A room that is large enough to allow the groups to work without disturbing one another.

Process

   I. The facilitator announces the goals of the activity.
  II. Participants are divided into teams of five to eight members each.
 III. Each participant is given a copy of the fact sheet, a pencil, and a sheet of blank paper.
  IV. Each team is given one set of the data cards. The cards are distributed approximately evenly among the members of the team. The participants are told not to reveal the information on their cards to anyone else at this point.

V. The facilitator instructs the participants to study the fact sheet and the cards that were assigned to them. (Five minutes.)

VI. The facilitator asks if anyone needs clarification and deals appropriately with any questions. (Five minutes.)

VII. The facilitator explains that the participants will be timed as they unscramble the bank accounts and match the name of each account holder with the appropriate bank, account number, size of balance, and occupation. Participants are told that during the activity they may discuss the information on the cards that were assigned to them, but they may not pass the cards around for others to see. The facilitator also explains the scoring system, tells participants that no more questions will be answered, and instructs participants to raise their hands when they arrive at a solution.

VIII. The facilitator starts the stopwatch and announces that it is time to begin the activity.

IX. When a hand is raised, the facilitator makes a note of the time and then checks the answer for accuracy. If any part of the answer is wrong, the facilitator merely tells the participant or team to continue working on the problem because the answer is not correct. (Twenty-five minutes.)

X. After all teams have found the correct solution, the answers are written on newsprint. The facilitator leads a discussion on the following questions:

1. What individual behaviors and problem-solving methods facilitated the team in solving the problem? What individual behaviors and problem-solving methods hindered it?

2. At what points were you tempted to leave the team and try to solve the problem on your own? What choice did you make? How do you account for your choice?

3. When an individual dropped out of your team, how did you feel? How did you feel when the individual rejoined your group?

4. What did you learn about conflict between individual objectives and group objectives and its effect on teamwork?

5. In what ways could you make teamwork more effective in your back-home situation?

(Twenty minutes.)

Variations

I. Each member of the team could be given a set of data cards.

II. A few wild cards (which do not include pertinent information) may be added to the set of data cards. The following are examples of wild cards:

1. Pat drives a 1974 Buick.

2. Eastern Bank has fewer branches than any of the other banks.

3. Western Bank waives its normal charges for customers who maintain a balance in excess of $500.

4. Central Bank offers special discounts to senior citizens.

Submitted by John E. Hebden.

John E. Hebden, Ph.D., *is a senior lecturer in the department of business and management studies at the University of Salford in Salford, England. He is also a consultant in organization development and management organization. His major interests include issues surrounding the development of participative management styles, team building, and conflict management; organizational socialization and the growth of organizational identity; and the cross-national comparison of organizational processes. Dr. Hebden is co-author of* Pathways to Participation.

UNSCRAMBLING THE BANK ACCOUNTS FACT SHEET

The following five people have bank accounts:
Rob, Jamie, Ivy, Leslie, and Pat.

The names of their banks, listed alphabetically, are as follows:
Central, Eastern, Northern, Southern, and Western.

The following account numbers, listed in numerical order, have been issued to the account holders:
727253, 1799351, 4219530, 10429538, and 42911786.

The accounts contain the following amounts (listed in descending order of size):
$1,347.40; $550.90; $222.12; $105.00; and $25.50.

The account holders have the following occupations (listed alphabetically):
Accountant, architect, attorney, doctor, and teacher.

Instructions for Scoring

Your task is to match the name of each person with the appropriate occupation, bank, account number, and account balance.

If your team solves the problem correctly in every aspect, it will receive a score of one hundred minus the number of minutes it took to find the answer.

Each time a team turns in an answer that is not correct in every aspect, five points will be deducted from its score as it continues to try to solve the problem.

At any time, you—as an individual—may drop out of the team effort and propose your individual solution. If the first individual solution that you submit is correct in every aspect, your score will be one hundred minus half the number of minutes that were taken to solve the problem. You may then share the correct answer with your team, and your individual score will become your team's score. If your score is not correct in every aspect, you may rejoin the team and deduct ten points from the team's score (i.e., one hundred minus the number of minutes required to solve the problem minus an additional ten points). This will be your only opportunity to rejoin the team. If you choose to continue to work on your own, deduct fifteen points from your individual score. For each additional time that you turn in an incorrect answer, deduct five points from your individual score.

UNSCRAMBLING THE BANK ACCOUNTS DATA CARDS

Prior to the structured experience, the facilitator should prepare the appropriate number of sets of data cards. Each set should contain one card for each of the following pieces of information:

Pat's account number and Jamie's account number contain the same number of digits.

Leslie is an attorney.

Jamie is not an accountant.

There is a balance of $105.00 in the doctor's account.

Western Bank accounts have six digits.

Pat does not have an account with Southern Bank.

The balance in the account at Eastern Bank is $105.00.

Rob does not have an account with Southern Bank.

The doctor's account number is 42911786.

The balance in account number 4219530 is $222.12.

The balance in the accountant's account is less than $200.00.

Pat is a teacher.

The balance in the Western Bank account is more than $100.00.

The balance in Jamie's account is $550.90.

The teacher obtained a special discount with Central Bank.

Rob's account number is 10429538.

UNSCRAMBLING THE BANK ACCOUNTS ANSWER SHEET
(For the Facilitator Only)

Name	Occupation	Bank	Account No.	Balance
Rob	Accountant	Northern	10429538	$ 25.50
Jamie	Architect	Southern	1799351	550.90
Ivy	Doctor	Eastern	42911786	105.00
Leslie	Attorney	Western	727253	1,347.40
Pat	Teacher	Central	4219530	222.12

University Associates

432. SOCIETY OF TAOS: GROUP DECISION MAKING

Goals

 I. To allow the participants to experience problem-solving and decision-making strategies within a group.

 II. To offer the participants an opportunity to study how task-relevant information is shared within a group.

 III. To demonstrate the effects that individual priorities can have on group decisions.

Group Size

 Several subgroups of six or seven participants each.

Time Required

 Approximately two hours.

Materials

 I. A copy of the Society of Taos Background Sheet for each participant.

 II. One set of Society of Taos Role Sheets for each subgroup (a different sheet for each of five members) and one set for each observer.

 III. A complete set of Society of Taos Site Listings (1 through 5) for each participant.

 IV. A copy of the Society of Taos Site Map for each participant.

 V. A copy of the Society of Taos Observer Sheet for each observer.

 VI. A copy of the Society of Taos Answer Sheet for each participant.

 VII. A pencil for each participant.

 VIII. A portable writing surface for each observer.

Physical Setting

 A room in which the subgroups can work without disturbing one another. Movable chairs should be provided; tables are optional.

Process

 I. The facilitator announces that the participants will be involved in a role play concerning problem solving and decision making.

 II. The participants are assembled into subgroups of six or seven members each (five role players and one or two observers).

III. Within each subgroup the facilitator distributes handouts: a background sheet to each member, a different role sheet to each of five members, a complete set of role sheets to each observer, an observer sheet to each observer, a complete set of site listings to each member, and a site map to each member. In addition, each participant is given a pencil, and each observer is given a portable writing surface.

IV. The facilitator asks the participants to start reading their handouts. The role players are also asked to spend a few minutes studying their roles and thinking about behaviors that might be consistent with those roles. While the role players are studying, the facilitator meets with the observers in private to answer any questions that they have about their assignment; after ensuring that the observers understand what they are to do, the facilitator sends them back to their subgroups to finish reading their handouts. (Ten minutes.)

V. The facilitator answers questions about the role-play task as necessary, emphasizes that the role players must maintain their roles throughout the upcoming meeting, and asks the subgroups to begin. If the facilitator notices that any subgroup completes the task early, its members may be instructed to (1) discuss among themselves how productive they were and/or (2) share their role sheets with one another. (One hour.)

VI. After each subgroup has completed the task and arrived at an answer, all subgroups are instructed to stop their role plays. The facilitator distributes copies of the answer sheet, announces the two wrong answers, and briefly explains why they are wrong.

VII. The total group is reassembled, and the observers are asked to share the contents of their observer sheets. (Ten minutes.)

VIII. The facilitator leads a concluding discussion by asking the following questions:
1. How satisfied were you with your group's decision?
2. How comfortable were you with the process your group used to arrive at the decision?
3. How is what happened in your group similar to what you have experienced in other decision-making situations? How is it different? What conclusions can you draw?
4. How might you have changed this process to increase your comfort and satisfaction and those of your fellow group members?
5. How might you use what you learned to improve problem solving and decision making at home or at work?

Variations

I. The facilitator can tell the subgroups that they are in competition with one another and that the first subgroup to submit a correct answer "wins."

II. One of the roles can be changed to incorporate a vested interest in choosing one of the two wrong sites (for example, by having one of the committee members own one of the sites).

III. If the group is large enough, the facilitator can assemble an executive board to whom the subgroups can appeal about altering some of the board decisions described in the role sheets, or the facilitator can create a role sheet for an executive-board member and include one such member in each subgroup.

IV. Criteria and site descriptions can be added to or deleted from the original activity to shorten or lengthen it.

V. The issues of power and influence can be addressed. In this case the facilitator can add the following questions to the observer sheet:
1. What individual priorities are taking precedence as the group makes its decision?
2. How would you characterize the influence that is being used?

Submitted by Michael W. Cooney

Michael W. Cooney is the assistant superintendent of manufacturing at the Delco Remy Division of General Motors Corporation in Anderson, Indiana. For several years he was a member of the design team for the Delco Remy plant in Albany, Georgia (the leading participative-management plant in the General Motors system). Mr. Cooney is a part-time consultant and former internal consultant and statistical-process-control coordinator.

SOCIETY OF TAOS BACKGROUND SHEET

You belong to the Society of Taos, a five-hundred-member social organization that is increasing membership at a rate of 10 percent each year. A maximum membership of one thousand was established two years ago. The rapid growth of the society is probably due to bylaws that make membership available to anyone, regardless of race, sex, or creed, provided that he or she pays a $1500 initiation fee and agrees to pay monthly dues of $90 as well as $50 per month for food services.

The lease on the society's present lodge runs out in nine months and will not be renewed; consequently, the society must find and relocate to a new lodge within this time frame. In an effort to address this problem, the society chose you and four other members to serve on a committee to select a different lodge. The selection must meet several criteria that are included in your handouts and in those distributed to your fellow committee members. Five site possibilities are on the market, and the committee is meeting today to make the selection from among these five. You will be given pertinent data about each of the five sites, and you are to assume that all of these data are correct. In making your final choice, you and your fellow committee members must work as a group; there must be substantial agreement when the decision is made. You should note that there is not one *right* choice, but there is at least one *wrong*choice.

SOCIETY OF TAOS ROLE SHEET 1

You have been a member of the society since it was formed in 1972. Having watched a steady growth in membership, you are glad to see plans to purchase a different lodge. You are not sure, however, if the $400,000 budget allocated by the society's executive board will allow the purchase and renovation of a site that will make all of the members proud. The issue of pride in the lodge has become quite important to you; you have lived on West Oak Avenue all of your life and have watched the neighborhood decline badly in the last ten years. As a result, the lodge has become your home away from home.

You have surveyed the membership and found that most members are more interested in the outside appearance of the lodge and its landscaping than in the number of rooms available. This is probably due to the fact that 35 percent of the members live on the west side of town and, like you, have suffered declining property values or are afraid they will in the near future. Although this is a large percentage of the membership, even more— almost 50 percent—live on the north side of town. Many homes on the north side are known for their elaborate landscaping, especially during the spring when thousands of flowers are in bloom.

University Associates

SOCIETY OF TAOS ROLE SHEET 2

You have been a member of the society since 1978. You decided to join when you found out that several members had handicaps similar to yours. You had polio as a child and now must use a walker. Being around others with similar problems, particularly the paraplegic Viet Nam veterans who belong to the society, helps you live with your handicap more easily. Although 5 percent of the society members are handicapped, not many use the present lodge during the summer because it is not air conditioned. The lack of air conditioning might also explain why older members seldom use the lodge in summertime.

You are hoping that more arts and crafts activities will be offered in the new lodge; in fact, you have volunteered to help set up a room for this purpose. The society's executive board has determined that the new lodge must have a minimum of 25,000 square feet, almost twice as much square footage as the present lodge; therefore, there should be plenty of space to set up the kind of room you envision.

Another of your concerns with regard to the new lodge is the composition of the parking lot. It is difficult for you and the other handicapped members to cope with unpaved or gravel surfaces.

_____

SOCIETY OF TAOS ROLE SHEET 3

You have been a member of the society since 1972. Having watched a steady growth in membership, you realize that lodge space is a problem. You are not sure if the budget for the new lodge is reasonable, though, since the average member is by no means wealthy. In addition, most members are over forty and are probably earning as much as they ever will. Still another problem is the fact that the society is barely able to pay the $1500-per-month utility bills for the present lodge, which is only about half the size of the proposed new lodge. Of course, money to pay the utility bills would be more available if all members would pay their monthly dues on time; last month almost 20 percent of the dues were delinquent.

Because you are a businessperson and believe that you have a lot of business sense, you are glad you are on the site committee. Maybe you can help the society avoid some legal problems. You have checked and found zoning to be no problem since no public sales will occur in the new lodge. However, if the arts and crafts activities continue to expand, there has been talk of opening a small consignment shop. You will push for such a shop to be located elsewhere and to stand on its own financially.

While checking zoning laws, you found an important city ordinance that you did not know existed. The city requires a building to have twelve parking spaces for every five thousand square feet. Your own business is located in a building with 15,000 square feet and only twenty parking spaces; the ordinance requirement means that you should have thirty-six. In addition, the new city administration is starting to get tough on illegal parking.

SOCIETY OF TAOS ROLE SHEET 4

You have been a member of the Society of Taos since 1980. You joined the society when you learned that "Taos" is an Indian word meaning *people*. You have always had an active social life, so it seemed right to join "the society of people." You have had no regrets.

A year ago you were named the society's social director. That happened after a referendum to get rid of the society's liquor license, an action that provoked over one hundred members to threaten resignation. When the issue finally came to a vote, 280 members voted in favor of keeping the license and fifty-seven voted in favor of relinquishing it. Ultimately, the society's executive board voted 6 to 0 to keep the liquor license.

As social director you have been active, but find it difficult to satisfy many of the members. The majority seem to want golf or tennis outings, so it is important to you that the new lodge be located close to an area of existing golf or tennis facilities.

Another of your concerns is the fact that in ten months you will be hosting a convention of members of your society and similar social organizations across the state. You plan on breaking in the new lodge with a dinner for over 1,400 people who have already made reservations for this convention; consequently, it is critical that the new lodge have adequate kitchen and dining facilities.

SOCIETY OF TAOS ROLE SHEET 5

You have been a member of the society for the past year. You are the newest member to be selected for the site committee. Your selection was probably more because you are a member of the City Council than because of anything you have done for the society. Ever since you joined you have heard how strong the society is and how rapidly it is growing. You have checked the records for the last three years and have found that almost 10 percent of the membership quits each year, while new members join in numbers that not only replace those who quit but also increase the total membership by 10 percent.

Due to the effort you had to put into your City Council work in the past several months, you have had little time to spend dealing with issues concerning the society. Your pet project on the City Council has been the sponsoring of a bill that makes it illegal to sell or distribute liquor or to hold a liquor license within ten blocks of a school, college, or church. This bill was just passed, and you feel good about your victory.

On the home front, though, you are not too crazy about your luck. Last year the Environmental Protection Agency started investigating rumors that Lake Pueblo was covering one of the largest toxic-waste dumps in the country. As the investigation uncovered more and more evidence, you deciced to move from the lake-front house that you built four years ago. Your new house is on the corner of Highway 101 and Arrowhead Drive, and last week it was broken into and vandalized. After this happened you learned that in the last few months your neighborhood has become the highest crime area of the city; statistics show that the crime rate began increasing with the opening of the new shopping center near your home.

SOCIETY OF TAOS OBSERVER SHEET

Instructions: While the group members are studying their roles prior to the beginning of the simulation, read your copies of the background sheet and their role sheets and review the site map so that you can become acquainted with the situation involved. During the simulation you are to observe the group members' interactions carefully and write answers to the following questions. Later you will be asked to share your answers with the total group. If you need clarification of this assignment, consult the facilitator in private; do *not* share the content of this sheet with the role players.

1. How are the members choosing to share relevant information from their role sheets?
2. How are the members weeding out irrelevant information?
3. What problems are arising because of individual priorities? How is the group resolving these problems? How are they going about the process of meeting one another's needs?
4. What problem-solving and decision-making strategies is the group using to make its final decision about a site?

SOCIETY OF TAOS SITE LISTING 1

Address: 2150 W. Poplar Avenue

Bldg. Size: 25,000 sq. ft.   # Rooms: 14

Const. Type: Brick   Year Built: 1970

Sewage: City   Heat: Gas

Water: City   Air Cond.: Yes

Gas: Yes   Wtr. Heater: Gas

Insul.: Yes   220: Yes

Approx. Util. Cost: $1600/mo.

Mortgagee: R & N   Mortgage Bal.: $123,450

Price: $250,000

Lot Size: 2.5 acres

Possession: Immediate

Rest Rms.: 8

Kitchen: Yes

Load Dock: No

Drive: Asphalt

Parking: 90 spaces

Total Assess.: $187,000

Remarks: Includes restaurant equipment. Renovation: $100,000.
Renovation time: 6 months. Renovation includes:
enlarging kitchen, replacing air conditioning unit.

SOCIETY OF TAOS SITE LISTING 2

Address: 3650 N. Arrowhead Drive
Bldg. Size: 30,000 sq. ft.
Const. Type: Brick
Sewage: City
Water: City
Gas:
Insul.:
Approx. Util. Cost: $1700/mo.
Mortgagee:

#Rooms:
Year Built: 1970
Heat: Gas
Air Cond.: No
Wtr. Heater: Gas
220: Yes

Mortgage Bal.: None

Price: $200,000
Lot Size: 2 acres
Possession: 90 days
Rest Rms.: 8
Kitchen: No
Load Dock: No
Drive: Asphalt
Parking: 75 spaces
Total Assess.: $90,000

Remarks: Renovation $200,000. Renovation time: 180 days (note renovation may begin before taking final possession).
Renovation includes: replacing and recaulking all windows, installing kitchen facilities, constructing dining facility and two large meetings rooms on first floor.

SOCIETY OF TAOS SITE LISTING 3

Address: 536 W. Oak Avenue
Bldg. Size: 25,000 sq. ft.
Const. Type: Brick
Sewage: City
Water: City
Gas:
Insul.:
Approx. Util. Cost: $1600/mo.
Mortgagee:

Rooms:
Year Built: 1945
Heat: Gas
Air Cond.: No
Wtr. Heater: Elec.
220: Yes

Mortgage Bal.:

Price: $175,000
Lot Size: 2 acres
Possession: Immediate
Rest Rms.:
Kitchen: Small
Load Dock: No
Drive: Gravel
Parking: 64 spaces
Total Assess.:

Remarks: Roof leaks. Renovation $200,000. Renovation time: 8 months.
Renovation includes: replacing roof, enlarging kitchen, replacing windows.

University Associates

SOCIETY OF TAOS SITE LISTING 4

Address: 2020 S. Arrowhead Drive		Price: $275,000
Bldg. Size: 30,000 sq. ft.	# Rooms: 17	Lot Size: 2 acres
Const. Type: Brick	Year Built: 1957	Possession: 90 days
Sewage: City	Heat: Elec.	Rest Rms.:
Water: Well	Air Cond.: Yes	Kitchen: 2
Gas:	Wtr. Heater:	Load Dock: 2
Insul.:	220:	Drive: Gravel/dirt
Approx. Util. Cost: $1800/mo.		Parking: 150 spaces
Mortgagee: HFCL	Mortgage Bal.: $175,000	Total Assess.: $245,000

Remarks: Loading docks front-left corner (could be removed later). Renovation: $40,000. Renovation time: 90 days. Renovation includes: adding 2 restrooms.

SOCIETY OF TAOS SITE LISTING 5

Address: 5300 S. Main Street		Price: $225,000
Bldg. Size: 25,000 sq. ft.	# Rooms:	Lot Size: 3 acres
Const. Type: Alum.	Year Built: 1923	Possession: Immediate
Sewage: City	Heat: Steam/water	Rest Rms.:
Water: Well	Air Cond.: No	Kitchen: Large
Gas:	Wtr. Heater:	Load Dock: No
Insul:	220:	Drive: Paved
Approx. Util. Cost: $1600/mo.		Parking: 107 spaces
Mortgagee:	Mortgage Bal.: None	Total Assess.: $177,000

Remarks: Heating system needs to be replaced. Building remodeled 1952. Renovation: $220,000. Renovation time: 8 months. Renovation includes: installing new electric heating system, replacing roof, and upgrading kitchen.

SOCIETY OF TAOS SITE MAP

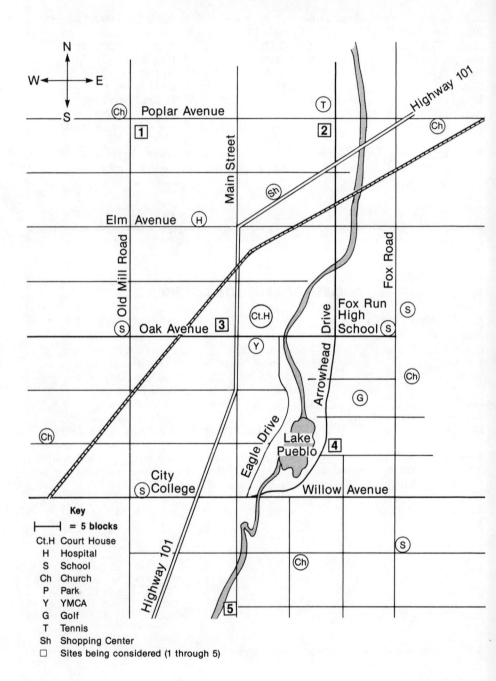

Key

├──┤ = 5 blocks

Ct.H Court House
H   Hospital
S   School
Ch   Church
P   Park
Y   YMCA
G   Golf
T   Tennis
Sh   Shopping Center
☐   Sites being considered (1 through 5)

SOCIETY OF TAOS ANSWER SHEET

Requirements (Needs)	Site 1	Site 2	Site 3	Site 4	Site 5
Occupancy in 9 months	6 months	Less than 9 months	8 months	6 months	8 months
Budget $400,000	$350,000	$400,000	$375,000	$315,000	$445,000
Liquor license	No	Yes	Yes	Yes	Yes
Building size Min. 25,000 sq. ft.	25,000 sq. ft.	30,000 sq. ft.	25,000 sq. ft.	30,000 sq. ft.	25,000 sq. ft.
12 parking spaces per 5,000 sq. ft.	90 Spaces	75 Spaces	64 Spaces	150 Spaces	107 Spaces
Kitchen facilities	Yes	Renovation	Yes/Renovation	2	Large

Site 1 is unacceptable. Church is less than ten blocks from building; cannot have liquor license.

Site 5 is unacceptable. Does not meet budget requirements.

Sites 2, 3, and 4 are all acceptable. Final selection depends on accommodating individual group members' needs.

433. QUANTITY VERSUS QUALITY: MATCHING PERCEPTIONS OF PERFORMANCE

Goals

VIII. To enable managers to compare their perceptions with those of peers regarding the way each of them views the relative importance of quantity and quality in productivity.

  II. To help managers assess the accuracy and consistency of their individual perceptions by determining how closely they align with the perceptions of their peers.

Group Size

Any number of triads of managers who work together in an organization or who know each other.

Time Required

One to one and one-half hours.

Materials

   I. One copy of the Quantity Versus Quality Information Sheet for each participant.

  II. One copy of the Quantity Versus Quality Matrix-Instruction Sheet for each participant.

 III. One copy of the Quantity Versus Quality Matrix for each participant.

  IV. A pencil for each participant.

   V. A portable writing surface for each participant.

  VI. A newsprint flip chart and a felt-tipped marker.

 VII. Masking tape for posting newsprint.

Physical Setting

A room that is large enough to allow triads to work without disturbing one another.

Process

   I. The facilitator explains the goals of the activity but is careful not to show a preference for either quality or quantity.

  II. The facilitator divides the group into triads and asks each participant to sit facing the other two members of the triad.

 III. Each participant receives a copy of the Quantity Versus Quality Information Sheet and is instructed to read it.

  IV. Each participant receives a copy of the Quantity Versus Quality Matrix-Instruction Sheet.

V. Each participant receives a copy of the Quantity Versus Quality Matrix, a pencil, and a portable writing surface.

VI. Participants are instructed to work independently to complete the matrix according to the instructions printed on the matrix-instruction sheet. The facilitator remains available to answer questions. (Ten minutes.)

VII. When all participants have completed their matrices according to the instruction sheet, the facilitator gives them the following additional instructions:

Share the ratings you gave the other two members of your triad with those members. They will copy the first three ratings that you selected onto their matrices in the column underneath your name. Members of your triad will take turns sharing their ratings until all of you have completed your matrices. Each person's matrix will then contain thirteen numbers.

VIII. When all participants have completed the task, the facilitator asks them to compare their matrices with those of the other members of their triads to determine the "accuracy" and "consistency" of the scores, using the operational definitions of "accuracy" and "consistency" that are listed on the matrix sheet. (Five minutes.)

IX. The facilitator gives the participants the following instructions:

1. Provide feedback to the other members of your triad on why you rated them the way you did.

2. Discuss the implications of the degrees of accuracy and consistency that were discovered in your comparison of matrices.

(Five minutes.)

X. The facilitator reassembles the total group, leads a discussion on the following questions, and records salient points on newsprint.

1. How did you feel about rating others?

2. How did you feel about being rated?

3. How did you react to the ratings you received?

4. How did you feel about the degrees of accuracy and consistency of the perceptions in your triad?

(Twenty minutes.)

XI. The facilitator leads a discussion on the importance of quantity and quality in the participants' organizations and asks the following questions:

1. In what ways does your organization value quantity? Quality?

2. How are quantity and quality rewarded in your organization?

3. What are the differences between the way your organization purports to value quantity and the way it is rewarded?

4. What are the differences between the way your organization purports to value quality and the way it is rewarded?

5. What can be done in your organization to improve the balance of quantity and quality?

(Twenty minutes.)

Variations

I. After step XI the facilitator can solicit examples of ways the participants have managed subordinates in order to enable them to produce a greater quantity on schedule without sacrificing quality or to enable them to maintain quality without sacrificing quantity. The facilitator can record the examples on newsprint and give the newsprint to one of the participants so that the examples can be reproduced later and distributed to the participants.

II. Variables in addition to quantity and quality can be used for perception comparisons.

Submitted by Allen J. Schuh.

Allen J. Schuh, Ph.D., is a professor of management sciences in the School of Business and Economics at California State University, Hayward. He also consults with public and private organizations in the areas of individual, group, and organizational practices. Dr. Schuh's primary interests are in effectiveness evaluation and the training of individuals, groups, and organizations. He has published over thirty articles in those subject areas.

QUANTITY VERSUS QUALITY INFORMATION SHEET

Assume that each person in your triad has been placed in charge of a task force that reports to top management. Although the problem that each task force is studying is not severe enough to cause the demise of the organization, top management has informed each of you that it expects your recommendations to be presented before it implements a new inventory system.

As the deadline for the recommendations approaches, it is obvious that none of the task forces can submit a complete report on time. Each task-force manager will have to decide whether to submit a substandard report on the date requested or to delay the report until after the new inventory system has been implemented. Task-force members are complaining that they have already given too much time to the task force and cannot continue to neglect their job responsibilities.

QUANTITY VERSUS QUALITY MATRIX-INSTRUCTION SHEET

Instructions: Consider how you believe each person (including yourself) in your triad would respond in the situation described on the Quantity Versus Quality Information Sheet. Rate each of them on a nine-point scale as follows:

1 = The person would submit a report on schedule regardless of the content of the report.

5 = The person believes in an equal balance between quantity and quality and would delay the report long enough to prepare an acceptable recommendation.

9 = The person would maximize the quality of the report even if doing so would delay the recommendations well past the due date.

The other numbers represent varying degrees of these tendencies, but any number over "1" means that the report would not be submitted by the due date.

Write the first names of all three members of your triad in alphabetical order as shown on the sample matrix. (Pat completed the sample matrix. The other members of Pat's triad are Lynn and Terry. The alphabetical order of their names ensures that each member's matrix will show the names in the same order. Notice that each name appears twice: once across the top and again down the side.) In this description of your task, the *vertical* columns are referred to as "columns," and the *horizontal* rows are referred to as "rows."

In the column underneath your name, write the numbers that you assigned to each person.

Now look at the column on the right, headed "I think they would rate themselves." Choose numbers from the nine-point scale that indicate the way you think the other members perceive themselves. Write those numbers in the rows that represent the other two members of your triad.

In the row labeled "I think they would rate me," write numbers underneath the names of the other members according to the way you think they are rating you. Your matrix should now contain seven numbers, as illustrated in the sample matrix.

Wait for further instructions from the facilitator.

Pat's Sample Matrix

		Names of members of Triad			I think they would rate themselves
		Lynn	*Pat*	*Terry*	
Names of Members of Triad	*Lynn*		4		5
	Pat		7		—
	Terry		2		1
	I think they would rate me	9	—	6	

QUANTITY VERSUS QUALITY MATRIX

	Names of Members of Triad			I think they would rate themselves
Names of Members of Triad				
I think they would rate me				

In comparing your ratings, use the following operational definitions:

Accuracy—the extent to which predicted ratings match actual ratings.

Consistency—the extent to which triad members agree on the ratings for any one member regardless of the accuracy of the rating.

434. INSTANT SURVEY:
CREATING AGENDA FOR TEAM BUILDING

Goals

I. To generate working agenda for a meeting in which the participants will discuss their concerns about work-group issues that will face them in the future.

II. To determine in a nonthreatening way the hidden needs and concerns of the participants.

III. To present for discussion the concerns of all the participants.

IV. To provide participants with a method for creating participant-owned, meaningful agenda that will assist facilitators in designing team-building sessions for the participants.

Group Size

From three to ten subgroups of three to seven members each. (Five members per subgroup is optimal.)

Time Required

From one and one-half to two hours.

Materials

I. One 3'' x 5'' index card for each participant.

II. One 5'' x 8'' index card for each participant.

III. One pencil for each participant.

IV. A newsprint flip chart and a felt-tipped marker for the facilitator and for each subgroup.

V. Masking tape for posting newsprint.

Physical Setting

A room that is large enough to allow the groups to work without disturbing one another.

Process

I. The facilitator announces the goals of the activity and explains that work units often fail to discuss the private needs and concerns of their members. The facilitator also explains that hidden agenda can interfere with productivity and a positive team climate.

II. Each participant is given one 3'' x 5'' card, one 5'' x 8'' card, and a pencil.

III. Participants are asked to think of the personal challenges they face as individual members of their basic work groups and to focus on their individual abilities to meet those challenges. Each participant is asked to silently identify one change in his or her abilities or characteristics that would enhance the effectiveness of his or her work group. Focusing on that change, the participant is instructed to express the need for the change by writing a sentence starting with "I need" on the 3" x 5" card.

IV. Participants are asked to think of the challenges their basic work groups face in performing their functions. Each participant is asked to silently identify one change in his or her work group's characteristics that is needed to enhance the effectiveness of the group's work. Focusing on that one need, the participant is instructed to express it by writing a sentence starting with "We need" on the 5" x 8" card.

V. The facilitator then randomly divides the participants into subgroups of three to seven members each and identifies each subgroup by a name or a number. (If the total group consists of fifteen or more participants, no subgroup should have fewer than five members.)

VI. Each subgroup places all its cards (both small and large) in one stack and writes the subgroup's name or number on the top card. Each subgroup trades its stack of cards with another subgroup.

VII. Each subgroup is given a newsprint flipchart and felt-tipped marker and is asked to think of itself as meeting to discuss the results of an anonymous survey about its needs and concerns.

VIII. Each subgroup is instructed to review the cards, discuss them, prioritize them, and plan a report on the findings. The facilitator asks participants *not* to deal with their own concerns but to consider only the concerns written on the cards. Each subgroup selects one member to report the findings, and the facilitator encourages the subgroups to use the newsprint flip charts in their discussions. (Forty-five minutes.)

IX. The total group is reassembled, and the representatives of the subgroups take turns reporting their findings. The facilitator summarizes the reports on newsprint and posts the newsprint. (Fifteen minutes.)

X. The facilitator leads a discussion about the findings, and participants are asked to identify the patterns that emerged. (Fifteen minutes.)

XI. The facilitator suggests that these needs could become the agenda for a team-building session and leads a discussion on the following questions:

1. In what ways would these agenda need to be changed for a team-building session with your basic work group?
2. How would you prioritize these agenda for a team-building session with your basic work group?
3. What items would need to be added for your basic work group?
4. What problems would be encountered if these agenda were presented to your basic work group as its agenda for a team-building session?

(Fifteen minutes.)

Variations

   I. In a team-building effort, this activity can be used as the first part of the first day's session. A second part could focus on the specific issues identified in the first part.

  II. If time is limited, the participants can make up only one type of card: either "I need" or "We need."

 III. The "I need" card can be used for generating agenda for any type of seminar. The card would read, "If this seminar is to be successful for me, I need..."

Submitted by Charles A. Cotton.

Charles A. Cotton, Ph.D., *is an associate professor in the School of Business, Queen's University, Ontario, Canada. He is also chairman of Queen's Programs for Management and is currently developing management and executive seminars within Queen's School of Business. Dr. Cotton specializes in leadership development, organizational behavior, and conflict management. He is a former head of the department of military leadership and management at the Royal Military College of Canada.*

435. WINTERSET HIGH SCHOOL: AN INTERGROUP-CONFLICT SIMULATION

Goals

 I. To provide participants with an opportunity to practice a conflict-management strategy.

 II. To examine ways that occupational stereotyping can contribute to organizational conflict.

Group Size

One or more groups of seven to fifteen members each.

Time Required

Approximately two and one-half hours.

Materials

 I. A copy of the Winterset High School Background Sheet for each participant.

 II. A copy of the Winterset High School Principal's Role Sheet for each participant who plays the role of principal.

 III. Enough copies of the Winterset High School Guidance Counselor's Role Sheet for approximately half of the other participants.

 IV. Enough copies of the Winterset High School Maintenance Staff's Role Sheet for the remaining participants.

 V. A pencil and several sheets of blank paper for each participant.

 VI. A clipboard for each participant.

 VII. A newsprint flip chart and a felt-tipped marker for the facilitator and for each team of guidance counselors and each team of maintenance personnel.

 VIII. Masking tape for posting newsprint.

Physical Setting

Movable chairs for participants and a room that is large enough to allow the groups to work without disturbing one another.

Process

 I. The facilitator explains the goals of the activity.

 II. Each participant is given a copy of the background sheet and is asked to read it. (Five minutes.)

III. The total group is divided into subgroups consisting of seven to fifteen members each. One member of each subgroup is selected by the group to play the role of principal. The facilitator assigns about half of the others to the role of guidance counselor, and the remaining participants are assigned to the role of maintenance staff. (From three to seven people can participate as guidance counselors, and from three to seven people can participate as maintenance personnel.)

IV. Each participant is given a copy of the appropriate role sheet, a clipboard, a pencil, and several sheets of blank paper and is asked to read the role sheet. Counselors and maintenance people are asked to write down some additional suggestions for solving the problem. (Ten minutes.)

V. The guidance counselors in each subgroup are instructed to discuss the conflict and plan a strategy for resolving the conflict, and the maintenance staff in each subgroup is instructed to meet separately and plan its strategy.

VI. While the counselors and maintenance staffs are planning their strategies, the facilitator meets in a separate area with all the principals to explain and clarify the process of the activity. A newsprint flip chart and a felt-tipped marker is given to each principal. The facilitator instructs the principals to copy the questions from their role sheets onto newsprint. Each principal copies the list twice (once for the counselors and once for the maintenance staff).

VII. About ten minutes into the discussion, the facilitator interrupts the counselors and asks each counseling team to meet with its principal. The maintenance staffs continue with their planning. Each principal meets with his or her counselors in a separate area and tries to persuade them to participate in an intergroup-development program with the maintenance staff. Each principal presents the team of counselors with the questions on newsprint. As the counselors respond to the questions, their answers are listed on the newsprint, and the newsprint is given to the counselors for further study and elaboration of answers. (Twenty minutes.)

VIII. The principals are instructed to meet with their maintenance staffs and make their presentations while the counseling teams continue their discussions. Principals try to persuade the maintenance staffs to participate in the intergroup-development program. They also present the staffs with the same questions on newsprint that they presented to the counseling teams. Answers are listed on the newsprint, and each principal gives the newsprint to the maintenance staff. (Twenty minutes.)

IX. Each counseling team exchanges newsprint with the corresponding maintenance staff. Each group works independently and makes notes on similarities and disparities in the answers proposed by the two groups. Members of each group are allowed to ask for clarification from the other group. Principals facilitate the clarification process. (Fifteen minutes.)

X. Each principal meets jointly with the team of counselors and the maintenance staff. The participants review the list of questions and determine which answers they can agree on and which remain as obstacles. (Ten minutes.)

XI. The total group is reassembled. As each subgroup of counselors and maintenance staff presents its agreed-on answers, the facilitator lists them on newsprint. The results are tabulated or summarized. (Five minutes.)

XII. As each subgroup presents its conflicting answers, the facilitator lists them on newsprint. Each subgroup is assigned one of these conflicting answers and is instructed to try to resolve the conflict. Principals ask their groups to consider the five items that are listed under item VI of the principal's role sheet. (Fifteen minutes.)

XIII. The total group is reassembled. As each subgroup presents its solutions, the facilitator posts them on newsprint. The facilitator leads a discussion of the following questions:

1. How would you describe your behavior and the behavior of others in this conflict situation?
2. What was the most difficult part of arriving at solutions that were acceptable to both factions? The easiest?
3. What was similar to or different from your experience in actual conflict situations?
4. How did occupational stereotyping contribute to the difficulty in arriving at solutions? In what other kinds of ways might such stereotyping cause or add to organizational conflict? What can be done to decrease occupational stereotyping?
5. What insights or methods arising from this activity might you be able to use in future conflict resolution?

(Fifteen minutes.)

Variations

I. Some of the counselors can be instructed to "side" with the maintenance staff, and some members of the maintenance staff can be instructed to "side" with the counselors.

II. One participant from each group could be assigned to play the role of a graduate student. The student would be instructed by the facilitator to try to persuade the maintenance staff that the project was worth the Saturday work.

Submitted by Charles E. List.

Charles E. List, Ph.D., *serves as an adjunct faculty instructor with four colleges and universities and provides management and organization development facilitation for a wide variety of organizations. His specialties include conflict resolution, performance standards, and team building. Dr. List is an accredited professional in human resources (Personnel Accreditation Institute, American Society for Personnel Administration) and is listed in* Who's Who in the Midwest.

WINTERSET HIGH SCHOOL BACKGROUND SHEET

Several graduate students from the sociology department of State University asked the principal of Winterset High School for permission to conduct a research project at the school. They wanted to open the school on Saturdays to teach remedial reading, writing, and mathematical skills to children who were having problems in these areas and to semiliterate adults.

Although no government funding was available for the project, the graduate students had been promised that school supplies would be donated by a local business. The graduate students would take turns bringing homemade chili con carne or other foods that could be stored in the refrigerator and heated on the stove in the school cafeteria. Fifteen classrooms would be needed, and graduate students would volunteer their time to teach the classes.

The principal was delighted with the offer and told the graduate students that the school's guidance counselors would have to be consulted but an answer would be forthcoming shortly. The principal wanted the counselors to coordinate the program with the graduate students.

The counselors liked the idea and developed an action plan and check list for implementing the program. One of the items on the check list was to arrange for the maintenance staff to provide necessary services (e.g., unlocking and locking the doors and cleaning the facilities at the end of the day) on Saturdays. They made an appointment to discuss the program with the supervisor and several other members of the maintenance staff.

When the counselors presented the proposal, the response from the maintenance staff was hostile. The maintenance staff refused to work on Saturdays and would not budge from this position.

After the counselors reported the maintenance staff's position to the principal, several meetings were scheduled. The principal was confident that the intergroup conflict could be resolved in a cooperative and collaborative manner. First, the principal would meet with the counselors; then the principal would meet with the maintenance staff; later, the principal would meet together with both groups.

WINTERSET HIGH SCHOOL PRINCIPAL'S ROLE SHEET

You hope that the counselors and maintenance staff can work out an acceptable solution and that the remedial school program can be implemented. However, you do not want to force either group to make concessions. Your objective is to facilitate a mutually agreeable solution.

As you review some notes you took in a consulting-skills laboratory, you notice the following paragraph, which expresses the way you feel:

Lawrence and Lorsch,[1] in their differentiation-integration model, have clearly demonstrated that units of organizations are and should be different. When units have differing tasks, goals, personnel, time constraints, and structures, the functioning of these units is bound to be different. The issue is not how to make all the units the same, but how to develop an integrated process that allows these contrasting units to work together. One strategy for developing greater integration between work units is an intergroup development program.

You plan to speak with each group individually and to persuade each group to participate in an intergroup development program. In planning the program, you devise the following intervention:

I. Establish the following ground rule: Both groups should agree to adopt a problem-solving stance, rather than to accuse or fix blame.

II. On newsprint, copy the following list twice for separate presentations to the two groups:

   A. What actions did the other group engage in that created problems for us in this Saturday-program situation?

   B. What actions did we engage in that might have created problems for the other group regarding the Saturday program?

   C. What characteristics have been evident in the other group's behavior in this problem?

   D. What characteristics have been evident in our group's behavior in this problem?

   E. How do we think the other group will describe our behavior in this problem?

   F. What would each group need to do to enable both groups to work together effectively?

III. Answers formulated by each group will be listed on newsprint, and the two groups will exchange newsprint.

IV. Each group will review the work of the other group and may ask for clarification on any point. Each group will note which answers from the other group are in agreement with its own answers and which are different.

V. Both groups and the principal will meet jointly to identify the answers on which both groups agree. Answers that still need work will be considered jointly by members from both groups.

VI. As the groups work jointly on solutions to answers that were different, they should consider the following items:

---

[1]P.R. Lawrence and J.W. Lorsch (1969). *Developing Organizations: Diagnosis and Action.* Reading, MA: Addison-Wesley.

A. What the problem is,
B. What actions should be taken,
C. Who will be responsible for each action,
D. What the schedule is, and
E. What can be done to keep the problem from reoccurring.

You plan to use all of your facilitating skills to make this intervention successful.

WINTERSET HIGH SCHOOL GUIDANCE COUNSELOR'S ROLE SHEET

You hold a master's degree and are one of several guidance counselors for Winterset High School. You not only counsel students about vocational opportunities, but you counsel problem students with whom the teachers are not qualified to deal. Therefore, you and the other counselors consider yourselves a special group of professionals. You do not teach any classes and enjoy a great deal of flexibility in your schedule. Your supervisor, who is referred to as your "group coordinator," reports directly to the principal of the high school. All the counselors consider themselves as liberals, and they advocate change that will benefit all the citizens in the community. You are enthusiastic about the proposed Saturday program.

You think the maintenance staff is overpaid. You perceive these employees as too conservative and believe they have an unsympathetic attitude toward disadvantaged citizens. Your private opinion of them is that they are "prejudiced common laborers."

Nevertheless, you expected them to welcome the opportunity to be paid overtime wages for working on Saturdays. After all (so you imagine), the extra money would help to pay for many of the things they must be striving for. You feel angry and frustrated about their refusal to work on Saturdays.

You, of course, would not be working on Saturdays and would not be present to deal with the maintenance people if they were forced to do the Saturday work. Therefore, you are concerned about problems they might create for the graduate students. You perceive these people as being arrogant because they belong to a union that is different from the teachers' union and are exempt from some of the requirements imposed on the teachers.

When the principal of Winterset High School asks for a meeting with the guidance counselors, you are obligated to attend. As the counselors search for a resolution to the problem, the following suggestions will probably be considered:

1. Make the maintenance staff understand the financial benefits of working on Saturdays.
2. Persuade the maintenance staff that the Saturday students are serious students who will not create a lot of work for the maintenance people.
3. Schedule only two maintenance people to work on Saturdays and hire high school students to assist.
4. Rotate the Saturday work so that no maintenance person will have to work every Saturday.
5. Use disposable plates, cups, and forks so that dishwashing is not necessary.
6. Give the maintenance staff a free lunch on Saturdays.

WINTERSET HIGH SCHOOL MAINTENANCE STAFF'S ROLE SHEET

You are a high-school graduate who has a well-paying job as a maintenance person at Winterset High School. The union you belong to is different from the teachers' union, and you do not consider yourself part of the school staff.

You think that the school staff is too liberal and that the students should be controlled. No one seems to care how the building is left at the end of the day. Everyone knows that the maintenance staff will clean it thoroughly before morning. Whenever you catch students writing on the wall or otherwise damaging the school, the counselors simply talk to them sympathetically and send them on their way.

This job was not your first choice, but you do not resent putting in five days a week in order to make a good living. But now the counselors are wanting you to work on Saturday. You will not even consider such a possibility. After all, the Saturday classes would be available to the worst type of people—problem students and adults who did not have enough initiative to complete their education. And when you think about how liberal the present teachers are, you wonder what might happen when those young "radical" university students try to teach the classes. You cringe when you imagine the condition of the school at the end of the Saturday classes. You are even more resentful when you realize that these liberal counselors—who are insisting that you put in the extra time—are not even planning to be there on Saturdays. And their nerve—insinuating that you would do *anything* for a little extra money!

When the principal of Winterset High School asks for a meeting with the maintenance people, you are obligated to attend. As the maintenance staff searches for a resolution to the problem, the following suggestions will probably be considered:

1. Arrange for the counselors to clean the school on Saturdays.
2. Ask the graduate students to clean the school.
3. Hire an extra union person to work on Saturdays.
4. Schedule the classes for a weekday and limit the number so that the few vacant classrooms will accommodate these special students.
5. Hold the classes for one hour per day five days a week immediately following the close of the regular school.
6. Tell the graduate students to find facilities on their campus.

University Associates

436. I REPRESENT:
A WORLD MEETING

Goals

   I. To facilitate the getting-acquainted process.

  II. To enable participants to express indirectly how they would like to be perceived.

Group Size

     Twelve to twenty-four participants.

Time Required

     One to one and one-half hours.

Materials

   I. A blank self-stick name tag for each participant.

  II. A narrow felt-tipped marker for each participant.

Physical Setting

     A room large enough for participants to move about and converse with one another.

Process

    I. The facilitator announces the first goal of the activity.

   II. Each participant is given a blank name tag and a felt-tipped marker.

 III. The facilitator asks each participant to select a country that he or she would like to represent at a world meeting and to write the name of that country on the name tag. Any country may be selected except the country in which the participant was born. Each participant is instructed to leave room on the name tag to write his or her own name and three more words.

 IV. After all participants have selected their countries, the facilitator asks each participant to write two or three words on the name tag to indicate why he or she would be a good representative of that country.

  V. Each participant is then asked to write his or her own first name on the name tag and to wear the tag throughout the rest of the activity.

 VI. The participants move about the room and ask one another questions about the personal importance or significance of the words on the name tags. (Two minutes per participant.)

VII. The facilitator reassembles the total group, explains the second goal of the activity, and leads a discussion on the following questions:

1. What kinds of words are on the name tags?
2. What were the reasons given for the choice of words?
3. What connections can you make between the person's choice of words and the way that person wants to be perceived?
4. What conclusions can be drawn about self-presentation from this activity?
5. What changes would you like to make in your initial self-presentation?
6. What back-home benefits could this experience have?

(Twenty minutes.)

Variations

I. The participants can be divided into small groups for the conversations.

II. Cities in the United States can be selected. The participants would be instructed to choose cities in which they were not born.

III. Participants can be instructed to select individual countries or states that they have visited. Each participant then shares an experience that he or she had in the chosen country or state.

Submitted by Patrick Doyle.

Patrick Doyle is the principal of High Impact Training Services, is an associate in Management for Tomorrow, and is a teaching master at St. Lawrence College, Ontario, Canada. He is active in the field of human resource development in retail, public administration, and public health organizations. Mr. Doyle's specialty is management techniques in evolving environments.

INTRODUCTION TO THE INSTRUMENTATION SECTION

The instruments that are included in this section are provided for training and developmental purposes. They are *not* intended for in-depth personal growth, psychodiagnostic, or therapeutic work. They *are* intended for use in training groups, for demonstration purposes, to generate data for training or organization development sessions, and for other group applications in which the trainer, consultant, or facilitator helps the group to use the data generated by the instrument to move the work of the group along.

One of the dilemmas of most people is that they lack an adequate vocabulary with which to describe other people in nonpejorative ways, especially if the behavior of others has had an adverse effect on them. One of the principal benefits of using instrumentation in human resource development is that instruments typically provide participants with new, relatively neutral words to use in describing others. With such a new vocabulary, one can begin to describe another person's behavior as "stemming from a strong need for inclusion" or "representing a weak economic value commitment" rather than in more subjective and emotionally laden terms that interfere with, rather than enhance, communication (especially communication with the person being described).

In addition to helping participants to identify behavior, the comparison of scores from an instrument provides group members with a convenient and comparatively safe way to exchange interpersonal feedback. The involvement with their own scores helps participants to better understand the theory on which the instrument is based—a typical reason for using an instrument in training. Thus, there are strong, positive reasons for using instruments in training and development work.

The important caveat here is that the trainer, consultant, or facilitator must recognize that the scores obtained by individuals on any instrument are the result of their answers to a series of verbal questions at one point in time, and that such scores should not be treated with any undue reverence. Such responses typically change over time, for a variety of reasons. The individual's interpretation of the question the next time may affect his or her answer, a variety of experiences may change the person's self-perception, and so on. HRD professionals are encouraged to use instruments simply as one additional means of obtaining data about individuals, with all the risks and potential payoffs that any other data source would yield.

There are four instruments in this *Annual*. The first, "Role Pics" by Udai Pareek, measures strategies for coping with role stress. The instrument contains twenty-four statements in cartoon format, and space is provided for writing each response in a "balloon." The statements represent eight types of role stress, and guidelines are provided for classifying the responses in eight categories of coping with role stress.

The next instrument, "The Learning-Model Instrument," provides ten situations regarding the way a person experiences life and ten situations regarding the way a person learns best. The respondent chooses from two alternatives the way he or she prefers to experience life or learn in each situation. The scoring process provides four categories of preferred learning styles based on two continua: cognitive/affective learning and concrete/abstract experiencing.

The "Communication Congruence Inventory," by Marshall Sashkin and Leonard D. Goodstein, provides an opportunity to measure skills in matching responses to fifteen initial statements, which use language that relates to vision, hearing, and physical sensation. Each of three alternative responses for each statement also includes visual, auditory, or kinesthetic language. A fourth alternative contains neutral language. Properly matching the responses entails choosing visual responses for visual statements, auditory responses for auditory statements, and kinesthetic responses for kinesthetic statements. In no case is the neutral response the most appropriate match. This instrument is especially useful in helping consultants become aware of the types of language used by clients and of the importance of communicating with a client in his or her own preferred style of language.

"The Individual-Team-Organization (ITO) Survey" is a relatively concise (52-item) instrument for determining employees' perceptions of an organization. As the title implies, it is divided into three sections. The respondent must decide how often each of the fifty-two situations occurs. The results will help individuals, teams, and organizations to determine and focus on the areas that most need improving.

Readers of earlier *Annuals* will note that the theory necessary for understanding, presenting, and using each instrument now is included with the instrument itself. This eliminates the necessity of referring to several sections of the *Annual* in order to develop a program based on any of the instruments. All scales or inventory forms, scoring sheets, and interpretive sheets for each instrument also are provided. This consolidation of all related materials should make the Instrumentation section even more useful than before.

ROLE PICS: MEASURING STRATEGIES FOR COPING WITH ROLE STRESS

Udai Pareek

When individuals and organizations experience role stress, they adopt ways of dealing with it. Neither an individual nor an organization can remain in a continual state of tension, so even if a deliberate and conscious strategy is not utilized to deal with the stress, some strategy is adopted. For example, the strategy may be to leave the conflicts and stress to take care of themselves. This is a strategy, although the individual or the organization may not be aware of it. We call such strategies "coping styles."

The word "coping" has been used in several ways; two meanings predominate in the literature. The term has been used to denote general ways of dealing with stress and also has been defined as the effort to "master" conditions of harm, threat, or challenge when a routine or automatic response is not readily available (Lazarus, 1974). In this article, we shall use the first meaning: dealing, consciously or unconsciously, with stress experienced.

It is useful for individuals and organizations to examine what strategies they are using to cope with stress. If no coping strategy is adopted, lack of effectiveness may result. Hall (1972) has reported that the act of coping itself, as opposed to non-coping, is related to satisfaction and is more important than any particular coping strategy.

Lazarus (1974) emphasizes the key role of cognitive processes in coping activity and the importance of coping in determining the quality and intensity of emotional reactions. As Monat and Lazarus (1977) point out, there is impressive anecdotal and research evidence that we are continually "self-regulating" our emotional reactions, e.g., escaping or postponing unpleasant situations, actively changing threatening conditions, deceiving ourselves about the implictions of certain facts, or simply learning to detach ourselves from unpleasant situations. Lazarus' emphasis is on the individual (i.e., the self) actively appraising the situation and what he or she can do, rather than on the environmental contingencies that presumably manipulate the individual's behavior.

A link between styles of living, coping, and somatic illness has been suggested by Friedman and Rosenman (1974), who argue that a primary cause of heart disease is a distinctive pattern of behavior. They call this "Type A" behavior; it involves continual, pressured interactions with the environment and a compelling sense of time urgency, aggressiveness, competitiveness, and generalized hostility. In a sense, this pattern is a mode of coping with societal values of achievement and the work ethic in which these values have been internalized by the Type A person.

Two different approaches to the study of coping have been pursued by various investigators. Some (e.g., Byrne, 1964; Goldstein, 1973) have emphasized coping traits, styles, or dispositions. This approach, often used by researchers in the study of personality, assumes that an individual will utilize the same coping strategy (such as repression or sensitization) in most stressful situations, creating for the individual a stable pattern or style. A person's coping style or disposition typically is assessed by means of personality tests, not by observing what the person says or does in a particular situation.

Other researchers (e.g., Cohen & Lazarus, 1973; Katz, Weiner, Gallagher, & Hillman, 1970; Wolf & Goodell, 1968) have studied active, ongoing, coping strategies in particular stress situations. According to Cohen and Lazarus (1973), many psychological traits, including coping styles, show very limited generalities and, thus, are poor predictors of behavior in any given situation. Therefore, they prefer to observe an individual's behavior as it occurs in a stressful situation and then infer the coping processes implied by the behavior. This approach has been relatively neglected in the study of coping; the Role Pics instrument is allied to this approach.

STRATEGIES FOR COPING WITH STRESS

Lazarus (1975) has suggested a classification of coping processes that emphasizes direct actions and palliative modes. *Direct actions* include behaviors or actions that, when performed in the face of a stressful situation, are expected to bring about a change in the stress-causing physical or social environment. *Palliative modes* are those thoughts or actions whose purpose is to relieve the emotional impact of stress, be it bodily stress or psychological stress.

Pareek (1976) proposed two types of coping strategies that people generally use to deal with stress. One is that the person may decide to suffer from, accept, or deny the experienced stress or to blame somebody (self or other) or something for the stressful situation or the individual's being in it. These are *passive* or *avoidance* strategies and are referred to as "dysfunctional" ways of coping with stressful situations. A second type of strategy is the decision to face the realities of the situation and to take some form of action to solve the problems, either individually or with the help of others. The active, *approach* style is regarded by social scientists as a "functional" way of dealing with stress.

People do not restrict themselves to using one type of coping strategy exclusively, and different people employ complex and varied combinations of strategies to deal with the same kinds of stress.

THE ROLE PICS INSTRUMENT

Role Pics (Projective Instrument for Coping Styles) is a semi-projective instrument for assessing the strategies or styles used by respondents to cope with role stress. The instrument has three forms. Form O (the one presented here) is to be used to assess coping styles in relation to stress resulting from *organizational* or job-related roles.

The instrument presents illustrations in which a role occupant is involved in conversation with another person and one of them makes a statement about a situation involving role stress. To maximize projection, the illustrations are presented in cartoon form, similar to the Rosenzweig Picture-Frustration Study (Rosenzweig, 1978). The respondent is required to write how the person to whom the statement is made would respond. It is presumed that the responses will be projective expressions of the way in which the respondent would cope with the particular role stress.

The instrument depicts eight role stresses: role overload, role ambiguity, role stagnation, role isolation, self-role distance, interrole conflict, role inadequacy, and role erosion (for definitions of these, see Pareek, 1982). Table 1 provides an analysis of the statements presented in the Role Pics instrument (indicated by numerals from 1 to 24) in relation to the various role stresses that they indicate and whether the statement is made *by* the role occupant or *to* the role occupant.

Role Pics Categories

The scoring of responses utilizes a system of categorization that employs a two-by-two cube; that is, the scoring system has three dimensions, and each dimension has two aspects. The three dimensions are as follows:

1. **Externality.** This dimension measures the degree to which the person places the responsibility for the role stress on external factors, resulting in aggression toward and blame placed on such external factors. This may include the tendency to expect the solution to the stress to come from external sources. Externality is measured as high or low.

2. **Internality.** This is the opposite of externality. One may perceive oneself as responsible for the stress and may therefore express aggression toward or blame oneself. Similarly, one may expect that the solution to the stress should come from oneself. Internality is measured as high or low.

3. **Mode of Coping.** There are two modes: avoiding the situation (a reactive strategy) or confronting and approaching the problem (a proactive strategy). McKinney (1980) has proposed the concept of engagement style, differentiating the perception that one has of oneself as "doing" (agent) or "being done to" (patient).

Combining the two aspects of each of the three dimensions results in eight possible strategies to cope with stress. Concepts have been borrowed from Rosenzweig (1978) to name the various strategies.

The *avoidance* mode is characterized by (a) aggression and blame, (b) helplessness and resignation, (c) minimizing of the significance of the stressful situation by accepting it with a sense of resignation, or (d) denying the presence of stress or finding an explanation for it. All these behaviors "help" the individual to *not* do anything in relation to the stress. The categorization scheme uses Rosenzweig's term "punitive" (e.g., im*punitive*) to denote three of the strategies in the avoidance mode. "Defensive" is used to denote the fourth strategy. These strategies are abbreviated with capital letters (M, I, E, and D).

Table 1. Analysis of Role Pics Statements

Type of Role Stress	Role occupant to		Role occupant from		
	Colleague	Supervisor	Colleague	Supervisor	Spouse
1. Role Overload		9	1	17	
2. Role Ambiguity		10	2, 18		
3. Role Stagnation	11		3	19	
4. Role Isolation	12			20	4
5. Self-Role Distance		5	13	21	
6. Interrole Conflict	6		14		22
7. Role Inadequacy	23	15	7		
8. Role Erosion		16	8	24	
Total	4	5	8	5	2

The *approach* mode is characterized by (a) hope that things will improve, (b) effort by the individual to solve the problem, (c) the expectation that others will help or asking for help, and (d) doing something about the problem jointly with others. Rosenzweig's term "persitive" is used to denote the four strategies in this mode. These strategies are abbreviated with lower-case letters (m, i, e, and n).

These eight strategies (M, I, E, D, m, i, e, and n) are further explained in the section on scoring the instrument.

ADMINISTERING THE INSTRUMENT

Role Pics can be administered individually or in a group setting, but each respondent should work independently in formulating the replies. Completing the form takes about twenty minutes.

The instrument depicts twenty-four situations; in nine of these the role occupant expresses some dissatisfaction to colleague or boss. In fifteen situations a colleague or boss or spouse makes a statement to the role occupant regarding some area in which the role occupant appears to be experiencing role stress. For each situation, the respondent is to write *on the picture* how the person *to whom the statement has been made* would reply.

After distributing the Role Pics Instrument (the series of pictures) the facilitator should describe it, announce the instructions, and then tell the respondents to read the instructions on the front of their instrument packages. The facilitator should announce that the instrument may result in new self-awareness but that it is not a "test." Respondents should be advised to attempt to *identify with* (rather than to judge) the stressed person in each role situation and to write the reply that he or she (the respondent) would give if he or she were the person in the situation. The respondents also should be told to write down their first responses to each situation and not to take the time to evaluate or censor their responses. A response must be provided for *each* situation, in the order in which they appear.

SCORING THE INSTRUMENT

If the respondents are being trained to administer this instrument, they may score their own answers or one another's answers. In some situations, however, the facilitator may wish to have the instrument scored by someone who is not acquainted with the respondents.

After the respondents have completed the instrument, letters should be assigned to the responses as indicated in the following paragraphs.

Scoring "Avoidance" Responses

Impunitive (M). This is a combination of low internality, low externality, and avoidance. Responses that indicate either simple admission of the stress or that the stress is unavoidable and that nothing can be done about it are scored as M to reflect this style. A fatalistic attitude falls in this category.

Intropunitive (I). This is characterized by high internality, low externality, and avoidance. Blame and aggression are directed by the respondent toward himself or herself. Responses that indicate self-blame, remorse, or guilt are scored as I.

Extrapunitive (E). This is characterized by low internality, high externality, and avoidance. Responses that indicate irritation with the situation and/or aggression and blame toward outside factors and persons are scored as E.

Defensive (D). This is characterized by high internality, high externality, and avoidance. With the involvement of both oneself and others, but in the avoidance mode, one avoids aggression or blame by using defense mechanisms. Responses that deny the stress, rationalize the stressful situation, or point out benefits of the stress are scored as D.

Scoring "Approach" Responses

Impersistive (m). This strategy is characterized by low internality, low externality, and the approach mode. Rosenzweig's "impersistive" category relates to "expression given to the hope that time or normally expected circumstances will bring about the solution of a problem; patience and conformity are characterized." Responses are scored m if they indicate this interpretation.

Intropersistive (i). This strategy is characterized by high internality, low externality, and approach. Statements indicating that the respondent would take action in response to a stress are scored i.

Extrapersistive (e). This strategy is characterized by low internality, high externality, and approach. Statements of request made to someone to solve the problem or those indicating the expectation that the solution will come from other people are scored e.

Interpersistive (n). This strategy is characterized by high internality, high externality, and approach. It is the opposite of the defensive (D) style. This strategy is indicated by statements that suggest joint effort, by the respondent and some others, to deal with the stress.

Some statements may be indicative of two or three categories. In such cases, it is best to select the two most appropriate categories and to assign a half score (.5) to each.

After letters have been assigned to the twenty-four responses, the letters are transferred to the "Item Scores" section of the scoring sheet. Capital letters are recorded in the "Avoidance" column, and lower-case letters are recorded in the "Approach" column. A tally is made of the letters in the following manner:

1. Count the number of times each letter appears in items 1 through 12. In the sample scoring sheet in Figure 1, the M appears two and one-half times (once of item 3, once for item 11, and a half point for item 12, which was split between M and i. Record each total in the appropriate box in the "Profile" matrix on the scoring sheet.

2. Repeat step 1 for items 13 through 24.

3. Record totals as indicated on the profile matrix.

The dominant style is the strategy with the highest score. The back-up style is the strategy with the next highest score. These styles should be recorded in the appropriate blanks on the scoring sheet.

An interpretation sheet is provided for the respondents.

Trends

Some individuals switch strategies while responding to Role Pics. For example, after responding to eight pictures, a person may decide that the selected strategies are not "right" and may start using other types of strategies. Trends are calculated by comparing the response patterns in the first half of Role Pics (situations 1 through 12) with those of the second half (situations 13 through 24).

The formula for calculating the value of a trend is (a − b) ÷ (a + b), where "a" is the total number of times that a strategy was used on the first half of Role Pics and "b" is the number of times the strategy was indicated in the second half of the instrument. If the value of "a" is greater than the value of "b," the trend is positive. If the value of "b" is greater than that of "a," the trend is negative. To be significant, a trend must be based on at least four responses scored as that strategy.

ITEM SCORES

	Avoidance	Approach			Avoidance	Approach
1.	D		13.		M	
2.	D		14.		D	
3.	M		15.		M,D	
4.	D		16.			e
5.		e	17.			i
6.	D		18.		M	e
7.	D	i	19.		M	e
8.	D		20.		D	
9.		i	21.		M	
10.		e	22.		M,D	
11.	M		23.		E	
12.	M	i	24.		E	

PROFILE

		Avoidance				Approach			
		Low Externality		High Externality		Low Externality		High Externality	
Low Internality	1-12	M	2½	E	0	m	0	e	2
	13-24	M	4	E	2	m	0	e	2
High Internality	1-12	I	0	D	5½	i	2	n	
	13-24	I	0	D	3	i	1	n	0

Totals from Profile:

Avoidance 1-12: __8__   Approach 1-12: __4__

Avoidance 13-24: __9__   Approach 13-24: __3__

TOTAL AVOIDANCE: __17__   TOTAL APPROACH: __7__

STYLES

Dominant: _Defensive_   Back-up: _Impunitive_

TRENDS

.23
→ M

(a − b) ÷ (a + b)

.29
← D

Figure 1. Sample Role Pics Scoring Sheet

USES FOR THE ROLE PICS INSTRUMENT

In using Role Pics as a feedback instrument, the facilitator can report to each individual on his or her scores for the various coping styles and can also present information about the relationship between coping styles and personality and role dimensions. The feedback itself may help the respondents to examine the implications of their behavior and to make some plans for change. Individuals and groups can also develop strategies for moving from one coping style to another. A highly significant positive relationship has been reported between approach styles and internality and between avoidance styles and externality (Sen, 1982; Surti, 1982). Approach styles have a high correlation with optimism and a negative correlation with alienation (Sen, 1982). Findings in relation to organizational roles indicate that approach styles have a significant positive relationship with role efficacy and effective role behavior involving needs such as achievement, power, extension, control, and dependency (Sen, 1982). There also is a significant positive correlation between approach styles and job satisfaction (Sen, 1982).

RELIABILITY AND VALIDITY DATA

Extensive reliability and validity data are available. Those interested in using this instrument for research may request such data from University Associates.

REFERENCES

Byrne, D. (1964). Repression-sensitization as a dimension of personality. In B.A. Maher (Ed.), *Progress in experimental personality research* (Vol. 1). New York: Academic Press.

Cohen, F., & Lazarus, R.S. (1973). Active coping processes, coping dispositions and recovery from surgery. *Psychosomatic Medicine, 35,* 375-389.

Friedman, M.D., & Rosenman, R.H. (1974). *Type A behavior and your heart.* New York: Alfred A. Knopf.

Goldstein, M.J. (1973). Individual differences in response to stress. *American Journal of Community Psychology, 2,* 113-137.

Hall, D.T. (1972). A model of coping with role conflict: The role of college educated women. *Administrative Science Quarterly, 17*(4), 471-486.

Katz, J.L., Weiner, H., Gallagher, T.G., & Hillman, L. (1970). Stress, distress and ego defenses. *Archives of General Psychiatry, 23,* 131-142.

Lazarus, R.S. (1974). Cognitive and coping processes in emotion. In B. Weiner (Ed.), *Cognitive views of human motivation.* New York: Academic Press.

Lazarus, R.S. (1975). A cognitively oriented psychologist looks at biofeedback. *American Psychologist, 30,* 553-561.

McKinney, J.P. (1980). Engagement style (agent vs. patient) in childhood and adolescence. *Human Development, 23,* 192-209.

Monat, A., & Lazarus, R.S. (1977). *Stress and coping: An anthology.* New York: Columbia University Press.

Pareek, U. (1976). Interrole exploration. In J.W. Pfeiffer & J.E. Jones (Eds.), *The 1976 annual handbook for group facilitators.* San Diego, CA: University Associates.

Pareek, U. (1982). *Role Stress Scales: Manual.* Ahmedabad, India: Navin Publications.

Rosenzweig, S. (1978). *Aggressive behavior and the Rosenzweig Picture-Frustration Study.* New York: Praeger.

Sen, P.C. (1982). *Personal and organizational correlates of role stress and coping strategies in some public sector banks.* Doctoral dissertation, University of Gujarat, India.

Surti, K. (1982). *Some psychological correlates of role stress and coping styles in working women.* Doctoral dissertation, University of Gujarat, India.

Wolf, S, & Godell, H. (1968). *Stress and disease.* Springfield, IL: Charles C. Thomas.

Udai Pareek, Ph. D., is a consultant, researcher, and author. He specializes in organizational behavior, organizational design, and human resource development. He is currently president of the Indian Society for Applied Behavioural Science. Recently he served as a US-AID consultant on management training system development to the government of Indonesia. Dr. Pareek has held the Larsen & Toubro Chair in Organizational Behavior at the Indian Institute of Management and has been a fellow of the National Training Laboratories. He is the author of numerous books, instruments, and articles.

ROLE PICS
Udai Pareek

Instructions: The purpose of this instrument is to discover how different persons perceive different situations involving organizational roles. There are no right or wrong answers.

Twenty-four situations are depicted. In each picture, two people are talking; the statement made by the first person is printed, and the space for the response made by the second person is blank. For each situation (picture), imagine what the second person is saying and *write this response* in the blank space.

Write down your first reactions to each situation. Do not leave any picture blank, and go on to each new situation as soon as you have responded to the previous one.

ROLE PICS SCORING SHEET

Instructions: The facilitator will give instructions to the person responsible for scoring the responses. This person may or may not be the respondent. After this person assigns a letter to each of the twenty-four responses, transfer those letters to the "Item Scores" section of the scoring sheet. Make sure you record capital letters in the "Avoidance" column and lower-case letters in the "Approach" column.

Count the number of times each letter appears in items 1 through 12. Record each total in the appropriate box in the "Profile" matrix. Then count the number of times each letter appears in items 13 through 24 and write those totals on the profile. Calculate other totals as indicated from the profile.

Your dominant style is the letter with the highest score. Your back-up style is the letter with the next highest score. Record these styles in the appropriate blanks. The facilitator will explain the concept of "trends." The formula for calculating a trend is $(a - b) \div (a + b)$, where "a" is the total number of times a strategy was used on the first twelve role pics and "b" is the total number of times the strategy was used on the other twelve role pics.

Name _____ Date _____

ITEM SCORES

	Avoidance	Approach			Avoidance	Approach
1.	_____	_____		13.	_____	_____
2.	_____	_____		14.	_____	_____
3.	_____	_____		15.	_____	_____
4.	_____	_____		16.	_____	_____
5.	_____	_____		17.	_____	_____
6.	_____	_____		18.	_____	_____
7.	_____	_____		19.	_____	_____
8.	_____	_____		20.	_____	_____
9.	_____	_____		21.	_____	_____
10.	_____	_____		22.	_____	_____
11.	_____	_____		23.	_____	_____
12.	_____	_____		24.	_____	_____

PROFILE

		Avoidance		Approach	
		Low Externality	High Externality	Low Externality	High Externality
Low Internality	1-12	M	E	m	e
	13-24	M	E	m	e
High Internality	1-12	I	D	i	n
	13-24	I	D	i	n

Totals from Profile:

Avoidance 1-12: _____   Approach 1-12: _____

Avoidance 13-24: _____   Approach 13-24: _____

TOTAL AVOIDANCE: _____   **TOTAL APPROACH:** _____

STYLES

Dominant: _____   **Back-up:** _____

TRENDS

$$(a - b) \div (a + b)$$

ROLE PICS INTERPRETATION SHEET

Your dominant style reflects the strategy that you use most of the time. It is indicated on your scoring sheet by the letter that appears most frequently. The letter that appears with the next highest frequency indicates your back-up style. When a person is under stress or working in an emergency situation, he or she generally uses the back-up style more than the dominant style.

Given below are interpretations of the various strategies:

Impunitive (M). This is a combination of low internality, low externality, and avoidance. Responses that indicate either simple admission of the stress or that the stress is unavoidable and that nothing can be done about it are scored as M to reflect this style. A fatalistic attitude falls in this category.

Intropunitive (I). This is characterized by high internality, low externality, and avoidance. Blame and aggression are directed by the respondent toward himself or herself. Responses that indicate self-blame, remorse, or guilt are scored as I.

Extrapunitive (E). This is characterized by low internality, high externality, and avoidance. Responses that indicate irritation with the situation and/or aggression and blame toward outside factors and persons are scored as E.

Defensive (D). This is characterized by high internality, high externality, and avoidance. With the involvement of both oneself and others, but in the avoidance mode, one avoids aggression or blame by using defense mechanisms. Responses that deny the stress, rationalize the stressful situation, or point out benefits of the stress are scored as D.

Impersistive (m). This strategy is characterized by low internality, low externality, and the approach mode. Rosenzweig's "impersistive" category relates to "expression given to the hope that time or normally expected circumstances will bring about the solution of a problem; patience and conformity are characterized." Responses are scored m if they indicate this interpretation.

Intropersistive (i). This strategy is characterized by high internality, low externality, and approach. Statements indicating that the respondent would take action in response to a stress are scored i.

Extrapersistive (e). This strategy is characterized by low internality, high externality, and approach. Statements of request made to someone to solve the problem or those indicating the expectation that the solution will come from other people are scored e.

Interpersistive (n). This strategy is characterized by high internality, high externality, and approach. It is the opposite of the defensive (D) style. This strategy is indicated by statements that suggest joint effort, by the respondent and some others, to deal with the stress.

THE LEARNING-MODEL INSTRUMENT: AN INSTRUMENT BASED ON THE LEARNING MODEL FOR MANAGERS

Kenneth L. Murrell

Although the learning model presented here was not designed exclusively for managers, the versatility and flexibility demanded by a managerial career require a knowledge of and experience with a variety of learning styles. The Learning Model for Managers introduces four domains of learning based on a person's preference for cognitive or affective learning and the person's preference for concrete or abstract experiences. Since it is important for managers to learn how to use a variety of learning styles, the manager will be given special attention as the model and instrument are discussed.

DEVELOPING THE MODEL AND INSTRUMENT

The idea that people will be able to live a better life if they understand who and what they are goes back at least to the early Greek philosophers. Many aids and guides have been created to help people in today's world to learn more about themselves. After reading *Freedom To Learn* (Rogers, 1982) and studying various learning-style models and instruments (e.g., Kolb, 1974, and instruments described in Peters, 1985, and Pfeiffer, et al., 1976), I saw a need for a different type of learning model and self-awareness instrument. The following goals were important in developing this new model:

1. Create a model that will help to explain the cognitive and affective learning styles in such a way that managers and trainers can gain an appreciation for and understanding of the various ways in which learning takes place.

2. Clarify conceptually what a learning environment is so that participants in a learning program can gain an understanding of what the learning environment is and of how experiential-learning methods differ from other learning methods.

3. Create an instrument, based on the model's assumptions, that will provide immediate self-awareness feedback to help individuals know more about how they learn.

4. Develop an instrument that will help individuals (a) to connect their awareness of their own learning preferences to the nature of what and how a manager learns and (b) to understand why experiential learning and management development must differ from traditional classroom learning.

5. Develop an instrument that will generate thought and discussion about the process of learning, so that program content will be seen as only a part of the total learning experience.

THE MODEL

The Learning Model for Managers (see Figure 1), which was based on these goals, has been used in industrial settings, in graduate and undergraduate courses on management and organizational behavior, and in offices in the United States and abroad. The instrument is simple to use and is designed to help the instructor or trainer explain the importance of being able to learn in many different ways, including experiential learning.

Learning comes not only through thinking or cognition, but also from experience and affect or feeling. Although some people have realized this fact for a long time, it is still "good news" for many when they discover that it is acceptable to be emotional and have feelings and that they can take pride in being able to learn from emotions and feelings. Although everyone probably has a mixture of learning preferences, a way was needed to identify a person's preferred position on a continuum from the cognitive to the affective.

The Learning Model for Managers assumes that the difference in a preference on the affective-cognitive dimension of learning is a key factor in how a person learns. This assumption is based on the idea that the affective and cognitive end points can be defined so that they correlate with a people-versus-task orientation (Blake & Mouton, 1984). Although empirical research may not show a strong correlation between a preference for the cognitive style of learning and task orientation, they seem to be closely related because of the similarity in their definitions.

This task-person and cognitive-affective correlation provides an opportunity to use this learning model for stressing the relationship of learning style and personality type to the behavior of a manager. Although managers, like other people, probably prefer learning in a particular way, it is important for them to develop the ability to learn by both thinking and feeling. The model can be used to illustrate this importance. In training managers, the trainer should thoroughly discuss this issue and show how the model correlates with the career changes the managers may expect to face.

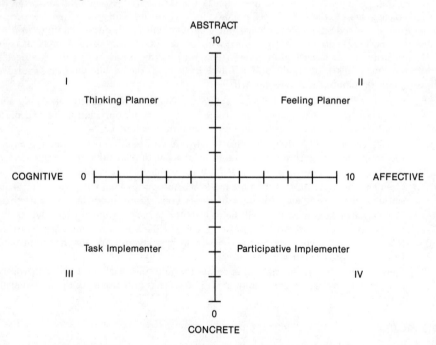

Figure 1. The Learning Model for Managers

The model's second dimension (the vertical axis) uses, as did Kolb, a concrete-abstract continuum. However, this model reverses the positions of the end points in order to place *concrete* (the down-to-earth point) on the bottom and *abstract* (the in-the-air point) on top. A preference for the concrete reflects a person's desire to come into contact with the real object, to touch it, or even to physically manipulate it. The abstract end of the continuum reflects a preference for dealing with the world in terms of thinking about it and for manipulating ideas or thoughts. The vertical axis represents the way people tend to experience life and is loosely associated with the psychology of Jung (1924). The preference for experiencing life in the concrete indicates a desire to experience through the direct senses.

The Learning Model for Managers, therefore, contains two primary axes, ranging from cognitive to affective in the horizontal dimension and from concrete to abstract in the vertical dimension. The axes divide the model into the following four domains: I, thinking planner; II, feeling planner; III, task implementer; and IV, participative implementer.

THE INSTRUMENT

The Learning-Model Instrument can be used in the following ways:

1. To give feedback to individuals on their own preferred styles of learning and domains of strength;

2. To help a new group of trainees or students to learn more about one another in order to work together more effectively; and

3. To provide an overall explanation of the learning environment so that participants will receive a conceptual understanding of the experiential approach to learning.

Validity and Reliability

Establishing validity and reliability of any model and instrument of this type is difficult or impossible. However, if the face validity is positive and if the learning value is apparent, then the material should be useful when it fits the training and learning goals. The results of the instrument are not intended to label the respondents, but simply to give them feedback on their preferred styles of learning.

Administering the Instrument

Although this instrument is particularly helpful to managers and prospective managers, it is appropriate for anyone who desires to know more about his or her own preferences for learning styles. A management-development program, which was built on the model and utilized the instrument, can be summarized in the following way:

The first session met in order to accomplish two things: (1) to allow the participants to become acquainted with at least four other participants and (2) to outline preliminary objectives for the program. To accomplish the getting-acquainted process, each person introduced one other person. Later, triads were formed to develop additional program objectives, which then became part of the program outline. The facilitator used a systems framework to explain the relationship of inputs, throughputs, and outputs. The facilitator also gave special attention to the feedback loop and discussed it in terms of the need for communication and self-control in order to make sure that the program was accomplishing its goals and that each participant was receiving what he or she needed.

The next focus was on the learning model. The facilitator explained how the program activities would by necessity be heavily oriented toward experiential learning and would deal directly with the feelings and emotions that would emerge as learning took place in domains II and IV of the model.

The model and instrument were valuable in helping participants to learn something about one another, which in turn helped them in working together more effectively. After the instrument was administered, the results of the last half of the instrument were used to form groups of participants with similar scores. Each group consisted of from five to seven members. Within each group, the members compared their responses and tried to determine whether or not the scores seemed valid. They also discussed the results of the first half of the instrument. Then all the groups held a joint discussion.

Topics for the joint discussion might include the way men are socialized to be more cognitive and women are socialized to be more affective; how background or academic interests can cause a bias; and how individuals can determine which domain they belong in if their scores place them on an axis. The discussions in both the small and large groups can help participants to be more aware of themselves, of the other participants, and of the kind of learning that will take place in the program.

This particular program was designed to place a heavy emphasis on and to give special skill-building attention to domains II and IV.

Scoring the Instrument

The scoring sheet indicates which answers receive a score of one point. The rest of the answers receive a score of zero. The total of the scores in the first half of the instrument is plotted on the vertical axis and a horizontal line is drawn through the point. The total of the scores in the last half is plotted on the horizontal axis and a vertical line is drawn through that point. The point of intersection of the two lines indicates the domain of the respondent.

Interpreting the Scores

The next four paragraphs give an interpretation of the four end points of the axes in the Learning Model for Managers. Following these are explanations of the four domains in the model.

Cognitive Learning

A person who scores low on the cognitive-affective axis shows a marked preference for learning through thought or other mental activity. People who grasp intellectually very quickly what they are trying to learn or who simply prefer to use controlled thought and logic will be found on the cognitive end of this axis. Rationality appeals to these individuals, as do logic and other thinking skills that are necessary for this type of learning. Although this statement is not based on hard research, it appears that a high cognitive orientation correlates with a high task orientation rather than with a people orientation. The research about possible left-versus-right brain functioning correlates a cognitive orientation to individuals who are left-brain dominant. Therefore, the left side of the axis was deliberately assigned to the cognitive orientation to serve as an easy reminder.

Affective Learning

A person who scores high on the cognitive-affective axis shows a marked preference for learning in the affective realm. Such an individual is more comfortable with and seeks out learning from his or her emotions and feelings. These individuals desire personal interaction and seek to learn about people by experiencing them in emotional ways. This type of learner would potentially be highly people oriented. A manager with this orientation would probably seek out social interaction rather than to focus exclusively on the task components of the job. In right-brain research, affective learners are said to be more intuitive, more spontaneous, and less linear. They seek out feelings and emotions rather than logic.

Concrete Life Experiencing

People with a preference for the concrete enjoy jumping in and getting their hands dirty. Hands-on experiences are important to them. As managers, these people want to keep busy, become directly involved, and physically approach or touch whatever they are working with. If they work with machines, they will get greasy; if they work with people, they will become involved.

Abstract Life Experiencing

Individuals preferring this style have no special desire to touch, but they want to keep active by thinking about the situation and relating it to similar situations. Their preferred interaction style is internal—inside their own heads.

The Four Learning Domains

A person is unlikely to be on the extreme end of either axis, and no one type of learning is "best." Any mixture of preferences simply represents a person's uniqueness. The model is useful in helping people differentiate themselves, and it offers a method for looking at the way different styles fit together. This section describes the four domains that are represented in the model.

The descriptions of these domains could be of special interest to managers, because they will help the manager understand the relationship between managerial action and learning style. A manager should be capable of learning and functioning well in all four domains, especially if he or she expects to face a variety of situations and challenges. The successful manager is likely to be the one who can operate in both a task and a people environment with the ability to see and become involved with the concrete and also use thought processes to understand what is needed. The normative assumption of the model is that a manager should learn how to learn in each of the four domains. In doing this, the manager may well build on his or her primary strengths, but the versatility and flexibility demanded in a managerial career make clear the importance of all four domains.

Domain I, the Thinking Planner. A combination of cognitive and abstract preferences constitutes domain I, where the "thinking planner" is located. This domain might well be termed the place for the planner whose job is task oriented and whose environment contains primarily things, numbers, or printouts. The bias in formal education is often toward this learning domain, and Mintzberg (1976) was critical of this bias. In this domain things are treated abstractly and often their socio-emotional elements are denied.

The domain-I learner should do well in school, should have a talent for planning, and is likely to be successful as a staff person or manager in a department that deals with large quantities of untouchable things. This domain represents an important area for management learning. Of the four domains, it seems to receive the heaviest emphasis in traditional university programs and in management-development seminars, particularly those in financial management.

Domain II, the Feeling Planner. A combination of affective and abstract preferences constitutes domain II, where the "feeling planner" is located. The managerial style associated with this domain is that of the thinker who can learn and who enjoys working with people but has limited opportunity to get close to them. This domain is important for the personnel executive or a manager with too much responsibility to interact closely with other employees.

Social-analysis skills are represented in this area. Managers in this domain should be able to think through and understand the social and emotional factors affecting a large organization.

Difficulties in this area sometimes arise when good first-line supervisors who have a natural style with people are promoted into positions that prevent them from having direct contact with others and are expected to determine without concrete experience the nature of and solutions to personnel problems.

Domain III, the Task Implementer. A combination of cognitive and concrete preferences constitutes domain III, where the "task implementer" is located. This domain contains decision makers who primarily want to understand the task and who can focus on the details and specifics of the concrete in a thoughtful manner. If these people are allowed to think about a situation, they can see the concrete issues and, after close examination, can make a well-thought-out decision. A person in this domain is often a task-focused doer. If the interpersonal-skill demands are low and if the emotional climate is not a problem, this person is likely to do well.

Domain IV, the Participative Implementer. A combination of affective and concrete preferences constitutes domain IV, where the "participative implementer" is located. The manager with people skills who has the opportunity to work closely with people is found in this category. This is the place where implementers and highly skilled organization development consultants reside. This domain is for those who like to become involved and who have the ability and interest in working with the emotional needs and demands of the people in an organization. This is the domain that is emphasized by most of the practical management programs, and it can be used to complement the traditional educational programs of domain I.

REFERENCES

Blake, R. R., & Mouton, J. S. (1984). *Managerial grid III* (3rd ed.). Houston, TX: Gulf.

Jung, C. G. (1924). *Second impression* (H. Godwin, Trans.). New York: Harcourt Brace.

Kolb, D. A., Rubin, I. M., & McIntyre, J. M. (1974). *Organizational pschology: An experiential approach* (2nd ed.). Englewood Cliffs, NJ: Prentice-Hall.

Mintzberg, H. (1976, July-August). Planning on the left side and managing on the right. *Harvard Business Review*, pp. 49-58.

Peters, D. (1985). *Directory of human resource development instrumentation*. San Diego, CA: University Associates.

Pfeiffer, J. W., Heslin, R., & Jones, J. E. (1976). *Instrumentation in human relations training* (2nd ed.). San Diego, CA: University Associates.

Rogers, C. R. (1982). *Freedom to learn*. Columbus, OH: Charles E. Merrill.

Kenneth L. Murrell, D.B.A., *is an associate professor in the managment department of the University of West Florida in Pensacola and is also an organization development consultant. He has worked with the United Nations, the World Bank, and USAID in developing management and institutional development plans and programs. Dr. Murrell has also served as an internal organizational development consultant for G.D. Searle in Chicago, and he is a co-editor of* Management Infrastructure for the Developing World.

THE LEARNING-MODEL INSTRUMENT
Kenneth L. Murrell

Instructions: For each statement choose the response that is more nearly true for you. Place an X on the blank that corresponds to that response.

1. When meeting people, I prefer

    _____ (a) to think and speculate on what they are like.

    _____ (b) to interact directly and to ask them questions.

2. When presented with a problem, I prefer

    _____ (a) to jump right in and work on a solution.

    _____ (b) to think through and evaluate possible ways to solve the problem.

3. I enjoy sports more when

    _____ (a) I am watching a good game.

    _____ (b) I am actively participating.

4. Before taking a vacation, I prefer

    _____ (a) to rush at the last minute and give little thought beforehand to what I will do while on vacation.

    _____ (b) to plan early and daydream about how I will spend my vacation.

5. When enrolled in courses, I prefer

    _____ (a) to plan how to do my homework before actually attacking the assignment.

    _____(b) to immediately become involved in doing the assignment.

6. When I receive information that requires action, I prefer

    _____ (a) to take action immediately.

    _____ (b) to organize the information and determine what type of action would be most appropriate.

7. When presented with a number of alternatives for action, I prefer

_____ (a) to determine how the alternatives relate to one another and analyze the consequences of each.

_____ (b) to select the one that looks best and implement it.

8. When I awake every morning, I prefer

_____ (a) to expect to accomplish some worthwhile work without considering what the individual tasks may entail.

_____ (b) to plan a schedule for the tasks I expect to do that day.

9. After a full day's work, I prefer

_____ (a) to reflect back on what I accomplished and think of how to make time the next day for unfinished tasks.

_____ (b) to relax with some type of recreation and not think about my job.

10. After choosing the above responses, I

_____ (a) prefer to continue and complete this instrument.

_____ (b) am curious about how my responses will be interpreted and would prefer some feedback before continuing with the instrument.

11. When I learn something, I am usually

_____ (a) thinking about it.

_____ (b) right in the middle of doing it.

12. I learn best when

_____ (a) I am dealing with real-world issues.

_____ (b) concepts are clear and well organized.

13. In order to retain something I have learned, I must

_____ (a) periodically review it in my mind.

_____ (b) practice it or try to use the information.

14. In teaching others how to do something, I first

    _____ (a) demonstrate the task.

    _____ (b) explain the task.

15. My favorite way to learn to do something is

    _____ (a) reading a book or instructions or enrolling in a class.

    _____ (b) trying to do it and learning from my mistakes.

16. When I become emotionally involved with something, I usually

    _____ (a) let my feelings take the lead and then decide what to do.

    _____ (b) control my feelings and try to analyze the situation.

17. If I were meeting jointly with several experts on a subject, I would prefer

    _____ (a) to ask each of them for his or her opinion.

    _____ (b) to interact with them and share our ideas and feelings.

18. When I am asked to relate information to a group of people, I prefer

    _____ (a) not to have an outline, but to interact with them and become involved in an extemporaneous conversation.

    _____ (b) to prepare notes and know exactly what I am going to say.

19. Experience is

    _____ (a) a guide for building theories.

    _____ (b) the best teacher.

20. People learn easier when they are

    _____ (a) doing work on the job.

    _____ (b) in a class taught by an expert.

THE LEARNING-MODEL INSTRUMENT SCORING SHEET

Instructions: Transfer your responses by writing either "a" or "b" in the blank that corresponds to each item in the Learning Model Instrument.

Abstract/Concrete		Cognitive/Affective	
Column 1	Column 2	Column 3	Column 4
1. _____	2. _____	11. _____	12. _____
3. _____	4. _____	13. _____	14. _____
5. _____	6. _____	15. _____	16. _____
7. _____	8. _____	17. _____	18. _____
9. _____	10. _____	19. _____	20. _____

Total
Circles _____   _____   _____   _____

Grand Totals _____   _____

Now circle every "a" in Column 1 and in Column 4. Then circle every "b" in Column 2 and in Column 3. Next, total the circles in each of the four columns. Then add the totals of Columns 1 and 2; plot this grand total on the vertical axis of the Learning Model for Managers and draw a horizontal line through the point. Now add the totals of Columns 3 and 4; plot that grand total on the horizontal axis of the model and draw a vertical line through the point. The intersection of these two lines indicates the domain of your preferred learning style.

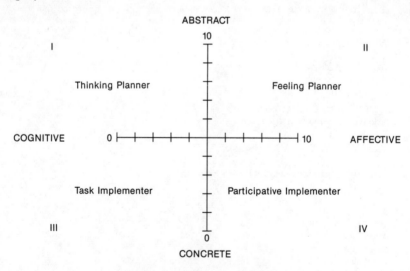

The Learning Model for Managers

THE LEARNING-MODEL INSTRUMENT INTERPRETATION SHEET

The cognitive-affective axis or continuum represents the range of ways in which people learn. Cognitive learning includes learning that is structured around either rote storing of knowledge or intellectual abilities and skills, or both. Affective learning includes learning from experience, from feelings about the experience, and from one's own emotions.

The concrete-abstract axis or continuum represents the range of ways in which people experience life. When people experience life abstractly, they detach themselves from the immediacy of the situation and theorize about it. If they experience life concretely, they respond to the situation directly with little subsequent contemplation.

The two axes divide the model into four parts or domains. Most people experience life and learn from it in all four domains but have a preference for a particular domain. Liberal-arts education has typically concentrated on abstract learning (domains I and II), whereas vocational and on-the-job training usually takes place in the lower quadrants, particularly domain III.

Occupations representative of the four styles include the following: domain I, philosopher or chief executive officer; domain II, poet or journalist; domain III, architect or engineer; domain IV, psychologist or personnel counselor.

Managerial jobs require an ability to learn in all four domains, and a manager's development depends on his or her ability to learn both cognitively and affectively. Thus, management education and development demand the opportunity for the participants to learn how to learn in each domain.

COMMUNICATION CONGRUENCE INVENTORY (CCI)

Marshall Sashkin and Leonard D. Goodstein

Many children retain more of what they hear than what they see, and vice versa. According to Fiske (1981), some even learn best when studying within the reach of food or when working with their hands, and a number of schools have built a variety of learning options into their classrooms so that students can gain knowledge within their preferred learning systems.

Grinder and Bandler (1976) propose that people also have preferences in their language behavior for one of three basic representational systems. That is, they suggest that individuals tend to prefer to think and communicate in terms of one of the three major sensory systems—seeing, hearing, and feeling (i.e., the sense of touch). Although most people are not limited to just one of these three, Grinder and Bandler argue that generally people use speech metaphors that center on either visual experience or auditory experience or kinesthetic experience, and they developed a model of communication styles that identifies three major approaches to the use of language. This concept is part of their larger model, which they call "neurolinguistic programming" (NLP).

A recent review of research on NLP (McCormick, 1984) indicated that there was little, if any, real support for the basic tenets of NLP. Although young children often display a preference for and even learn better through the use of one or another of the three major sensory systems, by the time they reach adulthood they generally do not have a dominant representational system. Even Bandler and Grinder (1975) note that such a limitation would be an indicator of pathology.

There was, however, one substantial research finding relevant to representational systems and their reflection in language. Brockman (1981) and Frieden (1981) found that therapists who matched their own style to that used by the client were more effective in establishing client trust and rapport. Rath and Stoyanoff (1982) describe the importance of matching language styles in the following way:

> If two people are having trouble communicating, the problem can be diagnosed by analyzing the principal representational system being used by each person. If it is discovered that these people tend to emphasize different types of imagery, their communication can be improved by involving a third person to translate for each in terms of his or her preferred system. As a result of this process, each of the original parties hears terminology consistent with his or her preference but based on the other's representational system. When such a process takes place in a group setting, the others who are present may point out and explain what is being observed. These explanations help the two parties to understand that their inability to communicate is based not on unwillingness to do so but rather on the fact that they have different styles of communication because they use different representational systems. Ultimately, each of the two may become sensitive to the other's style and may generalize this sensitivity so that the communications of others are more understandable and acceptable.
>
> Such sensitivity can be a valuable asset when communicating with supervisors, clients, family members, close friends, and fellow group members. The individual who can identify another's preferred representational system can employ that system to communicate effectively with the other person. (p. 169)

These findings and observations suggest that a consultant who uses a representational system that is congruent with that used by the client is more likely to have a positive effect.

In order to measure and improve on this congruence, the Communication Congruence Inventory (CCI) was developed. Although the CCI may indicate—as does the Language System Diagnostic Instrument (Torres, 1986)—whether or not the respondent has a particular style preference, the primary purpose of the CCI is to experientially demonstrate the concept of consultant-client communication congruence and to provide a method for improving the congruence.

ADMINISTERING THE CCI

The CCI consists of fifteen items. Each item includes one initial statement, and the respondent should select one of the four alternative restatements. One of the four alternatives is a neutral restatement and three are active-listening restatements that a human resource development or organization development consultant might make in response to the initial statement of the client. Of the fifteen client statements, five use auditory terminology; five, visual terminology; and five, kinesthetic terminology. The four alternatives include auditory, visual, kinesthetic, and neutral terminology.

This instrument is designed to provide consultants with experiential feedback on how they relate to clients in terms of clarifying specific client communications. Most consultants are familiar with the concept of active listening or listening with empathy for feelings and ideas and restating to the client those expressed feelings and ideas. Such restatements are used by the consultant to help clarify the client's own thinking as well as the client-consultant communications. The scoring system will help the respondent to explore the degree of congruence between the selected alternatives and the initial statements.

SCORING AND INTERPRETING THE CCI

A scoring form, which is already marked with the congruent responses, is provided. After the respondent has completed the instrument, his or her selections should be transferred to the scoring form by circling the corresponding letter on the scoring form for each of the fifteen items. Then the number of circles in each of the four columns should be written on the corresponding "total circles" line. Next, the number of squares that were circled in each column is written in the boxes underneath the "total circles" lines. The total of the scores in the three boxes becomes the final score. No credit is given for selections in column IV (the neutral alternatives).

A consultant who is able to use language that is congruent with the client's style should select the alternative that matches the initial statement in each item. That is, if the initial statement contains auditory terminology, the respondent should select the alternative that contains auditory terminology, and so on. In no case should the neutral alternative be selected.

After the scoring is completed, the facilitator can lead a discussion on (a) why the alternatives represented by the letters in the squares on the scoring sheet are congruent with the initial statements and (b) how a consultant can listen for particular types of language used by the client and attempt to rephrase the statement with the same type of language. The facilitator can also help respondents to discover whether or not their selections indicate a preference for auditory, visual, or kinesthetic terminology.

REFERENCES

Bandler, R., & Grinder, J. (1975). *The structure of magic* (Vol. 1). Palo Alto, CA: Science and Behavior Books.

Brockman, W.P. (1981). Empathy revisited: The effect of representational system matching on certain counseling process and outcome variables (Doctoral dissertation, College of William and Mary in Virginia, 1980). *Dissertation Abstracts International, 41*(8), 3421A.

Fiske, E.B. (1981, December 29). Teachers adjust schooling to fit students' individuality. *New York Times.*

Frieden, F.P. (1981). Speaking the client's language (Doctoral dissertation, Virginia Commonwealth University, 1981). *Dissertation Abstracts International, 42*(3), 1171B.

Grinder, J., & Bandler, R. (1976). *The structure of magic* (Vol. 2). Palo Alto, CA: Science and Behavior Books.

McCormick, D.W. (1984). Neurolinguistic programming: A resource guide and review of the research. In J.W. Pfeiffer & L.D. Goodstein (Eds.), *The 1984 annual: Developing human resources* (pp. 267-281). San Diego, CA: University Associates.

Rath, G.J., & Stoyanoff, K.S. (1982). Understanding and improving communication effectiveness. In J.W. Pfeiffer & L.D. Goodstein (Eds.), *The 1982 annual for facilitators, trainers, and consultants* (pp. 166-173). San Diego, CA: University Associates.

Torres, C. (1986). The language system diagnostic instrument (LSDI). In J.W. Pfeiffer & L.D. Goodstein (Eds.), *The 1986 annual: Developing human resources* (pp. 99-110). San Diego, CA: University Associates.

Marshall Sashkin, Ph.D., is a senior associate in the U.S. Department of Education, Office of Educational Research and Improvement, where he helps develop and guide applied research for school improvement. Dr. Sashkin has done extensive research in the areas of leadership and organization development and has published numerous books and research reports.

Leonard D. Goodstein, Ph.D., is executive officer of the American Psychological Association in Washington, D.C. His specialties are organizational behavior, consultation skills, and organization development and team building with executive groups. Dr. Goodstein is a diplomate in clinical psychology of the American Board of Professional Psychology and was formerly chairman of the board of University Associates.

COMMUNICATION CONGRUENCE INVENTORY (CCI)
Marshall Sashkin and Leonard D. Goodstein

Instructions: In each of the following fifteen items, a statement is presented that is typical of something a client might say to a consultant. Imagine that the client is speaking to you. How would you—as a consultant—rephrase the statement in order to let the client know you understood what was meant? Four alternatives are given for rephrasing each statement, and you should select one. When you have made your selection, write an X in the appropriate blank. After you have completed the fifteen items, wait for instructions from the facilitator.

1. It happened again in my division just the other day. I cannot help but feel angry when people get ahead by pushing themselves and climbing over others who are just as—or even better—qualified.

   _____ a. It makes you angry that people get ahead in this company by clawing their way up the ladder, passing over others who deserve as much or more consideration.

   _____ b. You believe that the organization's promotion policies do not always result in the best person being selecting for the job, that self-promotion often plays a big part.

   _____ c. You get burned up over people who are promoted because they blow their own horns and are heard while those who are just as qualified, or even more so, are silent.

   _____ d. You become angry when it appears that management is blind to the real qualifications of promotion candidates, promoting instead the ones most visible.

2. Roberts has been my mentor ever since I have been on this job, and I'm grateful that I can see things through the eyes of someone like that, someone who has seen it all and yet still has a real vision of the future.

   _____ a. You are thankful for a mentor who sees the situation and the future so clearly.

   _____ b. You feel grateful toward your mentor, who has helped you feel out your courses of action and move on the basis of experience and hands-on planning.

   _____ c. You are thankful for your mentor's words of widsom; by listening to and heeding Roberts' advice and stories of the future, you have benefited greatly.

_____ d. You are grateful to Roberts for giving you the benefit of both experience and good ideas of what is to come.

3. I often feel frustrated when I'm trying to build an effective team; it's like trying to conduct a symphony when each member of the orchestra wants to play his or her own tune—loudly!

_____ a. It's frustrating to try to lead and develop a team when everyone seems to be looking at a different map or seeing a different goal.

_____ b. You believe it is often difficult to develop a cohesive group when each member tries to be independent.

_____ c. You become distressed when you are trying to develop a team, because instead of listening to you, each member is shouting for attention.

_____ d. It frustrates you as a team leader when you feel the pressure of all the members straining to go their own ways.

4. It was bad enough that the error hurt the project; but when Adams made the error and tried to hide it with that transparent lie, I really saw red!

_____ a. You felt angry enough to tear into Adams, ripping apart the attempt to paper over the truth.

_____ b. You were so angry at hearing Adams speak a lie to hide the mistake that you wanted to literally shout out the truth.

_____ c. It was wrong for Adams to make such a mistake and then lie to you about it.

_____ d. It was easy to see through Adams' lie, and the attempt to cover up the mistake that way made you very angry.

5. When I received those figures, I felt so good I jumped for joy.

_____ a. You were delighted to hear the good news.

_____ b. You thought the results were excellent.

_____ c. You felt great and received a real boost from the impact of those figures.

_____ d. Seeing those great results made you feel wonderful.

6. The constant rumors that were flying around, the mudslinging, and the personal abuse on top of all that really got me down.

_____ a. The rumors and accusations seemed unending.

_____ b. It was depressing to know that people would listen to the rumors and talk about the vicious personal gossip.

_____ c. You were depressed that people could look at the rumors and accusations seriously and that you had to watch the lies about you spread around.

_____ d. The tales that were making the rounds and the impact of the accusations being hurled at you made you feel depressed.

7. I'm satisfied with this project, because it allows people to listen to information they are entitled to hear and that is beneficial to them.

_____ a. You feel glad that this project hands over to people information that really hits home.

_____ b. You believe that this project will provide people with beneficial information.

_____ c. You are satisfied because this project will let people hear what they need to hear and that your voices will not have been in vain.

_____ d. It's satisfying that when people see what you have done, they will have a clear picture of how the information can be usefully applied.

8. Anyone could see that Barnes was the best candidate. I was embarrassed because I had to go through the charade of interviewing him, look carefully at everyone, and then pick the person that the chief wanted.

_____ a. You felt embarrassed because you were forced to rubber-stamp the person the chief had already picked.

_____ b. You believed that there was no alternative but to accept the chief's choice.

_____ c. It was obvious to anyone with eyes to see that the chief had pointed out the decision in advance, and it was embarrassing to see the best choice was not made.

_____ d. You were ashamed that after hearing all the candidates, the only voice that counted was that of the chief.

9. I was worried about taking on this job after hearing all the horror stories about it, but I guess you can't always believe everything you are told. I'm really pleased with the way things have worked out.

_____ a. You believed that this job might have too many problems, but your concerns turned out to be unnecessary.

_____ b. Your initial fears about the job, based on what others had told you, were unfounded; now you're glad you didn't listen to them.

_____ c. You were initially concerned, but you soon saw that things were not as you feared, that none of the supposed problems were appearing on the horizon.

_____ d. Your hesitancy about taking the job was unfounded; moving ahead turned out to be the right action, and you're pleased that you turned down the advice of those who told you to back out.

10. When I saw that boot go under the press, I thought that Terry would come out looking like a sheet of paper. I can't tell you how relieved I was when I saw the automatic safety disengage.

_____ a. You were really upset when you thought of Terry smashed to a pulp under the tons of pressure, but you felt the tension ebb when the safety mechanism kicked in.

_____ b. It was frightening to see the accident happen right in front of your eyes, especially when you could do nothing but watch. You were very relieved when you saw that Terry was safe.

_____ c. You were certain Terry was about to die, but the safety release came on, saving Terry's life.

_____ d. You were distressed when you heard Terry cry out, expecting next to hear the sound of the press. The hiss of the safety mechanism disengaging was like music to your ears.

11. At first it sounded confusing, but I kept listening to the explanation and the instructions, and I finally realized why the new system sounded so great.

_____ a. Your initial uncertainty was resolved by your attention to what they were trying to tell you; the more you heard the better it sounded.

_____ b. Although you couldn't see it at first, you persisted until the confusion was cleared up, and it became apparent why the new system worked so well.

_____ c. You couldn't grasp it at first; but you grappled with the instructions until you finally mastered them.

_____ d. You were uncertain at first, but eventually you understood the way the new system worked and its advantages.

12. I've struggled to become a better coach to my employees, so when Carson came to me for help without being pushed, I felt really great.

_____ a. Hearing about the problem directly from Carson made you realize that the hours you spent talking and listening were really worthwhile.

_____ b. It felt great when Carson actively sought your help. You realized your struggles to become a good coach had made an impact.

_____ c. When Carson came to you for help, you realized your coaching skills had had a positive result.

_____ d. You saw the fruit of your efforts to put coaching in a positive light when Carson came to see you, and you felt great about that.

13. In a sense, I felt sorry for them. The concept they were trying to deliver has its good points. But the presentation was so poor and came across so badly that I thought I'd laugh so hard I'd fall out of my chair.

_____ a. Although sympathetic, you were amused when it was clear that the picture they were painting looked so ridiculous.

_____ b. Although you felt sorry for them, their performance was so poor that you almost fell over with laughter.

_____ c. You considered their presentation an amusing failure.

_____ d. The longer you listened to their presentation, the more your sympathy was replaced by amusement. Finally, it was so bad that you thought you would laugh out loud.

14. I wasn't sure that I should do it at first, but I showed my boss where to look for the flaws in the proposal and outlined my viewpoint. When my boss saw that what had been pictured was not really possible and that my view was correct, I felt vindicated.

_____ a. You believe you did the right thing by reviewing the flaws of the proposal with your boss, who agreed with your critique.

_____ b. Although you were uncertain, your boss listened closely to your analysis, hearing out your assessment of the proposal's problems and leaving you feeling pretty good.

_____ c. You are glad you overcame your hesitancy and extended yourself to make the presentation, because once you laid out all the facts and problems, your boss agreed with you.

_____ d. You feel great that you showed your boss the problems with that proposal, giving a more realistic view and a chance to review the options.

15. I was shocked by top management's announcement of the reorganization. I heard the words, but it took a while for me to hear all the implications.

_____ a. You were so surprised when they told you about the planned changes in the organization that you really did not comprehend what you had heard.

_____ b. You were taken aback by the news, because you hadn't seen it coming. When management suddenly unveiled the plan, you did not even understand it.

_____ c. You were knocked off your feet when they dumped the news of the reorganization on you. At first you could not even pick up what they were trying to get across.

_____ d. You were puzzled by the reorganization plan, because it was a complete surprise to you.

CCI SCORING SHEET

Instructions: After you have completed the Communication Congruence Inventory, transfer your answers to the scoring form in the following manner:

1. Circle the letter on the scoring form that corresponds to the response you selected for each of the fifteen items. You will notice that the letters on the scoring form are not in alphabetical order, so be sure to circle the *letter* that preceded the response you selected on the CCI.

2. Count the number of circles in Column I and write the total on the "Total Circles" line under Column I. Repeat this process for Columns II, III, and IV.

3. Count the number of squares that you circled in Column I and write the total in the box that appears above the word "Visual." Repeat this process for Column II and write the total in the box that appears above the word "Auditory." Repeat the process for Column III and write the total in the box above the word "Kinesthetic." (No squares appear in Column IV.)

4. Add the figures that appear in the three boxes and write the total in the triangle. This is your total score.

5. For a visual interpretation, transfer the scores from the boxes to the large triangle that precedes the interpretation sheet. The dot in the center of the triangle is zero. Each score should be plotted on the line in the direction of the corresponding corner of the triangle. When all three points have been plotted, connect each of them to the other two points with a line.

University Associates

CCI Scoring Form

Item	Column I	Column II	Column III	Column IV
1	d	c	[a]	b
2	[a]	c	b	d
3	a	[c]	d	b
4	[d]	b	a	c
5	d	a	[c]	b
6	c	b	[d]	a
7	d	[c]	a	b
8	[c]	d	a	b
9	c	[b]	d	a
10	[b]	d	a	c
11	b	[a]	c	d
12	d	a	[b]	c
13	a	d	[b]	c
14	[d]	b	c	a
15	b	[a]	c	d

Total Circles

Visual	+	Auditory	+	Kinesthetic	=	TOTAL

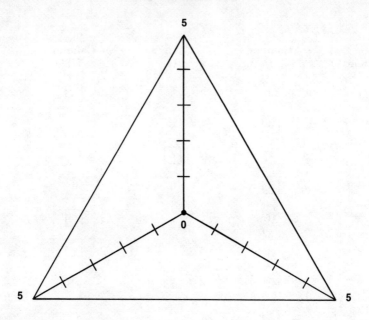

CCI INTERPRETATION SHEET

The Communication Congruence Inventory (CCI) is based on Bandler and Grinder's concept of predicate matching, which is derived from their theory of human communication. Bandler and Grinder argue that individuals generally prefer to think and communicate in one of the three major ways of representing thought and language: vision, hearing, and physical sensation (or *kinesthetics*). The CCI was developed because there is some research evidence that consultants are more effective when they match their linguistic modes to those used by their clients. Thus, when responding to a client who has just used visual terminology, the consultant would be more effective if he or she also used visual terminology. The same would be true about auditory and kinesthetic terminology. The CCI indicates how well you, as a consultant, are able to match your terminology to that of a client.

Each of the fifteen initial statements on the CCI is followed by four restatements, which represent auditory, visual, kinesthetic, and neutral terminology. The neutral statements play down or omit affective components, thus making them poor active-listening responses. A consultant who is attuned to the representational system used by the client will select the matching restatement for each of the fifteen items. That is, an auditory restatement would be selected for an auditory initial statement; a visual restatement, for a visual statement; and a kinesthetic restatement, for a kinesthetic statement. In no case should the neutral restatement be selected.

If the restatements are perfectly matched to the initial statements, the resulting score will be fifteen. The higher the score, the more effective the respondent is likely to be in building sound consultant-client communication relationships.

When you examine your scoring form, you can determine whether or not you have a bias toward a particular mode. Column I represents the visual mode; Column II, the auditory mode; Column III, the kinesthetic mode; and Column IV, the neutral mode. If you have circled more than five letters in any one of the first three columns, you may have a tendency to use that mode. Scores of ten or above for one of those columns suggest a strong bias for that mode. Scores above three for Column IV suggest that the respondent lacks active-listening skills.

Neither biases nor ineffective listening skills should be thought of as permanent problems. They can be improved through attention and practice.

THE INDIVIDUAL-TEAM-ORGANIZATION (ITO) SURVEY: CONSCIOUS CHANGE FOR THE ORGANIZATION

Will Anderson

THE ITO MODEL: GIVE-AND-TAKE AMONG INDIVIDUALS, TEAMS, AND THE ORGANIZATION

Organizations have three major components that share a give-and-take relationship: *individuals, teams,* and the *organization* itself (ITO). The ITO model (Figure 1) recognizes that give-and-take is a fact of organizational life, just as it is in many other human activities. It is the chief characteristic of the symbiotic relationship among the people, resources, structure, and goals that make up the organizational world.

The *individual* is the basic resource of any organization; most of the power with which an organization accomplishes its goals is ultimately derived from its individual members.

The *work team* is the mechanism through which individuals make their contributions. In any organization the team occupies a central and precarious position. On the one hand, it

INDIVIDUAL	TEAM	ORGANIZATION
Individual-to-Team Interface		
Individual Gives; Team Takes	*Team Gives; Individual Takes*	
Time Energy Creativity Skills and Expertise Information Dedication Loyalty Integrity	Income Recognition Job Satisfaction Growth Support Direction Structure Fulfillment of Social Needs	
	Team-to-Organization Interface	
	Team Gives; Organization Takes	*Organization Gives; Team Takes*
	Time Energy Dedication Group Strength Synergy Task Management People Management Individual-to-Organization Liaison	Policy and Goals Financial Support Material Resources Facilities Strategic Planning Structure Ethics Climate

Figure 1. The Give-and-Take Relationships of the ITO Model

must serve the individual members who do the work; on the other hand, it must serve the organization, which provides additional resources needed to accomplish the team's assigned tasks. Conflict can exist—sometimes in sharp form—when the interests of these two masters collide.

The *organization* interacts with its teams in a way similar to that in which the team interacts with its individual members. (For this reason the team and the organization can be perceived as one in a small organization.) Because the individual does not have a direct relationship with the organization, the organization can sometimes lose the perspective that it is a collection of individuals.

Each of the three components also interacts with the rest of the world: the individual in areas involving his or her own health and growth needs, family, and other interests and concerns; the team in areas that provide other needed expertise and resources; and the organization in a way that enables it to finance its operations and market its products or services. Although these external environmental factors are not as amenable to managed change as the internal ones are, proper responses to the environment are essential to the organization's success. These responses may involve issues and areas such as employee-assistance programs, community and state concerns, markets, technological advances, strategic planning, economic conditions, and the national and world political climate.

AGREEMENTS, PERCEPTIONS, AND ATTITUDES

The chief characteristic of relationships among the three components is the flow of energy, communication, and resources on which they are based. Underlying and directing this basic flow are agreements between and among individuals. These agreements, which may be written, spoken, or assumed, are the fundamental reasons that the individual works for the organization and that the organization hires the individual.

When agreements are consciously recognized and understood by all of the parties involved, the flow of energy, communication, and resources is free and the organization is healthy. Typical areas about which agreements are clearly recognized include salaries, job descriptions, time and cost agreements, and sales quotas. When agreements are hidden or unclear, the flow is restricted and the organization suffers in terms of lack of clear goals, inability to mobilize resources, and loss in productivity. Hidden or unclear agreements are not verbal or written and frequently are not in the conscious awareness of at least one of the individuals involved. An agreement can exist even when one of the parties feels coerced; he or she still agrees, although reluctantly. Some areas that can be affected by hidden agreements are influence, roles, and organizational norms.

Clearer agreements result in fewer gaps in expectations among individuals. An important objective in using the ITO model and its associated instrument, The Individual-Team-Organization (ITO) Survey, is to create greater conscious awareness of these agreements and the differences in people's perceptions of them. Once agreements and differences in perceptions have been identified, a step-by-step process can be employed to change agreements as necessary and to resolve differences in an informed way (Ackerman, 1984).

Perceptions, unlike agreements, are entirely individual; they can be gathered and used, however, as hard, numerical data with which to assess organizational effectiveness. Attitudes are another valuable organizational-assessment measure, but they cannot be gathered and used with the same precision as perceptions. It is important to note, though, that perceptions are not entirely divorced from attitudes. Clearly, we all see what we want to see to some degree. An individual's organizational reality is greatly affected by attitudes and thoughts that can "color" his or her conscious perceptions of the organization. Thus, conscious organizational change involves not only making changes in a conscious manner, but also altering people's conscious perceptions of organizational functioning.

The idea of conscious change has been an inherent part of the definition of organization development since its inception (French, 1984; Goodstein & Cooke, 1984). Terms such as *data-based* or *planned change* imply increasing the awareness of the individual involved in the change process. The starting point for the individual is an accurate assessment of his or her current perception of the organization. This assessment stage is the point at which the ITO model and the ITO survey become useful. The ITO survey is used not only to collect data about individual perceptions, but also, by feeding back the results and acting in accordance with them, to change these perceptions.

DESIGN OF THE ITO SURVEY

The design of the ITO survey is based on an individual's perception of the frequency with which certain conditions or behaviors occur in the organization. The survey consists of fifty-two items divided into three sections corresponding to the three components of the ITO model. Most of the categories dealt with in the survey conform to those traditionally used in organizational-assessment instruments, but two categories—risk taking and employee assistance—are relatively new. The emphasis given to risk taking acknowledges the need for innovation in the organization; the items on employee assistance recognize the growing use and importance of these programs in the work place. Three categories—time management, influence, and purpose—are of high concern at all three organizational levels; thus, they are dealt with in all three sections.

ADMINISTRATION OF THE ITO SURVEY

It is recommended that the ITO survey be administered to twenty to fifty people at a time, usually assembled in intact work groups. It is also recommended that the respondents be assembled and educated about the survey and how its data will be used prior to actual administration. The basic purposes of the survey can be stated as follows:

- To provide each employee with an opportunity to assess and influence the work environment;
- To provide work teams with information about their own functioning so that they can determine areas in which improvement might be needed as well as areas of particular strength; and
- To provide management with information that will be useful in designing future training and other programs intended to improve the work environment and productivity.

Plans for feedback of results also should be clearly announced.

FEEDBACK AND USE OF SURVEY RESULTS

After all respondents have completed the survey and the scoring sheet, the data are collected and averaged at team and higher organizational levels. If desired, an internal or external consultant may analyze the individual scores within each team and plot the overall team scores on a graph. Such a graphic representation of a team's data can be extremely helpful to the team members as they discuss which areas of their own or the organization's functioning may need improvement. Organization-wide data also can be plotted on a graph to illustrate how the organization is perceived by the various organizational components and levels. Individual anonymity can be preserved by reporting the results only as team or organizational averages.

The ITO survey uses comparisons rather than absolute scores. These comparisons can be made with what managers and/or nonmanagerial workers expect the scores to be; or, if the survey has been administered previously, comparisons can be made with previous scores. Equally useful is an examination of the "spread" of individual perceptions, that is, the differences or gaps between and among individuals in their perceptions of the same organizational characteristics. These gaps indicate the areas in which there is more or less confusion regarding individual perceptions of agreements.

Other ways to use the data for comparative purposes are as follows:

- To compare an individual's perceptions with those of his or her team and/or organization;
- To compare the perceptions of teams that are responsible for similar work (in conjunction with other productivity measures, if desired);
- To compare the perceptions of one or more teams with organizational norms; and
- To compare the perceptions of an individual, a team, or the entire organization with the perceptions that existed at some other point in time.

Although the analyzed ITO survey data reveal gaps in perceptions and areas of concern, the survey is not designed to yield specific information about the perceptions and agreements themselves or to provide answers about actions that might be taken in accordance with the results. For these kinds of specific information, each work team uses group-problem-solving techniques to plan action designed to address identified areas of concern. The resulting action plans can be used to institute, guide, and monitor a change process within the organization that is consistent with needed improvements indicated in the survey data. If desired, the organization can combine action plans with programs involving quality of work life, participative management, or other human resource development issues. In addition, the ITO survey can be administered yearly as part of an ongoing, evolutionary-change process based on continual review of changes in individual perceptions.

VALIDITY AND RELIABILITY

The ITO survey has face validity, and its results can serve as a useful base from which to start an organizational-change process. Because of the intended purpose of the instrument, no attempt has been made to establish validity and reliability beyond this point.

REFERENCES

Ackerman, L.S. (1984). The transformational manager: Facilitating the flow state. In J.W. Pfeiffer & L.D. Goodstein (Eds.), *The 1984 annual: Developing human resources.* San Diego, CA: University Associates.
French, W.L. (1984). *Organization development.* Englewood Cliffs, NJ: Prentice-Hall.
Goodstein, L.D., & Cooke, P. (1984). An organization development (OD) primer. In J.W. Pfeiffer & L.D. Goodstein (Eds.), *The 1984 annual: Developing human resources.* San Diego, CA: University Associates.

Will Anderson is the principal partner in the firm of Anderson & Associates, Washington, D.C. Prior to beginning his work in organization development, he worked as a research engineer and program manager for government and industry. For the last several years he has been supervising and conducting consulting and training in organizational change, strategic planning, management development, work-team development, and participative management.

THE INDIVIDUAL-TEAM-ORGANIZATION (ITO) SURVEY
Will Anderson

Instructions: This instrument consists of fifty-six statements. It is divided into three sections, each of which is designed to help you evaluate how you perceive a different aspect of your life at work. In addition, each section is divided into categories representing issues that are pertinent to that section.

On the same line with each statement are the numbers 5, 4, 3, 2, 1, and 0; these numbers correspond to the headings *Almost Always, Usually, Frequently, Occasionally, Seldom,* and *Almost Never.* For each statement, circle the number that most closely represents how often that statement is true for you. For example, if a statement is true for you almost always, circle 5; if it is frequently true, circle 3; if it is almost never true for you, circle 0. Be sure to read the information provided at the beginning of each section; it is intended to provide you with background on that aspect of your life at work so that you can more easily respond to the items in that section.

SECTION 1: INDIVIDUAL

The basic resource of any organization is its individual people. The items in this section deal with how you see *yourself and your co-workers as individuals* with regard to such issues as role clarity, satisfaction, rewards, communication, collaboration, risks, and influence.

**How Often
Statement Is True**

	Almost Always	Usually	Frequently	Occasionally	Seldom	Almost Never
Role Clarity						
1. I know what my job is.	5	4	3	2	1	0
2. The roles of my co-workers are clear to me.	5	4	3	2	1	0
Job Satisfaction						
3. I am satisfied with my job.	5	4	3	2	1	0
4. My work is meaningful to me.	5	4	3	2	1	0
Rewards						
5. I receive the recognition I deserve.	5	4	3	2	1	0
6. I believe that rewards are given fairly here.	5	4	3	2	1	0

	Almost Always	Usually	Frequently	Occasionally	Seldom	Almost Never

Communication

7. I know in plenty of time when anything important happens.

| 5 | 4 | 3 | 2 | 1 | 0 |

8. My co-workers and I communicate clearly and effectively.

| 5 | 4 | 3 | 2 | 1 | 0 |

Collaboration

9. I assist and help my co-workers.

| 5 | 4 | 3 | 2 | 1 | 0 |

10. When I need help, I can find someone who is willing and able to give it to me.

| 5 | 4 | 3 | 2 | 1 | 0 |

Time Management

11. I get things done in plenty of time to avoid a last-minute rush.

| 5 | 4 | 3 | 2 | 1 | 0 |

12. My co-workers have enough time to do a good job.

| 5 | 4 | 3 | 2 | 1 | 0 |

Risk Taking

13. I am supported in using unique and different approaches to problem solving.

| 5 | 4 | 3 | 2 | 1 | 0 |

14. In this organization failures are forgiven rather than held against people forever.

| 5 | 4 | 3 | 2 | 1 | 0 |

Employee Assistance

15. There are people here to whom I can go for confidential help when I have personal problems that affect my work.

| 5 | 4 | 3 | 2 | 1 | 0 |

16. If I or my co-workers had problems with drugs or alcohol, I would feel that I could use the resources my organization provides.

| 5 | 4 | 3 | 2 | 1 | 0 |

Influence

17. I have the authority I need to get my job done.

| 5 | 4 | 3 | 2 | 1 | 0 |

18. I feel that I have a significant impact on my work team and my organization.

| 5 | 4 | 3 | 2 | 1 | 0 |

How Often
Statement Is True

| | Almost Always | Usually | Frequently | Occasionally | Seldom | Almost Never |

Purpose

	Almost Always	Usually	Frequently	Occasionally	Seldom	Almost Never
19. I have a clear sense of what my goals are.	5	4	3	2	1	0
20. My work is important.	5	4	3	2	1	0

SECTION 2: TEAM

Your work team is the organizational environment in which you accomplish things most frequently. It is the vehicle through which you interact with the rest of the organization, and it can be an important source of social contact and support. The items in this section address issues such as leadership, meetings, conflict, problem solving, and productivity with regard to *your immediate work team.*

How Often
Statement Is True

Leadership

	Almost Always	Usually	Frequently	Occasionally	Seldom	Almost Never
21. My team has effective leadership.	5	4	3	2	1	0
22. My team leader is available to discuss issues and resolve problems.	5	4	3	2	1	0

Meeting Effectiveness

	Almost Always	Usually	Frequently	Occasionally	Seldom	Almost Never
23. When the members of my team meet, we accomplish what we set out to accomplish.	5	4	3	2	1	0
24. My team's meetings help me to get my job done.	5	4	3	2	1	0

Conflict Management

	Almost Always	Usually	Frequently	Occasionally	Seldom	Almost Never
25. My team is free of the kind of conflict that might affect its progress.	5	4	3	2	1	0
26. The members of my team have clear ways to resolve our differences.	5	4	3	2	1	0

How Often Statement Is True

	Almost Always	Usually	Frequently	Occasionally	Seldom	Almost Never

Problem Solving

27. My team solves problems in a timely fashion.

| | 5 | 4 | 3 | 2 | 1 | 0 |

28. My team has clear and effective decision-making procedures.

| | 5 | 4 | 3 | 2 | 1 | 0 |

Productivity

29. My team produces effective and valuable results.

| | 5 | 4 | 3 | 2 | 1 | 0 |

30. My team's productivity compares favorably with that of other teams here.

| | 5 | 4 | 3 | 2 | 1 | 0 |

Time Management

31. In my team we spend our time in activities that are directly useful to our work.

| | 5 | 4 | 3 | 2 | 1 | 0 |

32. The quality of my team's output is more important than any deadlines the members have to meet.

| | 5 | 4 | 3 | 2 | 1 | 0 |

Influence

33. My team's recommendations are given thoughtful consideration by management.

| | 5 | 4 | 3 | 2 | 1 | 0 |

34. The solutions that my team offers to management are implemented.

| | 5 | 4 | 3 | 2 | 1 | 0 |

Purpose

35. I have a clear sense of what the goals of my team are.

| | 5 | 4 | 3 | 2 | 1 | 0 |

36. My team has an important function here.

| | 5 | 4 | 3 | 2 | 1 | 0 |

SECTION 3: ORGANIZATION

Your organization provides you with the overall framework and resources with which you do your work. The items in this section address the issues of planning, structure, procedures, climate, stress, and purpose within *your organization as a whole*.

How Often Statement Is True

	Almost Always	Usually	Frequently	Occasionally	Seldom	Almost Never

Planning

37. My organization takes planning seriously. 5   4   3   2   1   0

38. The planning we do here is useful. 5   4   3   2   1   0

Structure

39. This organization has the flexibility needed for changing conditions and career growth. 5   4   3   2   1   0

40. The reporting system and accountability channels here run smoothly and effectively. 5   4   3   2   1   0

Procedures

41. People around here are more concerned about getting the job done than they are about accounting for time and cost. 5   4   3   2   1   0

42. Our company regulations make sense and support my work. 5   4   3   2   1   0

Climate

43. I enjoy working here. 5   4   3   2   1   0

44. I have positive feelings about my work relationships. 5   4   3   2   1   0

Stress

45. I can handle the amount of work I have to do. 5   4   3   2   1   0

46. People in this organization function so that they avoid crises and having to "put out fires." 5   4   3   2   1   0

	Almost Always	Usually	Frequently	Occasionally	Seldom	Almost Never

Time Management

47. I am able to take time to sit back and get a broader perspective on my work.

| | 5 | 4 | 3 | 2 | 1 | 0 |

48. Work flows easily here with no excessive delays.

| | 5 | 4 | 3 | 2 | 1 | 0 |

Influence

49. This organization can provide the resources needed to get the job done.

| | 5 | 4 | 3 | 2 | 1 | 0 |

50. This organization has a significant impact on its professional field and/or its marketplace.

| | 5 | 4 | 3 | 2 | 1 | 0 |

Purpose

51. I have a clear understanding of the organization's mission and goals.

| | 5 | 4 | 3 | 2 | 1 | 0 |

52. I am happy to contribute to the accomplishment of the organization's mission and goals.

| | 5 | 4 | 3 | 2 | 1 | 0 |

I think the following work areas need the most attention (circle up to five numbers).

1. Role Clarity
2. Job Satisfaction
3. Rewards
4. Communication
5. Collaboration
6. Time Management *(Individual)*
7. Risk Taking
8. Employee Assistance
9. Influence *(Individual)*
10. Purpose *(Individual)*
11. Leadership
12. Meeting Effectiveness
13. Conflict Management
14. Problem Solving
15. Productivity
16. Time Management *(Team)*
17. Influence *(Team)*
18. Purpose *(Team)*
19. Planning
20. Structure
21. Procedures
22. Climate
23. Stress
24. Time Management *(Organization)*
25. Influence *(Organization)*
26. Purpose *(Organization)*
27. _____
28. _____
29. _____
30. _____

THE ITO SURVEY SCORING SHEET

Instructions: When you have completed the survey, transfer the frequency number you circled for each item (5, 4, 3, 2, 1, or 0) to the corresponding blank on the scoring form. Next, add the two scores in each category and write the total in the appropriate square. The third step is to total all the squares in each of the three sections: *Individual, Team,* and *Organization.* Now check your copy of the survey to see which five categories you selected as needing the most attention; circle these five on the scoring form. (If you selected some categories that do not appear in the survey, write these selections at the bottom of this sheet.)

The ITO Scoring Form

Individual		Team		Organization	
1	___	21	___	37	___
2	___	22	___	38	___
Total Role Clarity	[ ]	Total Leadership	[ ]	Total Planning	[ ]
3	___	23	___	39	___
4	___	24	___	40	___
Total Job Satisfaction	[ ]	Total Meeting Effectiveness	[ ]	Total Structure	[ ]
5	___	25	___	41	___
6	___	26	___	42	___
Total Rewards	[ ]	Total Conflict Management	[ ]	Total Procedures	[ ]
7	___			43	___
8	___	27	___	44	___
Total Communication	[ ]	28	___	Total Climate	[ ]
9	___	Total Problem Solving	[ ]	45	___
10	___	29	___	46	___
Total Collaboration	[ ]	30	___	Total Stress	[ ]
11	___	Total Productivity	[ ]	47	___
12	___	31	___	48	___
Total Time Management	[ ]	32	___	Total Time Management	[ ]
13	___	Total Time Management	[ ]	49	___
14	___	33	___	50	___
Total Risk Taking	[ ]	34	___	Total Influence	[ ]
15	___	Total Influence	[ ]	51	___
16	___	35	___	52	___
Total Employee Assistance	[ ]	36	___	Total Purpose	[ ]
17	___	Total Purpose	[ ]		
18	___				
Total Influence	[ ]				
19	___				
20	___				
Total Purpose	[ ]				
Total Individual	[ ]	**Total Team**	[ ]	**Total Organization**	[ ]

THE ITO SURVEY INTERPRETATION SHEET

The scoring of the ITO survey helps individuals, teams, and organizations to focus on areas that need improvement. Comparisons can be made with what managers and/or nonmanagerial personnel expect scores to be; or, if your company has used the survey previously, comparisons can be made with previous scores. You may find it equally useful to examine the "spread" of individual scores (the gaps between individual perceptions of the same organizational characteristics).

Other ways to use the results of this survey for comparative purposes are as follows:

- To compare your perceptions (as shown by your scores) with those of your fellow team members or of the company population as a whole;
- To compare your team's perceptions with those of other teams that are responsible for similar kinds of work;
- To compare the perceptions of one or more teams with those of the company population as a whole; and
- To compare the perceptions of one person, a team, or the entire company with the perceptions that existed at some other point in time.

You and your fellow team members can work with your supervisor or a consultant to determine other uses of the survey results and how to address any areas of particular concern that you identify.

University Associates

INTRODUCTION TO THE
PROFESSIONAL DEVELOPMENT SECTION

This is the fourth year of the *Annual's* Professional Development section. In the 1984 *Annual* we inaugurated this section to bring together a variety of materials that would be useful to HRD professionals in their personal and professional development. These materials, written by professionals for professionals, provide information about the trends that are at the cutting edge of the rapidly developing, ever-changing field of human resource development: the directions in which the field is heading; new technologies (and new uses of old technologies); the personal and professional stresses and dilemmas experienced by HRD professionals in their daily work; new areas for application; new processes, perspectives, outlooks, and theoretical developments; and attempts to integrate specific content areas.

This section includes articles that HRD professionals can bring to the attention of others on the management team or use in a training session. Such articles often are useful in documenting or supporting a position or in explaining a complex or subtle point. These articles also can be used to help HRD professionals to "sell" a broader understanding of the HRD function to line managers who need distance, time, and documentation in order to modify their views or to support their emerging understanding.

The Professional Development section includes the contents that previously were found in the Lecturette, Theory and Practice, and Resources sections of the first twelve *Annuals*. When lecturettes are intended for specific structured experiences or instruments, they will appear in those sections. When lecturettes appear in the Professional Development section, they will include background information for the potential HRD user, together with information on when and where such a lecturette would be appropriate. Resource pieces will alert the reader to additional readings, educational programs, materials, groups, and other sources of further professional development in a wide variety of subject areas related to applied behavioral science, management, and human resource development.

The fourteen articles in the following section cover a wide range of issues and topics, and most of them incorporate how-to-do-it elements. The section begins with "Competence in Managing Lateral Relations" by Burke and Coruzzi. This article is exceptionally strong and rich with practical research data that have important implications for consultants. "Impact at Ground Zero," by Doyle and Tindal, discusses the point at which managers must convert the organization's philosophy into practice. It presents an eleven-point prescription to help managers turn theory into practice. Kaufman, in his article "Toward Functional Organizational Development," offers suggestions on "what to do after the search and the passion for excellence," and Crosby's article on "Why Employee Involvement Often Fails" tells what it takes to succeed.

In "Use of the Collaborative Ethic and Contingency Theories in Conflict Management," Taft presents a conflict-intervention process that relies on two dimensions (*conflict-content/conflict-process* and *abstract/concrete reframing*) for analyzing a situation. "Humanizing the Work Place," by Schindler-Rainman, brings to our attention some global developments and trends in the work place and also examines some challenges and possible interventions.

In the next article, "Diagnosing the Training Situation," Kay, Peyton, and Pike introduce an instructional-design grid to help trainers select appropriate instructional techniques. In "Forecasting the Economic Benefits of Training," Swanson and Geroy depict a model to help predict the cost of training programs. "Career Stages and Life Stages," by Feldman, outlines the stages in a person's life and career and examines the concerns that are present at each stage.

"The Lost Art of Feedback," by Karp, gives some guidelines for effective feedback and also presents some step-by-step feedback strategies. In "Improving Client-Consultant Relationships," Kellogg offers consultants some research-based suggestions on matching, contracting, and communication processes.

"A New Model of Team Building" describes a technology that can be used immediately and that will also be appropriate for the future as seen by the authors, Kormanski and Mozenter. Dimock's "Thirty Years of Human Service Education and Training—One Perspective" contains a valuable history of training in North America.

The Professional Development section ends with "Guidelines for Contributors to University Associates Publications." These guidelines delineate the types of material we are looking for, and they also include specific directions for typing and submitting manuscripts.

As usual, the range of topics covered in this section is broad, and we do not anticipate that every article will appeal to every reader. Nevertheless, the range and scope of what we offer should encourage a good deal of thought-provoking, serious discussion about where the field of HRD is now and where it is going.

COMPETENCE IN MANAGING LATERAL RELATIONS

W. Warner Burke and Celeste A. Coruzzi

Accomplishing things in a pyramidal organization is not quite as simple and effective a process as it was a number of years ago. It is fairly clear that the pyramid is not working as well as it once did, primarily because people have changed their values and attitudes about work. It seems that people who were teenagers in the Sixties are now more dedicated to their chosen professions than they are to their organizations.

This trend is made apparent by the steady increase in the number of individuals who are obtaining advanced degrees in a variety of professions. As a result, people are entering into organizations at older ages and with higher levels of expertise required to achieve work outcomes. In addition, they bring with them value systems that have been nurtured outside their organizations and that are not necessarily in accord with company policies and procedures. Consequently, corporate norms are being challenged.

As Douglas Bray (1986), formerly with AT&T Corporations, says, individuals are not choosing management as often as before; instead, they are choosing professions. This shift has great implications for the ways in which people are managed. We are in a different stage of the pyramid today than we were in the past, so the traditional focus on monetary rewards and obedience to authority needs to be altered. In order to cope with the shift, people in organizations need to be able to influence one another in ways other than those connected with monetary or position power.

With the recognition of this need, several important questions arise:

- How can work be accomplished through other people when one does not have a formal position of authority?
- How can one influence people who are at the same hierarchical level but whose motivations are different from one's own?
- How can one influence people who are higher in the organizational hierarchy?

Most formal education with regard to management development and training has focused on managing subordinate relationships. However, the changing attitudes just discussed require a different focus. One's effectiveness in leading people without being in a position of authority or status rests in his or her ability to influence. The issue of influence as a form of leadership is the focus of this paper; the authors' conclusions about how to develop and use influence are based on their study of program managers at the National Aeronautics and Space Administration (NASA).

THE NASA STUDY

The authors have been working with NASA since 1976. Their work has focused primarily on investigating the management competencies indicative of successful manager-subordinate relationships at two levels of management, the executive level and the middle level. Thus, management competence has been examined from a vertical standpoint. Recently, however, a new kind of manager has developed at NASA; and this individual, the "program manager," does not fit the traditional management mold. Management practices previously identified as related to effective interpersonal relationships are inappropriate for successful interaction involving these new managers.

The program-management function involves the accomplishment of a broad scientific or technical goal in NASA's long-range plan through the management of a series of related projects that continue over a period of time, normally years. Program managers are staff officials who are connected with all of the NASA administrative activities that their programs comprise. Their basic responsibilities include developing and administering the guidelines and controls within which projects are conducted; competing with other program managers for resources allocated; preparing testimony and justification for Presidential and Congressional authorization; and monitoring project execution and relating that execution to NASA's overall objectives (Chapman, 1973).

What is unique about this position is the fact that program managers must manage relationships between and among different organizational units without the power of position or the power to reward. Program managers must interact with managers who are of equal or higher status and who have responsibility and decision-making authority for their own organizational units. Therefore, program managers must be able to influence others if they are to accomplish their objectives. Without having direct control, they must affect different individuals' behavior and attitudes.

The program manager's dilemma is considerable. At the outset of a program, the manager goes to Congress to vie for that program, explaining the need to investigate the particular area of aeronautical and/or space research involved. Thus, the manager must present convincing and technically sound arguments for the pursuit of his or her objectives, explaining how these objectives fit within NASA's overall goals. Assuming that the program in question is funded, the program manager must see to it that the program plans go through the proper administrative channels for authorization. At this point the manager has funding for his or her program and, consequently, is in a position of power in NASA—at least temporarily.

Then the program manager determines which of NASA's field centers can best fulfill the program's technical and research requirements. Once this has been determined, the manager must "sell" the program plans to the personnel at the chosen center. Field centers have great latitude in choosing their assignments and projects; it is through negotiation and discussion that the program manager and the field-center director agree on the terms of managing the program. Subsequently, the field-center director assigns a technical manager to carry out the program objectives, and the program manager allocates resources to the center.

After this transaction has been completed, the program manager is left with little or no control over the spending of the money funded; however, he or she remains responsible for overseeing the program's development. The program manager's primary responsibility is managing the relationships between the technical managers, on the one hand, whose positions are hierarchically equivalent to his or her own, and the headquarters administrators, on the other, whose positions are higher but who view the program manager as the expert in managing the program concerned. In the absence of a traditional hierarchical reporting structure, the program manager's ability to influence other organizational units rests largely in his or her ability to understand the limitations and constraints of the work situations involved as well as what other people expect from him or her.

The authors' study focused on the following questions:

- How does the program manager influence individuals in other parts of the organization over whom he or she has no formal power?
- What competencies distinguish the program managers who are viewed as more successful from those who are viewed as less successful?

The authors asked people who are the objects of program managers' influence attempts to rate the effectiveness of these managers. This inquiry focused on the network of individuals who are at the same and higher status at NASA. Three conceptual models were used to analyze the influence attempts made by program managers: personal power strategies, transformational versus transactional leadership, and empathy versus perspective taking.

Personal Power Strategies

At OD '80, the University Associates conference on organization development held in New York, San Diego, and London in 1980, Harrison (1980) delivered a presentation and subsequently wrote a paper about his work on personal power. His presentation focused primarily on people in organizations who do not have the traditional forms of power that are associated with positions in the hierarchy. Such individuals include staff, product/program managers, and consultants who act as resources to operating managers. In the absence of positional power, these people have to rely on what Harrison calls *personal power*. Harrison states that in order to make optimum use of personal power, one must be responsive to the "psychological energy" of the individual, group, or organization with whom he or she interacts. When one person tries to change or affect another, something analogous to physical energy or force is involved; energy is required to overcome the inertia of the other person and to produce movement or change. Harrison describes four energy modes in interpersonal relationships on which a model of influencing behaviors may be based: joining, attracting, pushing, and *disengaging*.[1]

1. *Joining.* In joining, a person adds his or her energy to that of others in order to enhance or supplement it. Joining can be accomplished by encouraging, empathizing, understanding, reflecting the ideas of others, and expressing willingness to cooperate and reach agreement. By joining, one builds an atmosphere of trust, support, and personal acceptance. The influence strategy associated with a joining response is that of *facilitator*. Responding to another person's needs can result in a strong sense of power, and this method is used to a high degree by facilitators in the area of OD consulting.

2. *Attracting.* In attracting, an individual behaves in such a way that others are drawn to join or follow that person. One who attracts people functions as a *visionary*, inspiring and energizing others and creating a sense of common purpose. This person's vision about what *can be* is a strong source of influence based on ideals and values.

3. *Pushing.* In pushing, one directs energy toward influencing others to change in some way, to adopt different attitudes, or to perform according to certain standards. This person attempts to move, induce, teach, or control others by suggesting, prescribing, and directing. In its more extreme form, this behavior results in arguing and debating. The influence strategy associated with pushing is that of *expert*.

4. *Disengaging.* In disengaging, an individual avoids or deflects others' energies in order to diminish their impact. This behavior consists of trying to influence others by keeping them from doing what they want. One disengages by withdrawing, humoring, failing to respond, or changing the subject. For example, a conflict is postponed or delayed rather than dealt with; and conflicts are depersonalized by making reference to rules and regulations. Harrison refers to the influence strategy associated with disengaging as being that of "system worker"; but for the purposes of this paper, the authors prefer to label it *deflector*. This form

---

[1]The four paragraphs that follow have been adapted with permission from "Personal Power and Influence in Organization Development" by R. Harrison, in *Trends and Issues in OD: Current Theory and Practice* by W.W. Burke and L.D. Goodstein (Eds.), 1980, San Diego, California: University Associates.

of personal power can be extremely effective, especially if one is in a position in the organization to use it. Staff personnel are often seen as deflectors; this may be the case because preventing others from doing something is the only source of power these individuals believe they have. In other words, the source of their power comes from their feeling of powerlessness (Kanter, 1985).

In the authors' study, the Harrison schema was used, in conjunction with data received from initial exploratory interviews with a sample of program managers at NASA, as the conceptual basis for the establishment of program-manager practices. The authors developed an instrument that included the four influence strategies of *facilitator, visionary, expert,* and *deflector* as well as other personality measures. This instrument was administered to a sample of program managers and individuals with whom they interact on a continual basis (project managers, program-manager supervisors, project-manager supervisors, and headquarters associates).

The findings were simple and straightforward. Strong positive correlations were found between the effectiveness of program managers and their use of the first three influence strategies (facilitator, visionary, and expert). In other words, the more program managers used these three strategies, the more they were rated as effective by their associates and superiors. In contrast, a strong negative correlation was found for program-manager effectiveness and use of the fourth influence strategy (deflector). This finding suggests that the more program managers deflect others, the less effective they are perceived to be.

Transformational Versus Transactional Leadership

Another conceptual schema used by the authors to develop an understanding of program-manager effectiveness was the distinction between "transformational" and "transactional" leadership. *Transformational* leaders are characterized by their focus on change, influence, and inspiration. They are more interested in long-range issues than in day-to-day concerns, and they are more interested in ends than in means. In addition, they are creative and may be reluctant to accept traditional ways of viewing situations. *Transactional* leaders, on the other hand, are characterized by their concern for equity in their relationships with followers, the practical issues of work, the ensurance of clarity, and the completion of short-term goals. For them, leadership is a transaction: If you do this for me (follow), I will do this for you (promote).

Transactional and transformational leadership are not necessarily polar concepts. However, they are inversely related; they represent the types of thought processes indicative of all leaders, but practiced in inverse proportions.

The authors' hypothesis was that because program managers are not managers in the traditional sense (in that they are not responsible for planning, organizing, rewarding, and evaluating the work of others), their success would be characterized as transformational in nature rather than transactional. The findings supported this hypothesis. The more program managers were rated by others as transformational leaders, the more they were perceived as effective.

To confirm this conceptual distinction, the authors looked at transformational versus transactional leadership under various work situations. They found that under most conditions, those program managers who were rated as more effective scored higher on both transactional and transformational leadership. These relationships, however, were contingent on several factors, such as the development phase of a program, which ranged from "start-up" to "up-and-running" to "down-hill," and program stability, which ranged from "stable" to "unstable." For programs operating in a *start-up* phase, individuals viewed program managers acting as transformational leaders as more effective than those acting as transactional leaders. As programs matured to the *up-and-running* phase, the more effective program managers were seen as transactional leaders. Finally, as programs proceeded into the *down-hill* phase, effective program managers were viewed as transformational leaders.

In addition, the authors examined stable versus unstable program conditions and found that effective program management in *unstable* conditions was associated more with transformational leadership, while under *stable* conditions it is associated with transactional leadership.

Empathy and Perspective Taking

The authors' third step in studying program managers was to analyze the impact of empathy on perceived effectiveness. Two scales were used in the instrument to assess the multidimensional concept of empathy: the "empathic-concern scale," which taps a person's tendency to become emotionally involved while observing events in which others participate, and the "perspective-taking scale," which taps a more rational form of relating in which the person tends to understand the experiences of others without necessarily having strong emotions. The empathic-concern scale is predictive of helping behavior, and the perspective-taking scale has been shown to predict accuracy in interpersonal judgment and skill in bargaining situations.

The authors examined the impact of empathy on individuals' perceptions of program-manager effectiveness in stable and unstable situations. The findings suggest that under *stable* conditions, program-manager effectiveness is based on being empathic with another, sustaining and maintaining the other's energy and direction. However, under *unstable* conditions, program-manager effectiveness is associated with perspective taking and the ability to look at the overall picture.

IMPLICATIONS

More and more frequently it is the case that managers within organizations have no formal or traditional power and must accomplish things through personal power. Like the program managers at NASA, people are beginning to see personal power as a positive force in organizational life and are beginning to cultivate it. The results of the authors' study indicate that under stable work conditions, the individual who wants to be influential must maintain and sustain the flow of events. Facilitating, acting in a transactional-leadership role, and being empathic seem to be appropriate responses to stable conditions. However, when the work situation is unstable, such a manager might be perceived as more successful by acting as a visionary, taking a transformational-leadership role, and assuming perspective and examining the overall picture.

These findings may be generalized to other types of roles, such as that of organization development or human resource development consultant. It appears that people who are in the role of influencing others are not evaluated solely in terms of being facilitators. One who wants or needs to influence others in an organizational setting first should ascertain the particular conditions under which he or she must operate:

- Is the project involved characterized by stability or instability? (Under stable conditions, transactional leadership and an empathic approach may be more effective; under unstable conditions, transformational leadership and concentrating on the overall picture may be more effective.)
- Is the project in a "start-up," an "up-and-running," or a "down-hill" phase? (During the "start-up" and "down-hill" phases, transformational leadership may be preferable; during the "up-and-running" phase, transactional leadership may be a more viable approach.)

- Does the situation necessitate the role of facilitator, visionary, or expert? (All three of these roles can be effective, depending on the circumstances involved.)

As indicated in the results of the study, each of these situations requires a different emphasis and combination of influence strategies. It is the authors' belief that any person put in the position of influencing others can exert the appropriate strategy to elicit the appropriate response. Thus, the focus of attention should not be exclusively on how good one is at being a facilitator, visionary, or expert, or whether one by nature prefers transactional versus transformational leadership or an empathic approach versus one that emphasizes perspective; instead, the focus should be on how accurately one characterizes the situation so that the appropriate influence strategies are used.

REFERENCES

Bray, D. (1986, March). Management careers: Their nature and nurture. Presentation at *UA '86* in San Francisco.

Chapman, R.L. (1973). *The program management in NASA: The system and the men.* (SP-324, Stock No. 3300-00514). Washington, DC: Scientific and Technical Information Office, National Aeronautics and Space Administration.

Harrison, R. (1980). Personal power and influence in organization development. In W.W. Burke & L.D. Goodstein (Eds.), *Trends and issues in OD: Current theory and practice.* San Diego, CA: University Associates.

Kanter, R.M. (1985). *The change masters: Innovation for productivity in the American Corporation.* New York: Simon & Schuster.

W. Warner Burke, Ph.D., is the president of W. Warner Burke Associates, Inc., in Pelham, New York. In addition, he is a professor of psychology and education as well as the director of the graduate program in organizational psychology at Teachers College, Columbia University, in New York City. His specialties are organization development, managerial competence, management, and human resource development.

Celeste A. Coruzzi, Ph.D., is an organization development consultant with W. Warner Burke Associates, Inc., in Pelham, New York. Her specialties include researching organizational behavior and applying the results to company policies and programs. Her current research efforts are the identification of effective management practices, organizational climate, and culture within client organizations.

IMPACT AT GROUND ZERO: WHERE THEORY MEETS PRACTICE

Patrick Doyle and C.R. Tindal

> The best laid schemes
> o' mice and men
> gang oft aglee
>
> Robert Burns ("To a Mouse")

Ground zero is the point at which managers must convert the organization's philosophy or management "style" into management practices. It is the transition between what a particular management theory or concept says should happen and what the manager actually does. However, as Robert Burns pointed out two centuries ago, things often do not work out as expected. There are numerous examples in the HRD literature of implementation that have "missed the target."

- "Management by objectives works," says Peter Drucker, "if you know the objectives. Ninety percent of the time you don't" (Tarrant, 1976). This may be why management by objectives (MBO) has not always lived up to its advance billing.
- Many organizations have embraced new budgeting techniques such as program budgeting, PPBS (planning-programing-budgeting system), and zero-base budgeting, only to abandon each in disillusionment.
- Many systems of performance appraisal that look so impressive on paper often degenerate into meaningless exercises (McGregor, 1957) involving the completion of forms to satisfy the personnel department.
- Although Peters and Waterman (1982) and others have described various, common-sense approaches to organizational excellence, these approaches seldom are applied successfully.

The answers to these dilemmas are to be found at ground zero: the critical point at which any of these management concepts and approaches actually must be implemented. Although we have an abundance of theories, we appear to lack sufficient understanding of how any particular management approach should be introduced, implemented, measured, and monitored. We need to know more about what happens—and what should happen—at ground zero.

The first part of this article will list some of the problems in attempting to implement theories and describe the symptoms of those problems; the second part of this article will provide prescriptions for turning theory into practice more effectively.

PROBLEMS IN IMPLEMENTING MANAGEMENT THEORY

Everybody Has an Answer

Much of the confusion in the implementation of theory arises from the plethora of theories and concepts being advocated today. Theories change continually and often contradict one another. The following will help to illustrate this.

- There still is some controversy about the reasons for the effects cited in the Hawthorne Studies (Carey, 1967; Dickson & Roethlisberger, 1966; Hersey & Blanchard, 1982; Landesberger, 1958; Rice, 1982; Shepard, 1971), often cited as the beginning of humanistic management practices.
- Although the "Japanese style of management" (Theory Z) has been advocated as the wave of the future (Ouchi, 1981; Pascale & Athos, 1982), we have learned that the Japanese are only practicing management techniques about which Americans have known (Wheelwright, 1981) but which they have failed to practice (Hayes, 1981). In addition, we are told that Japanese management has its own problems and that many of the popular beliefs about Japanese management are either myths or are no longer true because of changes in the nature of the Japanese work force (Kobayashi, 1986).
- Characteristics of America's best-run companies were revealed in a search for excellence (Peters & Waterman, 1982; Peters & Austin, 1985), then some of these same companies experienced organizational problems.

Theories of Management Are Important

Even though their diversity presents problems, the need for management theories has been defended strongly (Granger, 1964). The concept that "practice is static, it does what it knows well," whereas "theory is dynamic" (Urwick, 1952) is important. Theory enables us to build contingency plans for future practices and to consider the influence of change on today's methods. We must appreciate the fact that theory and practice do not exist as independent extremes on the scale of management alternatives. Theory without practice is a luxury that organizations cannot afford. Practice without theory is a one-way ticket to obsolescence. To manage successfully in today's organizations, managers must understand theories of management and must be able to translate them into specific practices. Managers must learn to function effectively at ground zero, where theory meets practice.

Apart from the confusing array of highly touted theories, there are a number of other reasons for the frequent failures at ground zero.

Symbols over Substance

When Ouchi, Pascale, and others wrote about the benefits of the Japanese approach to management, many organizations immediately established quality circles; many announced their commitment to worker involvement in decision-making processes; and a few considered lifetime-employment practices. Most of them, however, adopted only the symbols of Japanese management styles. They did not change their basic attitudes or ways of operating.

In attempting to keep up with the latest management practices, organizations have engaged in a form of show and tell, embracing the terminology and the trappings of a fashionable theory but not (a) understanding the purpose and elements of the theory or (b) training those who were expected to implement the theory well enough to make the substantive changes that were necessary to support the new approach.

"Achiever" Managers and Change for Change's Sake

One of the reasons why many organizations superficially embraced one theory after another without giving sufficient attention and time to any of them is that managers today are expected to implement changes. Furthermore, a large number of managers have ascended the hierarchical ladder because they are achievement driven. Such managers require high reinforcement, accomplished by "doing" and "completing" things. Some of them are characterized by reaction (doing something) without proaction (planning what to do). Because achievers have the tendency to jump in and do things themselves, rather than to invest the time needed to train their subordinates (McClelland, 1976), they may be poor teachers, trainers, or mentors. But they are *noticed* in organizations; they usually are at the center of any activity, working toward its rapid completion. Being noticed is prerequisite to promotion.

In their search for reinforcement, achievers continually look for activities that they can *complete*. Activities such as conceptualizing and planning to meet the organization's needs fifteen years in the future do not have high visibility and, thus, are of limited interest to achievement-driven managers. They are more interested in something with a not-too-distant completion date and with high visibility. Although such behavior is understandable, so is its impact on the organization when achievers are promoted into senior management positions, which call for less doing and more planning.

When promoted, the achiever tends to look for a "new" approach to managing the organization, one that is highly visible or "high profile." Unfortunately, there is little interest in detailed follow-up or in monitoring activities on a daily basis. The achiever tends to be impatient with the lengthy time frames needed to implement most management theories. Thus, an organization that is led by achievers may be introduced to a new management theory or concept every two or three years, primarily to cater to the achievers' needs to be doing things.

The Search for the Simple Solution

In their desire to find solutions that will have predictable success, managers may seek simplistic answers. The search for the simple solution is likely to be based on several questionable beliefs.

* Simple solutions often are associated with rapid implementation and fast results. This psychology is part of management's belief that understanding a change is equivalent to acceptance of the change. The assumption is made that simple solutions are easily understood and, thus, easily accepted. As a result, when planned change is unsuccessful, the excuse often is that those involved failed to understand the purpose and importance of the change (presumably because it was too complicated). In fact, it is more likely that the individuals involved understood the purpose of the change but reached different conclusions about its validity. It also is unlikely that merely because a need and proposed solution is obvious to one person or group, it also will be obvious to others.

* Another complicating factor is the belief that one can simplify change by presenting it as *not* being change. When faced with the need to introduce change, managers may attempt to convince employees that they already are operating in the desired manner: For example, a manager may introduce MBO to a subordinate by claiming that

"All you do is write out as objectives the things that you are already doing; it's nothing more than a change in terminology."

Such an approach may be quite comforting to the employee in the short run. People often prefer stability and continuity—both of which are insinuated by the manager's comments. But this approach virtually ensures future complications and difficulties. The manager would be ignoring the need for innovative and problem-solving objectives that go beyond the basic job description of the employee and help to ensure the adaptability and survival of the organization. The manager would also be disregarding the fundamental change in the basis of evaluating the employee's performance that should now occur. These are but two of the major implications of MBO that are ignored when a manager attempts to pass it off as nothing more than a change in terminology.

Failure to Follow Through

Much of the difficulty at ground zero is caused by failure to audit the implementation of the theory being adopted. There are a number of reasons why the auditing and follow-up stages may be neglected or ineffective.

- Unless one is very clear at the outset about the objectives of the new approach and the results that are expected, there may not be much of a basis for measuring change.
- Even if the process begins with objectives, it still is difficult to translate objectives into measurable work standards that are suitable for auditing purposes.
- If one is able to follow through and measure results, one may not like what one finds. An effective auditing program may confront management with the fact that the planned change has not been successful; and if lack of success is documented rather than merely suspected, it is likely that someone will have to accept responsibility for the failure. Particularly if a change has been directed primarily for the sake of change, auditing the implementation of a theory may be seen as (a) too much trouble and (b) risky. Bad news does not ascend well and tends to become filtered or watered down at each successive level. Avoiding the follow-through phase avoids the strains and repercussions.

Without auditing and follow through, however, it is questionable whether there is any point in introducing any organizational change.

Failure To Focus on Strategy

Organizations tend to deal with isolated, specific changes rather than with an overall strategy of change—a framework within which change will take place. McConkey (1967) states that there must be a foundation of trust within the organization prior to the introduction of MBO. Ironically, MBO is often introduced as a solution to a lack of trust in an organization. Building trust is a slow, laborious undertaking that requires patience and the ability to accept disappointments when progress is not as rapid as anticipated (Argyris, 1971). It requires meticulous consideration of detail in dealing with others. These requirements have a striking contrast to typical characteristics of achiever managers. The search for a quick and simple solution often leads to the adoption of MBO before the organizational climate is prepared for it.

Another problem is that the installation of MBO requires a great deal of time (Odiorne, 1972; McConkey, 1972). From three to four years are necessary to implement the concept successfully. Such long-term results are generally beyond the time focus of the achiever managers to whom the implementation of change is assigned. Typically, such managers would anticipate two or three major changes in responsibility in that period of time. As a result, the implementation of MBO may be passed to several different managers, each of whom is anxious to see the task completed as quickly as possible.

Other Examples

There are many other examples of a misdirected focus on specifics rather than on overall strategy. Many organizations have responded to the publication *In Search of Excellence: Lessons from America's Best-Run Companies* (Peters & Waterman, 1982) by instituting awards nights and service pins for employees without otherwise changing the ways in which they treat their employees. Similarly, the concept of management by walking around (MBWA) has encouraged some managers to try to avoid spending more than 25 percent of their time in their offices. However, most of them are not sure what to do with the other 75 percent of their time, resulting in a new version of MBWA: management by wandering aimlessly. The specifics may be there, but the overall strategy is missing.

THE SOLUTIONS

The following prescriptions can increase a manager's effectiveness at ground zero—turning theory into practice.

1. Plan Before You Plunge

The change process should begin with the development of a comprehensive plan for implementation. The following questions—along with others, of course—need to be answered in an implementation plan: Who will be responsible for implementing the change? Will the change be introduced throughout the organization simultaneously? When will the change be introduced? What resources will be required to handle the implementation? What follow-up steps will be needed to monitor progress toward implementation?

2. Don't Crusade Alone

It is foolish to introduce a new management system or concept unless there is strong commitment from senior management. Interest in and support for the change need not be unanimous. Under certain circumstances, it may be effective to begin with a pilot project in a department or section that is most enthusiastic about the proposed change. However, to introduce a change when opinions are sharply divided or when key members of the management team are strongly opposed is almost certainly futile.

3. Bring Everyone on Board

Training programs should be developed to familiarize all concerned with the change being introduced and with the specific ways in which they (or their responsibilities) will be affected. In general, managers do not respond favorably to being told to attend a seminar or read a book about an imposed change. Customized training should take into account the distinctive features of the organization, in order to ensure a common understanding of the nature and purpose of the change.

4. Be Sensitive to the Various Impacts of Change Within the Organization and Among Individuals

The introduction of new management theory does not affect all parts of the organization equally. Some individuals are more directly affected than others. Obviously, the nature of the impact on the person's work will influence the degree of reaction and resistance that can be anticipated. Those responsible for implementing change should attempt to assess its probable impact and should develop appropriate strategies to deal with those who are likely to feel threatened (Doyle, 1985). The insights gained from such analysis should be reflected in any implementation plans and training programs.

5. Implement the Entire Change Strategy, Not Just Slogans

Specific management practices take place within a strategy, and both the strategy and the practice must remain within the focus of the manager. For example, a program to generate a positive customer orientation in employees requires that the employees also be treated in a positive, adult manner. In the same vein, superficial compliments or rewards will not enhance productivity if employees are otherwise managed in a dictatorial or competitive environment.

One organization had been attempting to develop excellence and had placed great emphasis on "concern for employees," evidenced by forms of recognition such as service pins and awards. An employee of this organization stated that he found it more productive to work part of the time at home because of the convenience of his microcomputer and research materials there. His manager, however, was unable to cope with this exception to the normal working arrangements. Not surprisingly, the negative effect of the manager's refusal to consider alternatives more than offset the positive effect to the employee (and his colleagues) of the awards and service pins. Although the awards were symbolic, the manager's actions were seen as substantive and as indicative of the organization's real attitude toward employees.

6. Measure, Monitor, Modify, and Maximize

If changes are to be implemented effectively, there must be follow through. "People respect what you inspect" (Argyris, 1982).

In one organization, a training auditor was appointed to ascertain that the practices of the managers were consistent with the training that had been conducted. The auditor met periodically with the operating managers to determine, through discussion and review of documents, whether the training was having an impact on their activities (at ground zero). Managers who had attended a seminar on reinforcing employees were asked to show any recent letters of appreciation sent to their subordinates. Samples of performance-appraisal documents were examined in the case of managers who had attended a seminar on this topic. As a consequence of this follow-up, managers applied the training suggestions more faithfully than is the norm in organizations that do not conduct such an audit. In addition, the findings of the auditor led to improvements in the training program.

7. Use Time As a Tool

The implementation of almost any theory is measured in years, not months. Do not expect quick results or allow staff members to expect overnight improvements. Such expectations lead only to disillusionment and often result in loss of commitment and the eventual abandonment of the attempt. Time is a tool in implementing any change; as one thing "takes," it makes it easier for others to follow. People must become accustomed to new ideas and new procedures and they must be allowed time to learn ways to implement them most effectively. Feedback on progress and mid-course correction should be built into the change process.

8. Reinforce Desired Behavior and Highlight Progress

Because the successful implementation of change can be a long, slow process, it is important to demonstrate that progress is being made. In the early stages of the implementation of a theory, employees may place more emphasis on the lack of change or the negative aspects of the change (Schein, 1969) than on its positive aspects. Managers must be sensitive to the fact that their actions will be scrutinized closely by employees for evidence of the new strategy. Managerial behavior that is inconsistent with the theory is likely to override the organization's intended message.

A systematic follow-up procedure makes it possible to measure progress. Through the use of reinforcement techniques, individuals can be encouraged to continue their efforts in the desired direction. Moreover, the evidence that progress is being made may help to win over some of the doubters and resisters.

Although specific changes in management approaches can be highly visible in a short period of time, overall strategies are not as visible and take place over a longer period of time. Therefore, reinforcement efforts must highlight the relationship between the two so that the gradual progression of theory into practice (the transition at ground zero) is recognized and appreciated by all employees.

9. Confront and Deal with Dysfunctional Behavior

It is important that dysfunctional behavior not be tolerated or ignored. The difficulty here is that in many organizations low performance levels and other problems have been tolerated for a long time by managers who are eager to avoid conflict. Faced with the task of implementing change, such managers still will be inclined to avoid confrontation if it is at all possible. Although they may be in favor of the change and willing to encourage those who perform in the desired manner, they will try to avoid taking action in connection with the nonperformers.

If managers are allowed to ignore dysfunctional behavior, the organization again is sending out conflicting messages to its employees. In such a situation, the momentum for change may be checked, and the entire effort may be undermined. This problem has been described as "the folly of rewarding A, while hoping for B" (Kerr, 1975).

10. Beware the Half-Way Blues

As Yogi Berra once remarked, "It ain't over 'till it's over." Following the rules outlined here and proceeding well with implementation for a year or so is gratifying; the danger is that it can lead to a false sense of complacency—a feeling that the battle has been won. At this point, an organization is likely to experience the "half-way blues" and a loss of commitment. The newness of the change effort has worn off, and the desire of the achiever managers for instant success has made them restless and anxious to try something new. A well-designed implementation plan and follow-up procedure can help to head off this midpoint slump.

11. Nail Down the Implementation: Integrate the Change into the System

The challenge at this point is to ensure the continuance of the change. Too often an initiative is introduced with great fanfare, superficially accepted, and yet gradually eroded as time passes (Watson & Glaser, 1965). There may not have been open resistance. The change may not be officially withdrawn. It just does not last!

What is needed is continuing positive reinforcement and efforts to make the new approach a familiar and routine part of the day-to-day activities of the organization. In addition, provision should be made for continuing evaluation of the change and continuing maintenance efforts to prevent erosion and backsliding (Watson & Glaser, 1965).

Summary

The secret to effective utilization of new management theories is to avoid change simply for change's sake and to attempt to implement only those practices that will aid the organization in accomplishing its mission more effectively—those for which there is a need. Dabbling with management theories does more harm than good. If a change is determined to be wise, the substance of the theory must be understood and promoted, not just the trappings. Saying that something will be done does not do it; special attention must be paid to the specific implementation plan. Implementation must be consistent; the process of implementation must be monitored; and follow-up procedures must be installed. Finally, sufficient time must be allowed (without a slackening of effort and with the provision of positive reinforcement) for the change to become part of the procedure of the organization. A long time ago, someone said, "Anything worth doing is worth doing right."

A Check List for Managers

An organization that is introducing new management practices imposes additional demands on its managers, who must understand not only the new theory but also the strategy used to implement it and the implications for the organization of various changes in behavior. The check list that follows is designed to stimulate a manager's thinking about how he or she might proceed when called on to take part in the introduction of a new theory or management system.

Reviewing this check list may help the manager to think of other questions that need to be asked. The challenge is to relate the overall strategy for the proposed change to the actual operating capabilities of the organization.

Characteristic of the Strategy	Implication for Practices
1. Does the strategy assume that a specific type of groundwork has been laid (e.g., that trust exists within the organization)?	Given my present managerial practices, do the employees have reason to believe that the groundwork is in place?

If not: How can I begin to establish that foundation so that the strategy will have an increased probability of success?

What is a reasonable amount of time for this activity?

2. Does the strategy assume specific managerial skills? (E.g., many strategies require good communication skills.)	Do I have those skills to the degree necessary for successful implementation of the strategy?

If not: Am I able to acquire those skills to the degree required?

How will I acquire the skills?

What is a reasonable amount of time for this activity?

3. What assumptions does the strategy make about employees? (E.g., maturity level, ability to cope with ambiguity, commitment to organizational goals, level of needs, desire to improve the situation, etc.)	In the case of my organization, are these assumptions valid?

If not: How serious are the discrepancies?

Will they significantly influence the outcome of the change effort?

Must the discrepancies be handled before implementation or can this be part of the implementation design?

What is a reasonable amount of time for this activity?

Characteristic of the Strategy	Implication for Practices

4. What assumptions does the strategy make about the operational climate of the organization? (E.g., does it assume a "Theory X" or "Theory Y" approach?)

Does the operational climate of the organization coincide with that assumed by the theory?

If not: How important is the climate to the success of the theory?

Do changes need to be made prior to implementation or can they be attempted as part of the implementation effort?

If changes are required prior to implementation, what is a reasonable amount of time for this activity?

---

5. What assumptions does the strategy make about the economic environment of the organization? (E.g., is the organization currently experiencing reductions in staff, shortage of needed resources, arguments about priorities, or other major problems?)

Is the economic environment of the organization conducive to successful implementation?

If not: Can the economic problem be overcome during implementation?

How long would implementation be delayed if we were to wait until a more conducive economic environment exists?

What can be done to change the situation? How long will this take?

---

6. What assumptions does the strategy make about the commitment of top management? (E.g., is the support of top management critical or just desirable? Can this approach be forced from the bottom up?)

Is the level of top-management commitment sufficient to ensure the success of the approach?

If not: How necessary is the support?

Would communication with top management increase the level of support or would it be better to proceed and then demonstrate positive results to top management?

Should time and effort be spent in trying to convince top management of the value of the strategy or would this effort be in vain?

Characteristics of the Strategy	Implication for Practices

7. What level of resource commitment does the strategy assume? (E.g., time demands for both managers and employees, financial and staff resources for training, etc.)

Does the organization have sufficient resources to allocate what is needed to the change effort?

If not: Are there less costly ways in which to implement the change?

Are various levels of implementation feasible, given the present allocation of resources?

Can the theory be implemented (i.e., can management practices be changed as desired) with less commitment of resources?

REFERENCES

Argyris, C. (1971). *Management and organizational development.* New York: McGraw-Hill.

Argyris, C. (1982). *Reasoning, learning and action.* San Francisco: Jossey-Bass.

Carey, A. (1967). The Hawthorne studies: A radical criticism. *American Sociological Review, 32,* 403-416.

Dickson, W.J., & Roethlisberger, F.J. (1966). *Counseling in an organization: A sequel to the Hawthorne researches.* Boston, MA: Division of Research, Graduate School of Business Administration, Harvard University.

Doyle, P. (1985). Considerations for managers in implementing change. In L.D. Goodstein & J.W. Pfeiffer (Eds.), *The 1985 annual: Developing human resources.* San Diego, CA: University Associates.

Granger, C.M. (1964, May-June). The hierarchy of objectives. *Harvard Business Review,* pp. 63-74.

Hayes, R.H. (1981, July-August). Why Japanese factories work. *Harvard Business Review,* pp.57-66.

Hersey, P., & Blanchard, K.H. (1982). *Management of organizational behavior: Utilizing human resources* (4th ed.). Englewood Cliffs, NJ: Prentice-Hall.

Humble, J.W. (1973). *How to manage by objectives.* New York: AMACOM.

Kerr, S. (1975). On the folly of rewarding A, while hoping for B. *Academy of Management Journal, 18,* 769-783.

Kobayashi, M.K. (1986). *Japanese management: Myth and reality* (video package and booklet). San Diego, CA: University Associates.

Landesberger, H.J. (1958). *Hawthorne revisited.* Ithaca, NY: Cornell University Press.

McClelland, D.C. (1976). *The achieving society.* New York: Irvington.

McConkey, D.D. (1967). *How to manage by results.* New York: American Management Association.

McConkey, D.D. (1972, Winter). How to succeed and fail with MBO. *Business Quarterly,* pp. 58-62.

McGregor, D. (1957, May-June). An uneasy look at performance appraisal. *Harvard Business Review.* Reprinted in *The performance appraisal series,* No. 21143, (1972), pp. 5-10.

Odiorne, G.S. (1972). *Management by objectives: A system of managerial leadership.* New York: Pitman.

Ouchi, W. (1981). *Theory Z: How American business can meet the Japanese challenge.* Reading, MA: Addison-Wesley.

Pascale, R.T., & Athos, A.G. (1982). *The art of Japanese management: Applications for American executives.* New York: Warner Books.

Peters, T., & Austin, A. (1985). *A passion for excellence: The leadership difference.* New York: Random House.

Peters, T.J., & Waterman, R.H., Jr. (1982). *In search of excellence: Lessons from America's best-run companies.* New York: Warner Books.

Rice, B. (1982, February). The Hawthorne defect: Persistence of a flawed theory. *Psychology Today,* pp. 70-74.

Schein, E. (1969). The mechanisms of change. In W. Bennis, K. Benne, & R. Chin (Eds.), *The planning of change* (2nd ed.), (pp. 98-107). New York: Holt, Rinehart and Winston.

Shepard, J.M. (1971). On Alex Carey's radical criticism of the Hawthorne studies. *Academy of Management Journal, 14,* 23-31.

Tarrant, J.J. (1976). *Drucker: The man who invented the corporate society.* London: Barrie & Jenkins.

Urwick, L.F. (1952). *Notes on the theory of organization.* New York: American Management Association.

Watson, G., & Glaser, E.M. (1965, November). What have we learned about planning for change. *Management Review, 54*(11), 34-46.

Wheelwright, S.C. (1981, July-August). Japan: Where operations really are strategic. *Harvard Business Review,* pp. 67-74.

Patrick Doyle is the principal of High Impact Training Services, is an associate in Management for Tomorrow, and is a teaching master at St. Lawrence College, Ontario, Canada. He is active in the field of human resource development in retail, public administration, and public health organizations. Mr. Doyle's specialty is management techniques in evolving environments.

C.R. Tindal, Ph.D., is the president of Tindal Consulting Limited, is an associate in Management for Tomorrow, and is a teaching master at St. Lawrence College, all in Ontario, Canada. Dr. Tindal has extensive experience as a municipal consultant and trainer and is involved in management training for social-service organizations in the public sector.

TOWARD FUNCTIONAL ORGANIZATIONAL DEVELOPMENT: WHAT TO DO AFTER THE SEARCH AND THE PASSION FOR EXCELLENCE

Roger Kaufman

INTRODUCTION

The concept of organizational excellence is currently popular among organizational developers and managers. Organizations throughout the world are looking at what "excellent" organizations do and are copying many of their practices and approaches, because the "excellent" organizations are seen as delivering desired payoffs.

However, what the experts on excellence, management, and human resource development are providing are *processes*, not results; and processes are just possible ways of obtaining results. Emulating others' processes or simply searching and having the passion for excellence is not enough. Organizations that are continually successful define where they are going and why they are going there. Then they find proper pathways to achieve sustained organizational effectiveness. Copying is appropriate for clones but not for unique organizations with unique cultures and missions.

Rather than blindly playing follow the leader, an organization can adopt whatever works generically in all successful organizations and adapt those to the unique things that have in the past led organizations to unparalleled strength and success; for example, defining and determining (a) where society is going and why, (b) what the organization is now contributing, (c) the gaps between the organization's current and required contributions and/or results, and (d) what—including assumptions and methods—has to be continued or changed to close the gaps. This approach provides a rational alternative to "knee-jerk" responsiveness to client wishes, politics, and conventional wisdom as the basis for policies and decisions. Organizations must strive both to be responsive to current clients and to define what will be required in the future.

This article presents an approach for identifying and meeting needs (defined as gaps between current and required results); it links this model to policy implications; and it suggests ways to integrate policy, planning, and organizational success. Specific suggestions are provided for a Western alternative to Japanese management and for what to do after searching and acquiring a passion for excellence. It shows why and how to link means with useful ends.

Several options exist for the organizational developer: (a) keeping things the way they are, (b) making quick-fix changes to reap here-and-now improvements, or (c) deliberately fashioning future sustained improvements that are tailored to each unique organization and its environment. The pressures of day-to-day organizational marketplaces and political realities tempt one to substitute rhetoric for risk, but the demands for personal and organizational survival and contribution make the no-change or quick-fix options the most risky of all. Although it is convenient to be in mode with current "hot" ideas, a sensible leader will fashion responsive and responsible tools, techniques, ideas, and methods from that which is available; fit these to organizational characteristics and internal and external needs; and orchestrate these to meet current and future goals and objectives.

EXCELLENCE, THE JAPANESE MANAGEMENT APPROACH, AND WESTERN VALUES: IMPROVING OUR HERE-AND-NOW SUCCESS

So-called Japanese management has been successful. In fact, the Japanese management approach has been so successful that organizations the world over have studied it and have begun to copy its ways and means. Recent study (e.g., Pascale & Athos, 1981; Peters & Waterman, 1982) has indicated that many excellent non-Eastern organizations have common characteristics with their Asian counterparts. The employee value systems of these excellent organizations—Eastern or Western—integrate work and meaning as the basis for seeking success in terms of world good and improved contribution to world culture. Furthermore, excellent organizations, both foreign and domestic, recognize the importance of the client and the client's welfare, involve people constructively as participating partners in the business, take care of basics, and pay close, constructive attention to the day-to-day operations. They care about what they do and what utility it has for the clients.

Both the search and a passion for excellence are characterized by sensible factors, including an emphasis on leadership over management, vision, closeness to clients, unqualified client orientation, keeping in touch with associates as well as customers, enthusiasm, trust, zest, being a good coach, innovation in terms of client feedback, and thinking small. A number of attributes (actually processes or means) of excellence and passion for excellence are discussed by Peters and Waterman (1982) and Peters and Austin (1985).

Not all organizations have adopted the new leadership and excellence processes. Tough-minded, bottom-line-oriented Westerners still tend to target on increased productivity, efficiency, and accountability while downplaying the softer side of enterprise (such as human relations, commonly shared societal visions, group decision making, quality circles, and closeness to clients). Although efficiency and streamlined delivery count, they alone will not consistently deliver positive, sustained corporate payoff. When conventional organizations include both the softer skills and the harder ones, they often harvest success (Kanter, 1985; Kaufman & Stone, 1983; Peters & Austin, 1985; Peters & Waterman, 1982).

The Importance of a Shared Vision

Excellent Western and Japanese employees work simultaneously for themselves, their own organizations, and for the clients. Their classical-organization counterparts typically strive only for themselves; they assume that the organization can take care of itself. The conventional manager does the same, turning the organization into an adversarial battlefield.

One of the critical elements in achieving individual and collective success resides in having shared *superordinate purposes*: an agreed-on individual and organizational North Star toward which all may steer (Kaufman, 1984; Pascale & Athos, 1981; Peters & Austin, 1985; Peters & Waterman, 1982). More responsive and responsible organizations can be built when organizational efforts, organizational results, and societal impacts are aligned. If East-West excellence is to be shared, it will be through adopting the concern for superordinate goals.

This shared vision provides guidance at each level of the organization concerning what to do and what not to do, and it orchestrates individual efforts and results in a larger overall good. It allows each small piece, each breakthrough, and each product to combine and become integrated into a useful whole.

DOING WHAT IT TAKES TO BE SUCCESSFUL
TODAY AND TOMORROW...AND THE YEAR AFTER

Being Successful Today

If an organization wants to improve only in its here-and-now efficiency in meeting existing organizational purposes, it can copy the excellence blueprints and reap some quick-fix payoffs. The means, processes, how-to-do-it guidelines, and activities recommended by popular leadership-and-management authors may provide immediate results. In fact, some solid suggestions for improving here-and-now efficiency can be found in the works of Hersey (1985), Hersey and Blanchard (1982), and Peters and Waterman (1982), and in University Associates' Human Resource Development *Annual* series (1972-1987).

A first step on this road could include expanding the current planning and organizational-improvement focus from a preoccupation with unitary organizational splinters to a holistic view. For example, instead of dealing with only productivity, training, or cost cutting, the organization could be oriented toward achieving positive organizational impact in and for society as well as improving organizational efficiency. By encouraging small breakthroughs and taking the advice of excellence experts, an organization may be able to make it through today quite well. However, this does not mean the organization will be around tomorrow (Who's Excellent Now, 1984).

Caring About Tomorrow

Improving today while building for tomorrow demands some additional concerns for societal requirements and payoffs for the future; providing what the customer wants is not enough. Drivers in the United States wanted large automobiles even though the coming high prices for fuel were visible; later, when Detroit had few small cars to offer, consumers bought cars imported from foreign countries, which had dealt with the problem years earlier. Customers ask for sweet soft drinks, empty-calorie foods, and miracle drugs; then they ask why business and government did not protect them from obesity, poor diet, and drugs that adversely affect two in one million. They opt for low-priced, low-quality gadgets and complain about a throwaway economy. They demand lower taxes and more social services. In other words, they act like people.

Although the customer is not always right, the customer is always the customer. Being responsive to them is important for today and even for tomorrow. Nevertheless, a responsible organization must define what will be required for the self-sufficiency, self-reliance, and well-being of its clients, their world, and the organization. Even though building teams, developing ownership, and being responsive to clients are important, an organization must make certain that it will have products and/or services that will be required tomorrow in a world that is only beginning to show its shadow today. Listening only to clients or doing only what they suggest means operating in a reactive mode. Making clients' visions the sole source of organizational innovations is suicide.

Perceptions and judgments must be considered, but empirical evidence and hard data must also be used in making decisions. Relying solely on perceived realities can be tragic. For example, many airplanes have crashed because the pilots—even experienced ones—refused to believe their instruments and relied on their perceptions.

Combining perceived needs and those based on hard data (see Figure 1) will help an organization to be proactive and to create new areas of organizational goods and services. "Skunks" (Peters & Austin, 1985)—or off-line innovators—can be valuable if they are allowed to create products, not just solve knotty problems in existing products. Creative contributions come from finding a need and filling it, not just filling needs that are already apparent. The following guidelines will help in combining perceived data and hard data:

1. Seek and listen to the client's feedback and advice.
2. If the suggested changes are sensible, implement them. If they are not feasible, tell the client why you are not making the changes.
3. If one client's suggestion is good for other clients, generalize it.
4. Compare the perceived needs or wants of the client (e.g., increased production, increased sales, or more competent supervisors) with hard performance data and the

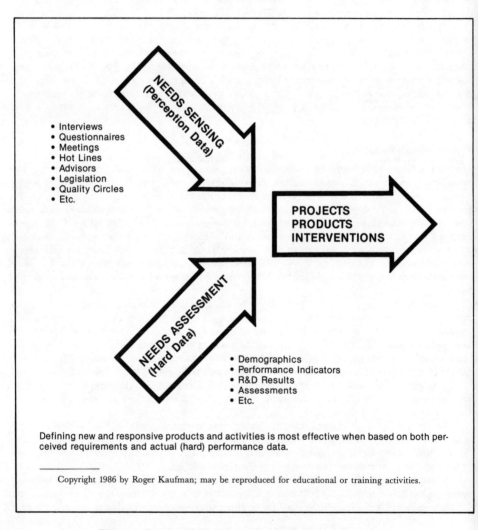

- Interviews
- Questionnaires
- Meetings
- Hot Lines
- Advisors
- Legislation
- Quality Circles
- Etc.

NEEDS SENSING
(Perception Data)

PROJECTS
PRODUCTS
INTERVENTIONS

NEEDS ASSESSMENT
(Hard Data)

- Demographics
- Performance Indicators
- R&D Results
- Assessments
- Etc.

Defining new and responsive products and activities is most effective when based on both perceived requirements and actual (hard) performance data.

Figure 1. Results of Combining Perceptions and Hard Data

resulting actual needs. (For example, the hard data may show that current profits were $100,000 when they should have been $1,000,000; forty grievances were filed against supervisors and there should have been none; or 25 percent of the shipments were rejected because of defects and there should have been none.) If the client's perceived needs and the actual needs agree, then make the necessary changes.

5. If the perceived needs and actual needs do not agree (e.g., if increasing sales without correcting the defects would not increase profits), then collect more data (e.g., determine why the defects are occurring and if the rejections are related to incompetent supervisors). Some sources for hard data might be production records, the file of grievances, profitability reports, and recorded reasons for rejections. Probe the data deeply and clarify points with the client. If disagreements still exist, either the opinions are wrong or sufficient data have not been collected. If it becomes obvious that the opinions are wrong, educate the client.

Coping with Politics

Politics has been defined as the substitution of power for rational, data-based decisions. Politics may be one of the roadblocks to a successful tomorrow, because politics is frequently another quick-fix alternative to rational goal setting and problem solving. Whether in government or in business, politicians attempt to move people toward a common ground—usually the politician's ground. By invoking statements designed to rally the troops and by appealing to "logic" (and carefully avoiding any recognition that the logic is not the same as rationality), the power broker attempts to bring about a solution that maintains the current power without necessarily responding to the organization's internal and external partners and clients.

Political decisions can be correct, of course, and may be useful when more reliable data are unavailable. Nevertheless, basing decisions on current crises and politicians' territorial imperatives or simply copying someone else is a poor alternative to finding a rational, justifiable basis for goal setting and operational activities.

One element that is required to replace politics with rationality is the determination of hard data on where the organization is going and why. For example, one chief executive expanded the employees' training program simply because he was badgered to do so by a supervisor. A closer examination, however, revealed that the employees were being asked to do hazardous work with malfunctioning tools and equipment. In another case, a supervisor purchased minivans with cages for luggage storage so that the company could "pick up clients at the airport." His real agenda, however, was that he wanted the company to provide appropriate vehicles for his show dogs. Clients arriving at the airport were so few that an ordinary automobile could be dispatched for each one.

Fortunately, people do not have to put up with politics and politicians indefinitely. They may choose to steer another course toward their common North Star.

Defining Where the Organization is Going and Why

Organizations and their policies and goals are not perfect. Most do not have any measurable statement of purpose, nor do they have useful criteria for measuring internal contributions or effectiveness in meeting organizational and societal goals. Even the best of organizations have a mixture of politics and useful purpose. This, of course, is a description of "what is" and not "what should be" (Kaufman, 1982).

Enduring, continuing, successful organizations require both the appropriate North Star toward which common effort may be directed and also policies and procedures that allow them to follow the star. Providing society with new and successful goods and services—not just improving on yesterday's successes—necessitates a shift from defining needs as wish lists to defining them as gaps between what is and what should be for both internal and external results (Kaufman, 1982; Kaufman & Stone, 1983). The world is not standing still for our convenience, and our tomorrow is not assured by simply increasing our current efficiency toward today's (and yesterday's) goals (cf. Nussbaum, 1983).

Overcoming the Passion for Process:
Relating Means and Ends

Another roadblock to a successful tomorrow is the passion for process and the assumption that processes guarantee results. Processes must be chosen wisely if they are expected to deliver useful ends. When a list of sixteen processes (from Peters & Austin, 1985, and Peters & Waterman, 1982) were analyzed, fifteen of them seemed to relate best to organizational means. Four of them were linked to organizational results, and only two of the sixteen could possibly be related to client and societal payoffs. As important as means and processes are, they make sense only when they are linked with results for the client and the world of today and tomorrow. The following steps outline a way to select means that will help produce desired results:

1. Read current books and articles on improving organizational effectiveness. Abstract and list the gems of advice, methods, and strategies.

2. Divide the list into three parts: those that deal with organizational means (the how-to-do-it items); those that deal with organizational results within the organization; and those that have an impact on outside clients, customers, and the world.

3. Define the organization's mission and objectives in a short statement of where the organization is going. Then add some indicators that will help determine when an impact has been made on clients.

4. Compare the list of item 2 with the objectives of item 3. Select the methods and strategies that appear to be able to yield results important to the organization. Gain the acceptance of associates and put the methods into practice.

5. After using the methods, evaluate their usefulness in obtaining both organizational and external results. If they are not effective, be ready to change quickly.

6. Continually collect information about future requirements. Become a "futures junky." Identify possible changes to the organization's goals and mission, and recommend such changes along with justifications. Care enough about the organization to take a risk and innovate for the future.

POLICY, PLANNING, AND PAYOFFS

Policy—the decision criteria that are used to decide what to do and deliver—should be more than good intentions. In most organizations, policy provides loose definitions of organizational purpose (e.g., "make a profit," "provide the best service in Clinksdale Corners," or "earn our wings everyday") and strict guidance only on procedures to follow. Unfortunately, policies are frequently the results of good intentions coupled with political machinations that were created when influential individuals moved into the vacuum created by the lack of rational information about where the organization was going and why it was going there.

Policies are useful to the extent to which they provide specific guidance on deciding where to go and what must be done to arrive there. Policies that restrict themselves to processes and procedures are bound to fail, because a poorly defined problem has an infinite number of solutions; or to paraphrase Mager (1975), if you don't know where you are going, just about any road will get you there.

Planning can identify where the organization is going and what must be accomplished to go from what is to what should be. However, such planning must also identify useful and realizable ends. This does not necessarily mean compromise. Rather it means recognizing the intermediate payoffs that must intervene between the methods and the ultimate results. An organization's avowed ends may be ambitious but also realizable if all agree to eventually reach them. Realizability may simply mean that the achievement of the ends must progress at a rate that allows all the players to go from what is to what should be—often step by step with a little progress each time. Patience, policy, cooperation, progress, and payoff are functional partners.

Payoffs, including profits, usually come more easily to organizations that define useful and progressively achievable purposes and then attain them. Linking policy, planning, and desired payoffs seems a sensible way to operate an organization.

EXPANDING THE FOCUS

By simply adding a positive societal impact to its current focus, an organization would be taking the stereotypical "excellence" approach (with its major concern about how to improve on "what is"). Ingenuity often achieves success by proactive and creative innovation. Therefore, organizations should continue to create a useful "what should be."

If an organization wants to develop a better tomorrow for itself, its workers, and the world, its policies, planning, development, implementation, and evaluation must include *all* elements of concern (see Table 1) for the twin dimensions of "what is" and "what should be" (Kaufman, 1982; Kaufman & Stone, 1983). A holistic perspective would include that which the organization uses (inputs), what which it does (processes), its en-route or building-block accomplishments (products), the results that it delivers to clients (outputs), and the impact for clients and society (outcomes). Together, these five components form the organizational elements; when used with the dimensions of what is and what should be, they allow an organization to orchestrate and link its efforts, accomplishments, and societal impacts.

By seeking ways to measure societal impact, however imperfect initially, an organization will be able to provide a better target for defining and following its North Star. The basic criteria for positive societal impact is that each person be self-sufficient and self-reliant, not under the care or control of another person or agent, and not addicted to other people or agencies (Kaufman & Carron, 1980). Organizations must learn not only to "do it right," but also to "do what's right" (Drucker, 1973). For example, an automobile manufacturer should strive to provide safe transportation that does not pollute the atmosphere.

Achieving societal good is not only moral, it is good business. Sooner or later, whatever an organization delivers is judged on the basis of quality, price, and its contribution to the public. If it delivers shoddy or irrelevant products, no amount of rhetoric, politics, or excuses can make up for a failed business.

REFERENCES

The *Annual* series for HRD practitioners. (1972-1987). J.W. Pfeiffer, J.E. Jones, & L.D. Goodstein (Eds.). San Diego, CA: University Associates.

Drucker, P. (1973). *Management: Tasks, responsibilities, practices.* New York: Harper & Row.

Hersey, P. (1985). *The situational leader: The other 59 minutes.* New York: Warner Books.

Hersey, P., & Blanchard, K.H. (1982). *Management of organizational behavior: Utilizing human resources* (4th ed.). Englewood Cliffs, NJ: Prentice-Hall.

Kanter, R.M. (1985). *Change masters: Innovation for productivity in the American corporation.* New York: Simon & Schuster.

Kaufman, R. (1982). *Identifying and solving problems: A system approach* (3rd ed.). San Diego: University Associates.

Table 1. Elements of Concern[1]

Element Name	Examples	Scope	Cluster
INPUTS (raw materials)	Ingredients, existing human and physical resources, existing needs, goals, objectives, policies, laws, money, values, state-of-the-world.	INTERNAL (Organization)	Organizational Efforts
PROCESSES (how-to-do-it)	Means, methods, procedures, how-to-do-its, techniques, "Japanese" management training, manufacturing, organizational development (any "doing" activity).		
PRODUCTS (en-route results)	Fenders completed, services delivered, reports completed, surgery completed, skills acquired, production quota met, tellers trained, disc drive produced, etc.		Organizational Results
OUTPUTS (the aggregated products of an organization which are delivered or deliverable to society)	Delivered automobile, delivered computer system, patients discharged, delivered finance package for municipal airport, etc.		
OUTCOMES (the effects in and for society indicated by self-reliance, contribution)	Profit, not on welfare, no addictive relationships with others and/or society, having financial credit, contributing to self and society, customer satisfaction.	EXTERNAL (Societal)	Societal Results/ Impact

Kaufman, R. (1984, October). Improving organizational impact: A Western alternative to Japanese management. *Performance and Instruction Journal*.

Kaufman, R., & Carron, A.S. (1980, Fall). Utility and self-sufficiency in the selection of educational alternatives. *Journal of Instructional Development, 4*(1).

Kaufman, R., & Stone, B. (1983). *Planning for organizational success: A practical guide.* New York: John Wiley.

Mager, R.F. (1975). *Preparing instructional objectives* (2nd ed.). Belmont, CA: Fearon.

Nussbaum, R. (1983). *The world after oil: The shifting axis of power and wealth.* New York: Simon & Schuster.

Pascale, R.T., & Athos, A.G. (1981). *The art of Japanese management: Applications for American executives.* New York: Warner Books.

Peters, T., & Austin, N. (1985). *A passion for excellence: The leadership difference.* New York: Random House.

Peters, T.J., & Waterman, R.H., Jr. (1982). *In search of excellence: Lessons from America's best-run companies.* New York: Harper & Row.

Who's excellent now? (1984, November 5). *Business Week.*

---

[1]Used with permission. Reprinted from R. Kaufman, "Improving Organizational Impact: A Western Alternative to Japanese Management." *Performance and Instruction Journal,* October, 1984.

Roger Kaufman, Ph.D., *is a professor and the director of the Center for Needs Assessment and Planning at Florida State University in Tallahassee. His interests include needs assessment, needs analysis, system planning, marketing (societal and holistic), and evaluation. Dr. Kaufman also does research and consulting in strategic planning, tactical planning, organizational development, and system renewal.*

WHY EMPLOYEE INVOLVEMENT OFTEN FAILS AND WHAT IT TAKES TO SUCCEED

Bob Crosby

Just as one was bombarded a few years ago with enthusiasm about employee-involvement efforts, such as those in connection with Japanese quality circles, today one is bombarded with stories of the failures of such efforts. The occasional success story whets our appetite, but more often than not we hear comments such as "Three-fourths of all such efforts fail," "We tried small employee groups at our company, and they bombed," or "Employee-involvement groups seemed to work for a while, but they don't even exist in our company anymore."

Paradoxes abound. We know that the resources of each individual employee need to be used as fully as possible, but American adaptations of Japanese quality circles do not seem to be the answer for most organizations.

The first step toward success in an employee-involvement effort is to define what is meant by the term "employee involvement." At one level, employees have always been involved merely by virtue of being employed. Similarly, companies have always hoped to derive the most from the time and talents of their employees. But an employee-involvement effort in today's terms necessitates a fundamental shift in attitude from viewing employees as workers who need to be prodded toward viewing them instead as people with valued skills who want to do excellent work and to contribute to the well-being of their companies.

Modern employee involvement is based on attempting to use employees' talents and experience for the greatest possible good of the company. The economic sense of this goal is clear to everyone, just as is the fact that it makes for a better work environment. However, the notion that the goal *can* be accomplished is not at all clear, nor is it obvious how to go about accomplishing it.

Supervisors and their subordinates do not want to be in conflict or adversarial situations at work. On the contrary, they have many goals in common. There is ample support for the notion that people have pride of craft; they want to do quality work and achieve a high sense of self-esteem. Nobody joins a company in order to do poorly; people join, by and large, with good intentions. From direct experience with some fifty organizations and the second-hand reports of more than four hundred companies over the last several years—noting both stark failures and striking successes—the author has formulated twelve guidelines for achieving success in an employee-involvement effort, thereby negating the notion that an adversarial relationship is a natural one.

1. COMMIT TO TOTAL INVOLVEMENT, A POSITIVE OUTLOOK, AND ECONOMIC FEASIBILITY

The terms in which employee involvement is discussed are critical. Ideally, employee involvement encompasses *every* employee. The process of involvement is intended to use fully the talents and experience of everyone.

To be effective, employee involvement also must be implemented in an environment of making results happen rather than finding fault or blaming. If this is not the case, the process can easily deteriorate. In a results-oriented environment, anything can be discussed with quick feedback and minimal defensiveness. This leads to searching for new opportunities for productivity and facing up to persistent problems. Companies that do not know how to shift from focusing on what is wrong to focusing on identifying opportunities need to seek help from consultants who can help them make this shift.

In addition, any employee-involvement effort must make economic sense. When the objective is one of "loving thy neighbor," the effort cannot succeed; failure is precipitated because the executives who initiated the effort are either naive or distorting the truth. An employee-involvement effort done well is productive; that it also creates a better and more humane work place is an added benefit.

2. USE A TOP-DOWN STRATEGY

Beginning at the top of the organizational hierarchy when implementing employee involvement is a strategy that sets up a success-oriented cycle. Those at the top can demonstrate that the effort is for everyone, that it works, and that it is not simply another program being tried but rather a new way of life for the company. With this approach, top management, middle management, and front-line supervisors are allowed to experience success before they are asked to enable their subordinates to have similar successes. The process begins when top managers have learned how to deal with the tough issues they face with their bosses as well as the tough issues they face with the people beneath them in the hierarchy. Before the involvement effort moves to hourly wage earners, top and middle management have already witnessed and experienced its potential for success.

Philosophizing by itself is not effective; simply holding an orientation session with the top people in a company to announce an employee-involvement effort for hourly wage earners does not work. The importance of employee involvement is measured by how seriously it is integrated into the ongoing structure of the company, including the top echelons.

3. TRAIN MIDDLE MANAGERS

The entire management of a company undertaking an employee-involvement effort needs to clearly understand the function of middle managers. With the exceptions of the church and the military, middle management did not exist at the turn of the century. Most industries were home industries, in which parents were executives and children were front-line workers. But as home industries merged and became larger, someone in each of these enterprises—perhaps the oldest child—became a supervisor. Those who became supervisors immediately discovered that they had been thrown into the muddy waters of human problems. They were no longer involved mainly with technical issues; now they had to figure out a way to manage people effectively.

When people become middle managers, they need expanded knowledge of policies and procedures. They may continue to provide expertise in technical areas, but by necessity they become more and more dependent on their subordinates for technical expertise. An effective middle manager soon discovers that his or her primary function is the use of human resources. If this fact is not discovered, the middle manager competes with the most intelligent of the front-line workers, fearing that their technical expertise will become so well known in the company that they will be promoted, replacing the middle manager. Therefore, it is critical to any employee-involvement effort that companies train their middle managers in the use of human resources; through such training people will be able to clearly understand their jobs, obtain the information they need to do a good job, and obtain the authority to do what they are given the responsibility to do. These human factors, when managed well by middle managers, will lead to greater productivity and foster collaboration and a spirit of cooperation among all levels of the organization. In order for this to happen, top managers need not only to arrange for training, but also to make it very clear that they are rewarding their middle managers and their first-line supervisors primarily for their ability to use the resources of the people they supervise.

4. EMPOWER SUPERVISORS TO MAKE DECISIONS AND NONSUPERVISORY PERSONNEL TO INFLUENCE

The success of an employee-involvement effort is dependent on two different kinds of empowerment: empowering supervisors to make decisions and empowering nonsupervisory personnel to influence the decision-making process (to be heard). When supervisors are appropriately empowered to make decisions, they are able to supervise better; they are able to use their authority more clearly and quickly; they are even able to make authoritarian decisions and be followed more surely than ever before. In addition, they are better able to listen because they are sure that their authority is accepted; when supervisors are secure in their positions, they can listen well and be influenced because they know who will make the ultimate decisions. In daily decisions, then, maximal effort can be made to use the experience and talents of anyone in the company who has knowledge about how a particular decision will affect the company's productivity.

Empowering nonsupervisory workers is also essential to an employee-involvement effort. All employees need to have the power to influence the work place as it affects them, as it affects productivity, and as it relates to their talents and experience. In this context it is important not to confuse *influencing* with *decision making*. Nonsupervisory personnel need the power to influence the decision-making process by ensuring that they are heard; supervisors need the power to make final decisions. Clarifying the difference between the two kinds of empowerment is essential in an employee-involvement effort. Otherwise, top managers will resist the effort for fear that they will lose their decision-making authority; also, employees from lower hierarchical levels may erroneously think that they are being asked to make decisions rather than offer their opinions. Real empowerment means that people understand, more clearly than ever before, how they influence and who makes the final decision.

5. USE A DATA-BASED APPROACH

The most common complaint about employee-involvement efforts is that they degenerate into gripe sessions. Employee-involvement efforts that work best begin with a data base, such as that derived from the administration of a survey.[1] The most effective data base is one that identifies the human factors:

- How clearly do people understand their roles?
- Are they obtaining the information they need to do a good job?
- What sense do they have about their futures in the company?
- Are they appreciated for what they do?
- If their work groups are unproductive, can they influence these groups to become more productive?

---

[1]See, for example, *People Performance Profile: An Organization-Effectiveness Survey* by B. Crosby and J. Scherer, 1985, San Diego, California: University Associates.

- Do they clearly understand the larger picture, or are they expected to be robots without any sense of the company's direction?
- When plans are made, do they hear about them in time to implement them appropriately?
- When decisions are made in areas in which they have experience and expertise, are they consulted?

There are many similar questions about human factors that need to be answered. When employees are presented with data that they have helped to generate, these data constitute a starting point for successful employee involvement. When employees then discuss issues indicated by these data, it becomes permissible to talk about the aspects of work that often are not even noticed or clearly conceptualized by anyone in the organization.

A common error is to gather data and keep these data at the top-management level. In fact, this practice is detrimental to productivity. Effective employee-involvement efforts require that data be shared. Not all data from all groups need to be known to every group; however, the people who work in shipping, for example, should examine the data about shipping that they generated, should work through the meaning of these data, and should come up with recommendations for effective ways to address any issues that need resolution. Perhaps no change process is more effective than that which occurs when data are gathered and fed back to the work force. Employees then can respond systematically to the data, develop recommendations to which management can respond, and share in the monitoring of the follow-through.

6. DEVISE A CUSTOMIZED STRUCTURE

Employee involvement needs to be tailor-made for each organization. The people within each company must be the ones who bear primary responsibility for developing the kind of structure that will make it work. Only when a customized structure is established and constantly monitored will employee involvement become a way of life—a way of doing daily business. The organization needs to decide about the birth and death of groups, leadership of groups, the issue of intact work groups versus task forces to deal with certain concerns, the kinds of report forms that need to be developed and made available, and the kinds of training that will support ongoing employee involvement. These issues are unique to each company. Although it is useful for an organization's management to know what other companies have done, that organization is most likely to succeed when its management develops unique ways of implementing employee involvement instead of buying another company's prescription. Employee involvement can be started quickly with the survey-feedback method, after which the effort quickly moves from the general to the specific in its focus. Outside people can help start employee involvement, but management must make its own unique adaptation.

7. ADDRESS SYSTEM ISSUES AT THE TOP LEVEL

An effective data-gathering process makes it clear that many issues permeate all groups in an organization and are, therefore, *system* issues. For example, if all groups in the organization score low on a survey item involving role clarity, then role clarity is a system issue and must be addressed at the top level of the company. Such issues cannot be addressed as successfully at lower levels. Sometimes a group can create its own environment and succeed in addressing system issues at its own level; however, this approach does not promote system-wide productivity. System issues can be identified easily with an effective data-gathering tool.

8. CONDUCT TRAINING IN PROBLEM SOLVING AND PROVIDING FEEDBACK

In order for employee involvement to work, a large proportion of people in the organization have to be trained in simple problem solving. A clear procedure for solving problems is needed; employees at all levels need to know exactly what they are to do when working on problems. At the very least, it is essential that they have the ability to distinguish between interpretive and concrete statements so that information provided to management and recommendations based on this information are as clear as possible. Note the difference, for example, between a recommendation that says "Improve sanitation in department B" and one that says "Department B's hoses are leaking from broken connecting joints, and the drain is partially clogged; therefore, we recommend that the connecting joints be replaced."

Supervisors also need skill training in completing the feedback loop, that is, in returning to their subordinates with information about what has happened to their recommendations and in doing so in a supportive, intelligent way. One of the major reasons for employee-involvement failure is that no response is made to worker suggestions.

9. USE THIRD-PARTY INTERVENTION TO ADDRESS DYSFUNCTIONAL SUPERVISOR-SUBORDINATE RELATIONS

Effective employee-involvement efforts make use of the services of third parties when necessary to handle dysfunctional supervisor-subordinate situations. For example, if the company has determined that a poorly functioning supervisor is to be kept in his or her position, then, as part of the employee-involvement effort, a third party needs to intervene between the supervisor and the subordinates who are affected. Third-party work of this type requires the services of someone who knows how to bring two individuals together, prepare them for a meeting, deal with the issues directly and quickly, and keep the two people from dealing with the issues as if a personality conflict were the basis of the problem.

The term "personality conflict" is, in itself, a dysfunctional concept. It is a Twentieth Century way of framing an interpersonal problem. When people choose to think in this way, they are usually deciding to be locked into a hopeless stalemate. Rather, an effective third party can help people to make the commitment necessary to achieve success, identify precise and concrete changes that need to take place in the relationship, and follow through with the individuals involved for a period of time to ensure that these changes are happening.

An effective third party can remedy 80 to 90 percent of all supervisor-subordinate situations that are perceived as dysfunctional. A highly skilled negotiator can usually reverse even chronic situations in a few weeks. If such a turnaround does not occur, employee involvement is imperiled, at least with respect to any group that is experiencing negative relationships.

Turnaround is dependent on whether the people involved are committed to improving the quality of their work relationship; if they are not committed, change is unlikely. However, a skilled third party usually knows how to foster commitments as well as take steps toward resolution.

10. ACKNOWLEDGE THAT DISAPPOINTMENTS ARE INEVITABLE BUT NOT DEVASTATING

People need to be informed and reminded repeatedly that disappointments will occur in an employee-involvement effort, no matter what precautions are taken to prevent them. When people are disappointed, they have two choices: to convince themselves that the effort is not working and abandon it altogether or to fix whatever has gone wrong. If employee involvement is to be a way of life for a company, a long-term commitment is necessary and must be begun by focusing on core, important issues. People should be told that they will have to take one step at a time, addressing one issue at a time and occasionally experiencing disappointment in the process. Eventually these disappointments will be overcome, and employee involvement will become a natural part of organizational life; when this point has been reached, the focus will shift from *problems* to *opportunities*.

11. VIEW INVOLVEMENT AS CULTURAL TRANSITION

Employee involvement needs to be seen in the context of a gradual transition of the company. Table 1 illustrates how one company expressed the directions toward which it preferred to move. The situation described in this table emphasizes the transitional nature of an employee-involvement effort. Employee involvement is not a three-month, magical program for accomplishing grandiose goals; instead, it becomes a standard way of functioning for a company while it is pursuing directions that, over time, will represent a significant cultural shift.

12. COORDINATE THE EFFORTS OF INDIVIDUALS, GROUPS, AND THE ORGANIZATION ITSELF

For employee involvement to succeed, it must be seen in the context of the three interrelated components that contribute to the effort: the *individual,* the *group,* and the *organization.* Each individual in the company must have a commitment to making employee involvement work, and so must each group. All groups within the organization establish norms that either support or work against employee involvement. Norms are generally unspoken rules that govern behavior; for example, norms tell us what is permissible to wear and what language is permissible to use. Similarly, people achieve a sense of the norms regarding whether it is permissible to favor employee involvement, to favor using people's resources, and even to be hopeful

Table 1. Cultural Transition Within One Company

From (The Way It Once Was)	Toward (The Way We Want It to Be)
Authority related primarily to status and role.	Authority primarily related to knowledge and competence, yet with clear lines of status and role authority when needed.
Low trust.	High trust.
Engineering design decided at the top without conferring with people who will work with the equipment.	All employees who will use equipment will be able to influence engineering design.
Supervisors feeling attacked, criticized, or threatened by hourly workers' suggestions.	Supervisors feeling supported by hourly workers' suggestions.
Supervisors holding onto notion that they have to know the most about technical matters.	Supervisors experiencing power from effective management of subordinates who are freed to use their technical knowledge and experience.

about an employee-involvement effort. An effective employee-involvement effort deals with such norms in groups and helps people understand how norms are shaped and how one keeps from becoming a victim of group norms.

The third component, the organization itself, is the basic ground for the whole effort. All three components are important, but the other two can work in support of employee involvement only if the organization truly demonstrates consistent commitment to the use of human resources. This commitment is demonstrated in statements from top management, in the presence of top managers in training sessions held for workers, and in a visible attempt to make the effort work. When the chief executive officer joins workers and middle managers in learning how to develop and recognize a recommendation that is specific and concrete, for example, the chances of effecting change increase considerably.

RESULTS

When all of the guidelines discussed in this paper are attended to, dramatic economic results are produced. Other changes also occur. Safety improves, even though safety may not be addressed directly. People feel free to submit requests for resources that they need, to disagree with their supervisors, to bring up viewpoints that are not popular, and to identify safety problems. In most cases, prior to an employee-involvement effort, these same people would have believed it better to "play it safe" and not mention such concerns.

Productivity usually strikingly increases in companies with an effective employee-involvement effort, and so do other kinds of improvements. The following are some examples from the author's experience:

- Turnover in a fast-food restaurant was reduced from 43 to 21 percent.
- A law firm billed 27 percent more clients than the previous year.
- A car dealership reduced the time necessary to repair a car and increased maintenance results.
- A manufacturer with two hundred and fifty employees increased sales 23 percent and saved $50,000 by lowering the number of accidents that occurred.

Sometimes such results happen even when the effort has been haphazard and has not fully taken into account the twelve guidelines. However, for those companies that want to outperform their competitors, employee involvement of the scope described in this paper needs to incorporate these guidelines so that it becomes a way of life.

Bob Crosby is a consultant with Management Analysis Company (MAC) in San Diego, California. His specialties are organizational effectiveness, employee involvement, and conflict utilization. Bob founded the Leadership Institute of Seattle (LIOS) as well as the Master of Arts in the Applied Behavioral Sciences program that operates out of Seattle. In addition, he co-authored the People Performance Profile: An Organization-Effectiveness Survey, *an instrument that has been used in over four hundred organizations.*

USE OF THE COLLABORATIVE ETHIC AND CONTINGENCY THEORIES IN CONFLICT MANAGEMENT

Susan Hoefflinger Taft

As American organizations are changing, social forces from within and international pressures from without are causing managers to re-examine the basic principles of management practice. In an era of rapid change and high uncertainty, the management of conflict and differences assumes an important role in assuring organizational viability.

The appreciation of differences is a central tenet of conflict management. Organizations are becoming increasingly diverse and are grappling with ways and means to capitalize on the diversity. At the same time, the open-system nature of organizations requires a receptivity to the inputs and forces of the environment. Openness requires a respect for and understanding of differences.

In the absence of important stakes—resources, opportunities, power, and control—differences between people are rarely a cause of conflict. In the presence of these stakes, however, and usually in direct proportion to them, conflict arises and escalates. The form of the conflict can be as simple as a difference of opinion between two colleagues, a supervisor and a subordinate, or two groups with differing core tasks; or it can be as complex as differences among U.S. senators who are trying to formulate international policy and pass legislation. The management of conflict in widely varying contexts requires a complex set of interpersonal and cognitive skills to locate and manipulate the key stakes.

Only recently has research in conflict management taken full account of the complex nature of conflict and the wide range of stakes to which incumbents may be attached. The call in the literature for more contingency theories (Filley, 1978; Robbins, 1978; Thomas, 1978; Thomas, Jamieson, & Moore, 1978) reflects our developing interest in finding comprehensive and flexible tools. This article reviews some of the theoretical heritage of conflict management. Based on the ideas of this heritage, a conflict-intervention process will be described.

Two schools of thought in conflict management are useful for the intervention process described later in this paper. These are the "collaboration ethic" (Thomas, 1977, 1978) and "contingency" approaches. The intervention process draws on the creative usefulness of working with several different frames of reference—collaboration as a value position and contingency approaches as tools of flexibility.

Collaboration has been "variously called 'confrontation,' 'problem solving,' 'integrating,' and 'integrative bargaining.' This behavioral mode seeks joint optimization of the concerns of two or more parties, with an emphasis on openness and trust. Advocates for this mode have often lapsed into absolutism" (Thomas, 1977, p. 485). This reference to absolutism implies that collaboration has been taken as a single-value stance without an

The author gratefully acknowledges the interest and support of David A. Kolb in the development of this article. She also thanks William Pasmore for his critiques of an earlier draft of the manuscript.

acknowledgement of the benefits and efficacy of multi-value stances. The second school, contingency theory, addresses this limitation.

Contingency theories acknowledge complexity. They direct the manager to an appreciation of the multiple factors—the contingencies—involved in a conflict, because a suitable strategy can often be derived by considering these contingencies. The strategy may be collaborative, it may involve accommodation, or it may alter power relationships or adjust resources.

THE COLLABORATION ETHIC

Collaboration as an approach to conflict management was first elaborated by Mary Parker Follett in the early years of the Twentieth Century. Because her classic work influenced many subsequent theorists and became the underpinning of the collaborative ethic, a closer look at some of her ideas is appropriate. In the collection of her papers by Metcalf & Urwick (1940, p. 30), her simple definition of conflict—"the appearance of difference, difference of opinions, of interest"—suggests that conflict results from the richness of diverse human interaction. She delineates three primary methods for dealing with conflict.

The first of these methods is *domination,* synonymous with the current-day term "competition," which provides for the victory of one side over the other. This method is easiest in the short run, requiring relatively little expenditure of time or energy, but it is often unsuccessful in the long run. The issues leading to the original conflict will often resurface later under the domination mode.

The second method is *compromise,* which is a common way to settle controversy. In compromise, each side gives something up for the sake of peace or resolution. Since some degree of sacrifice is involved, unsatisfied needs and wants are likely to resurface again later, as with domination.

Follett's third method of resolving conflict is *integration*, which is synonomous with "collaboration." Integration is a dialectical process: both parties speak to their needs, desires, and visions. As clarity emerges around the issues of both sides, inventiveness is used to seek an original, higher-order synthesis. The integration process supports and encourages diversity. Follett asserts the need for both sides to be highly self-interested; for without this characteristic, the data supplied will be insufficient to enable both parties to find a creative solution. Integration eliminates a win-lose attitude. Follett believes that "there are always more than two alternatives in a situation, and our job is to analyze the situation carefully enough for as many as possible to appear" (Metcalf & Urwick, 1940, pp. 219-220). Diversity is united, the integrity of both parties is protected, and creative problem solving is advanced; these benefits accrue to the parties in conflict as well as, in a ripple effect, to society in general (Metcalf & Urwick, 1940). Follett considers integration a qualitative adjustment and compromise a quantitative one. An integrative experience is a progressive experience, because it moves both parties forward.

Integration, however, as a method for conflict resolution is not always possible. Follett (1951, p. 163) admits that "not all differences...can be integrated. That we must face fully, but it is certain that there are fewer irreconcilable activities than we at present think, although it often takes ingenuity, a 'creative intelligence,' to find the integration." Other writers agree that integration is not always possible, but it may be useful more often than most people realize (Deutsch, 1969; Katz & Kahn, 1966). Many people find it easier to fight than to work constructively toward mutually satisfying conflict solutions.

Follett emphasized examining the conflict process as part of integrative resolutions. Messages between parties in conflict may include subtle or nonverbal cues, and a look at only the content of the message may lead one on a convoluted chase. Process cues can, at times, help to locate key issues quickly. Attending to both the content and the process enhances the likelihood of a collaborative solution.

Intellectually analytic activities are necessary in the pursuit of successful collaborative outcomes. Eiseman (1977, 1978) uses the development of a conceptual framework for looking at the parties' desires, beliefs, experiences, and behavior. The issue in contention is *reframed* intellectually so that opposing sides locate a perspective compatible to both. Reframing can involve moving toward more *abstract* ideals (e.g., "What is our common vision of what is best for the organization as a whole?") or toward more *concrete* concerns (e.g., "If we implement this policy, how are employees likely to respond?"). Moving between the abstract and concrete poles will assist in seeing the total situation. True to the spirit of collaboration, Eiseman (1978, p. 134) considers a conflict resolved "only when each party is convinced that his or her final way of thinking about the conflict embodies not only his initial position, but also those of his adversaries."

The manner in which individuals engage in conflict tends to draw on a few preferred behaviors. One model for identifying conflict style is oriented along two axes representing self-interest and concern for others (Thomas, 1976). Collaborative problem solving requires both a high degree of concern for self and a great amount of empathy for the other party. This view incorporates and synthesizes potentially opposing desires: the desire to win and the need to cooperate. Five conflict-handling orientations are plotted on the model, with collaborative behaviors initially representing the ideal orientation (high self-interest and high concern for others).

Subsequently, Thomas began to question the ideal status of collaboration, and his views illustrate the rising popularity of contingency theory. Differing values and situations may call for the functionally useful application of modes other than collaborating: competing, compromising, avoiding, and accommodating (Thomas, 1977). Although collaborating may be an idealized and valued strategy, it is not always possible or efficacious. A simplistic normative prescription for collaboration denies the inherent variability and complexity of life in modern-day organizations.

The foregoing views were selected to illustrate some of the history and ideas on the collaborative ethic. Although collaboration is a rich and provocative heritage and useful in managing many forms of conflict, it has limitations, which include the following:

1. An assumption basic to collaboration theory is the existence of two clearly defined sides or camps. In reality, the network of allies may take the form of a meandering chain with various degrees of wants and needs centered around multiple foci.

2. The collaborative ethic fails to address power inequities that are frequently present in conflict situations. For example, it is naive to believe that a collaborative spirit is all that is necessary to solve every conflict between a supervisor and subordinate.

3. The collaborative ethic assumes that both parties have good will and a desire to achieve the best possible outcome. However, conflict—by definition—assumes the presence of stakes; therefore, even the most honorable intentions may be derailed as parties examine their differences.

CONTINGENCY APPROACHES

The complexity of society—local, national, and international—is paralleled in organizations. It is a rare organization that does not need to cope with extensive social diversity and worldwide economic forces while pursuing its mission. Contingency theory takes into account variation, diversity, and complexity. Instead of advancing a normative prescription, it assists in the analysis of situations based on a range of intervening factors.

A contingency view of the collaborative ethic suggests that collaboration may be the best alternative when certain conditions are present: power equalization between parties; present and future interdependence; mutual interest in solving the problem; openness; organizational support and procedures for collaboration; and a desire to defeat the problem rather than the opponent (Derr, 1978; Phillips & Cheston, 1979). When sufficient conditions are not present for collaboration, other modes may be more useful. The absence of motivation to resolve a conflict may lead logically and functionally to an avoidance posture. Sharply differing value systems within an organization may be best coaxed into peaceful coexistence through compromise. The need for quick action may call for, at least temporarily, competing behaviors. Social credits and debits can be tallied through accommodation maneuvers, to be drawn on in the next conflict. Varying demands of a situation influence the choice of conflict strategy (Derr, 1978; Filley, 1978; Phillips & Cheston, 1979; Robbins, 1978; Thomas, 1977, 1978). Choices are contingent on a range of relevant factors, and managers are denied a quick and simple prescription for conflict interventions.

Power inequities make a major impact on conflict situations, and contingency theorists recognize this dynamic influence. Successful collaborative outcomes in the absence of power parity are difficult, and yet power differentials between conflicting parties are quite prevalent. Power may be associated with a host of factors: significant resources (money, information, connections to important people), legitimate authority, social demographic characteristics, alliances and positioning, facility with language, knowledge, and more.

Fisher and Ury (1981) explicitly address power inequities in negotiation. Much of their work is based on collaboration theory, for example, working to surface basic interests of parties rather than taking positions (which tend to become hardened and entrenched during negotiations). They propose using the following strategies when the opponent wields power:

1. Develop your best alternative to a negotiated agreement. Protect yourself from making an agreement that is not in your best interest.
2. Focus on the merits (i.e., the principles you and they wish to obtain in the outcome) rather than on positions.
3. Avoid defensiveness and counterattacking. Invite their criticism and advice. Ask questions.
4. Consider bringing in a third party.

Their book is rich with techniques and methods for conflict management. Although their philosophy is consistent with the collaborative ethic, it extends one's options for dealing with a variety of common contingencies. A limitation to the theory is the continued exploration of conflict between two parties without addressing the phenomenon as a disparate, multi-focused, ubiquitous resident of organizations.

Locating and defining the most germane conflict in an organization is a first and difficult task confronting the conflict manager. Behind every conflict there may lurk a small army of disparate employees, each with individual beliefs, perceptions, and stakes. Choosing the pertinent issue and addressing the most relevant interests are not simple tasks; frequently managers are caught in this bog and try to solve the wrong problem. What may look on the surface like a classic case of conflict between two stakeholders, and therefore between two parties, may take on subtle and varied nuances as the manager digs deeper to find the real sources of tension experienced by organizational members. Elusiveness of clearly definable sides in a conflict is common in real organizations.

The complex nature of conflict in organizations and the need for analytic tools are addressed in Brown's (1983) comprehensive theory. An extensive contingency framework is developed to assist managers and organizational theorists in the management of conflict.

Focusing on a conflict interface, Brown conducts an in-depth examination of the fields or clusters of people grouped around the conflict. His most significant contribution is to tackle, ambitiously, the complexity of organizational conflict and to suggest "countervening" strategies tailored to the situation. Because of the extent of detail, Brown's theory is difficult to summarize; yet a few words on the framework are necessary for any review of contingency theories.

A central tenet of Brown's theory is that conflict may exist in different quantities in organizations: too much, too little, or a productive amount. The dynamics of conflict may lead to problem solving or bargaining (productive), escalation (too much), or suppression or withdrawal (too little). An initial diagnosis by the manager should determine if conflict is at the right level. Too often conflict is attended to only when in abundance. It is, however, unhealthy for an organization to have too little conflict, because this condition means that the natural and creative diversity of the entity is not being expressed. Brown also addresses in-depth intervention strategies relevant to the diagnosis at hand: redirecting behavior, reallocating resources, reframing perspectives, and realigning underlying forces.

Brown's theory is an important and long-awaited addition to the conflict-management literature. It helps in understanding why the use of limited tools in conflict management may lead to frustration, at worst, or incomplete success, at best. His theory views organizations as multifaceted and multifocused and recommends a fully-equipped tool chest in searching for optimum outcomes. A criticism of his work, however, is that practicing managers find the complex theory difficult to comprehend and use.

Although contingency theories address some of the limitations of the collaborative ethic, they still have shortcomings, including the following:

1. Guiding values, although present, are less apparent in contingency approaches than in the collaborative ethic. Approaches to conflict management may become driven by pragmatics rather than by values, leading to a "whatever works" attitude.

2. Many contingency theories are complex and difficult to remember, making them less accessible and useful than are simple frameworks.

3. Little has been done to integrate contingency theories, leaving students of conflict resolution with confusing choices. The respective strengths and weaknesses of the theories have not been examined in any comprehensive way, and no guidelines exist to direct the choices. Often the theories seem to say only "it depends."

A CONFLICT-INTERVENTION PROCESS

A set of approaches—based on the theories that have been reviewed—have been designed to assist managers in conflict management. The approaches suggest a process that supports both collaborative outcomes and the use of choices based on relevant contingencies. The process includes analyzing, diagnosing, and intervening.

Four Approaches to Conflict Inquiry

Most conflict phenomena in organizations are complex, with multiple stakeholders, goals, group interests, and personal motivations behind any significant conflict. Resolving a conflict without having a broad information base on which to make decisions almost ensures that some form of the same conflict will emerge again. The process described in this article helps to expand the information available to managers by surfacing needs, wishes, goals, role issues, and the nature of the interactive process between conflicting parties. It is also useful for extending one's conceptualization of the dimensions of a conflict process and the range of access points for intervention. The process is simple enough to be remembered and used with ease.

This conflict-intervention process relies on the use of two dimensions in analyzing a situation: the *conflict-content/conflict-process* dimension, and the *abstract/concrete reframing* dimension.

1. *Conflict content* refers to the nature of the disagreement, the stakes involved, and what is being kept or given up.

2. *Conflict process* refers to the nature of the interaction over the content and to the way the parties conduct themselves with each other, vis-a-vis the content, both verbally and nonverbally.

3. *Reframing toward the abstract (up)* refers to the use of cognitive processes to search for higher principles or more generalized ways of conceptualizing the issues than are currently being exhibited.

4. *Reframing toward the concrete (down)* refers to the use of cognitive processes to bring the conflict "home" (i.e., to the parties' own felt needs and motivations), to review practical implications, and to increase ownership of the problem.

These dimensions provide direction for diagnosing conflict and intervening in it. They can be illustrated with a matrix, as shown in Figure 1, in which four approaches emerge.

	Conflict Content	Conflict Process
Reframing Toward Abstract (Up)	Content Reframing Up	Process Reframing Up
Reframing Toward Concrete (Down)	Content Reframing Down	Process Reframing Down

Figure 1. Approaches Emerging from Content/Process and Reframing Dimensions

Figure 2 illustrates how each of the four approaches could be used in reframing a conflict between two departments of an organization. This situation involves interdependencies.

Figure 3 illustrates how each of the approaches could be used when the conflict involves two employees of equal rank.

Figure 4 illustrates the approaches when the conflict is between a supervisor and subordinate.

The examples in Figures 2 through 4 illustrate the flexibility one can enjoy by using a reframing approach along the process/content and abstract/concrete dimensions. The use of new dimensions in a conflict situation may assist the conflicting parties to view and respond to the conflict with fresh and potentially creative perspectives. The conflicting parties would then be able to provide more accurate answers to the following questions: Is collaboration possible and desirable? What contingencies influence the situation? Is this a focused conflict or a multifocused, elusive conflict? Are major changes needed to resolve the issues? Can the perspectives be altered through reframing activities? Such an inquiry process, which draws on both collaborative and contingency-based methods, would help to clarify the parameters of the conflict and the extent of the intervention needed to manage the situation.

"Production won't manufacture our widgets fast enough to meet customer orders."

"The Sales Department does not understand our pressures. We cannot respond to the whims of every customer."

Content reframing up: "What do you think is best for the organization as a whole?"

Content reframing down: "What would be the best possible situation for sales? For production?"

Process reframing up: "What is a better way for your two departments to manage your demands on each other?"

Process reframing down: "How do you communicate your needs to each other?"

Figure 2. Two Departments in Conflict over Meeting Each Other's
Organizational Needs (Interdependencies)

"We should implement a performance-appraisal system that is focused on developing our employees."

"Nonsense. We are not a welfare agency. What we need is a better way to account for work that should be getting done."

Content reframing up: "What is our philosophy of management?"

Content reframing down: "What kinds of messages might be communicated to employees by each proposed system?"

Process reframing up: "What are the management processes that psychologically encourage maximum effort in the employees?"

Process reframing down: "What types of appraisal processes have increased your own performance? What types have discouraged you?"

Figure 3. Two Managers in Conflict over a Performance-Appraisal System

SUPERVISOR	SUBORDINATE MANAGER
"Our production figures need to increase dramatically in the next six months."	"If we don't improve some of our management systems—like promotion policies, equipment maintenance, and fringe benefits—we will soon have a very demoralized group of employees."

Content reframing up:	"What kind of climate and incentives do you envision as necessary for meeting organizational goals?"
Content reframing down:	"Each of you seems to have different perspectives and different goals. Describe the sources of your respective concerns."
Process reframing up:	"Is it possible to devote effort and resources to the pursuit of both goals? What would need to happen for that to occur?"
Process reframing down:	"What do you need from each other in order to realize your own goals?"

Figure 4. Conflict Between Supervisor and Subordinate Manager over Organizational Priorities

Guidelines for Choosing an Approach

The following guiding principles are helpful in choosing a reframing approach:

1. Try reframing the content when:
   - The inherent stakes are unknown,
   - The social context is relevant but incompletely acknowledged,
   - Differences in goals or roles have not been examined,
   - A win-lose or we-they battle line has been drawn, and/or
   - Relevant reference groups influence the thinking of the parties.
2. Try reframing the process when:
   - Power inequities exist,
   - Parties exhibit exaggerated posturing toward one another,
   - Behavior seems to be occurring without much reflective thought,
   - Responsibility for personal behavior and experience is missing from the interchanges, and/or
   - Ongoing interdependence is necessary.
3. Try reframing toward the abstract (up) when:
   - Disagreement at a personal or parochial level is present,
   - Narrow values are being served, and/or
   - Personal feelings have served to paralyze progress.

4. Try reframing toward the concrete (down) when:
- Arguing over principles is creating a stalemate,
- Sweeping generalizations or stereotypes serve to separate personal experience from the discussion, and/or
- The dilemmas of the parties' own feelings have not been explored.

The conflict-intervention process that has been described is most easily implemented when conflict is focused, as in dyadic conflict. It can also be useful in multifocal conflicts as a method by which information is surfaced and the problem elaborated, enabling parties to improve comprehension of the phenomenon and choose strategies based on full information. The simplicity of the framework makes it easy to remember and therefore readily useful to managers.

The reframing process helps to facilitate conflict management, regardless of whether collaborative or contingency approaches are subsequently pursued. It is rooted in the values and processes of collaboration (i.e., attention to both process and content, the seeking of a higher-order synthesis, creative outcome, and attention to both personal and social values), which discourage a "whatever works" mentality. At the same time, contingency thinking is a natural outcome of the reframing process, because complex intervening factors are surfaced and examined.

A search for new and more refined uses of contingency strategies should not disregard the values, principles, and ideals behind the collaborative ethic. In fact, collaboration is more than an ethic; it is a fundamental human drive and is critically needed in complex social forms of organizations. As an ideological orientation, collaboration actualizes many preferred values: mutualism, acceptance of diversity, common vision, and dialectical creativity. Nevertheless, more comprehensive tools for conflict management are still needed. Much remains to be done in the way of testing, altering, and expanding theories that have recently appeared. Differing theories may be needed for different contexts. The question still remains, for example, about the differences in conflict-management strategies among various types of organizations (e.g., manufacturing plants, high-technology service organizations, and government agencies).

In the meantime, the author hopes that this discussion will assist the reader in recognizing different schools of thought that are available for conflict management and that it will provide useful tools for diagnosing conflict and making appropriate interventions.

REFERENCES

Brown, L.D. (1983). *Managing conflict at organizational interfaces.* Reading, MA: Addison-Wesley.

Derr, C.B. (1978, Summer). Managing organizational conflict. *California Management Review,* pp. 76-83.

Deutsch, M. (1969, January). Productive and destructive conflict. *Journal of Social Issues,* pp. 7-42.

Eiseman, J.W. (1977). A third-party consultation model for resolving recurring conflicts collaboratively. *Journal of Applied Behavioral Science, 13*(3), 303-314.

Eiseman, J.W. (1978). Reconciling incompatible positions. *Journal of Applied Behavioral Science, 14*(2), 133-150.

Filley, A.C. (1978, Winter). Some normative issues in conflict management. *California Management Review,* pp. 61-66.

Fisher, R., & Ury, W. (1981). *Getting to yes.* Boston, MA: Houghton Mifflin.

Follett, M.P. (1951). *Creative experience.* New York: Peter Smith.

Katz, D., & Kahn, R.L. (1966). *The social psychology of organizations* (2nd ed.). New York: John Wiley.

Metcalf, H.C., & Urwick, L. (Eds.). (1940). *Dynamic administration: The collected papers of Mary Parker Follett.* New York: Harper Brothers.

Phillips, E., & Cheston, R. (1979, Summer). Conflict resolution: What works? *California Management Review*, pp. 76-83.

Robbins, S.P. (1978, Winter). "Conflict management" and "conflict resolution" are not synonymous terms. *California Management Review*, pp. 67-75.

Thomas, K. (1976). Conflict and conflict management. In M.D. Dunnette (Ed.), *Handbook of industrial and organizational psychology*. Chicago: Rand McNally.

Thomas, K.W. (1977, July). Toward multi-dimensional values in teaching: The example of conflict behaviors. *Academy of Management Review*, pp. 484-490.

Thomas, K.W. (1978, Winter). Introduction to special section: Conflict and the collaborative ethic. *California Management Review*, pp. 56-60.

Thomas, K.W., Jamieson, D.W., & Moore, R.K. (1978, Winter). Conflict and collaboration: Some concluding observations. *California Management Review*, pp. 91-95.

Susan H. Taft *is a doctoral candidate in the department of organizational behavior, Weatherhead School of Management, Case Western Reserve University. Prior to her doctoral work, she held various managerial positions in health-care organizations, and she taught in the Frances Payne Bolton School of Nursing at Case Western Reserve University. She is currently doing research, teaching, and consulting with a variety of organizations.*

HUMANIZING THE WORK PLACE

Eva Schindler-Rainman

Major changes are taking place in the world, our nation, and our communities. Usually with societal changes there is also turmoil. It is a time of challenge and choices as well as a period of creativity, initiative, and collaboration; it is a time to take stock of the human resources in the work place and to find meaningful ways to tap into and renew these resources. This paper deals with some of the major issues that are affecting and will affect the work place, some creative initiatives that are being taken or can be taken, and the challenges still to be met in the field of human resource development.

GLOBAL DEVELOPMENTS

A number of issues are developing on a global scale:[1]

1. *Competition, Economic Issues, and Power.* Competition is one of the major changes that is occurring globally. In addition, the pull of free trade versus protectionism is being felt. Deficits, currency fluctuations, and contemplated tax reforms all have a significant impact.

Another global issue is the change of power balances, with China emerging as a competitor and a producer. The changes are and have been very rapid in that large country and will affect the power balance of other nations. Certainly they will affect trade and the work places of the world.

2. *Population.* The increase in populations in many countries is also notable. Some of these countries can integrate more people; but for many others the implications include a subsistence economy, hunger, illness, and unmet human needs.

3. *Environmental Concerns and Insecurity.* Issues of pollution are constantly being brought to our attention, including concerns about acid rain, polluted rivers, and excessive noise. Terrorism and conflict are present everywhere, making the world less secure and safe. Nuclear build-up and threats to world peace prey on the minds of many people.

4. *Technology, Displacement, and the Ownership of Information.* Modern technology is displacing people in many cases, giving rise to still other issues. It is said that in Sweden employers pay the same tax for robots that is paid for employees, and in Japan some companies pay union dues for robots. Thus, the issues of displacement and underemployment become of prime concern in any considerations related to humanizing the work place.

Another consideration is the ownership of information. Because information equals power, there may well be a move to protect it in the same way that products are protected.

5. *Immigration and Emigration.* The compositions of the populations of countries are changing due to increasing immigration and emigration. For example, the West Coast of the United States is becoming heavily Pacific Asian and Latin. Demographic changes pose many implications for the work place.

---

[1]See also *Transitioning: Strategies for the Volunteer World* by E. Schindler-Rainman (V. Adolph, Ed.), 1981, Vancouver, British Columbia: Voluntary Action Resources Centre.

6. *Breakthroughs*. There is work being done to enable us to get food from the bottom of the ocean; computers are being developed that will surpass and supplant those currently in use; and artificial intelligence is being created. Surely we cannot consider humanizing the work place without taking into account these positive global developments.

TRENDS IN THE WORK PLACE

The following trends are having or will have a significant effect on the work place:

1. *Uncertainty of Employment*. Several subissues are critical with regard to the trend of uncertainty: temporary versus relatively long-term employment; automation; early retirement; mergers and changes of ownership; and competition between older, long-term employees and younger, newly trained, often "less-expensive" employees. Certainties and stable systems no longer exist. Litigation of all kinds is a reality in the work place. The bases for litigious action vary from physical and mental injuries to sexual harassment and age discrimination. Immigrants also can pose a threat to employees because so many are available for lower pay and fewer benefits; still other immigrants may be as well or better educated than the people who are already employed.

2. *Health and Wellness Issues*. Concern and action are increasing with regard to health maintenance and illness prevention. It is clear that employee wellness is directly related to productivity, and organizations are beginning to respond to this realization. In many work places there are prevention and treatment programs available for employees whose lives are affected by substance abuse. Even when such programs are unavailable in an organization, generally the organization can refer its employees to community programs for help. In addition, stress and burnout are health concerns for which companies sometimes provide counseling. Occasionally organizations enter into collaborative arrangements with local social agencies such as the YMCA in order to address health problems and needs.

3. *Noise Pollution*. Included in this concern is the invasion of hearing and physical space by new instruments, more people, thin or low walls, open offices, and "white" noise. Noise pollution has not been dealt with much in the work place, but it is and will become even more a major deterrent to creative thinking and effective work.

4. *Redesigning of Benefits*. Questions to be considered in connection with this issue are as follows:

- Who is eligible and when and for what kinds of benefits?
- Where and under what circumstances is job sharing possible?
- Is it possible to offer both full- and part-time employment opportunities?
- Would "flex time" be a help or a hindrance to the productivity of the system?
- What should the range of health benefits be?
- Should an employee-assistance program be implemented? If so, what should it include and who would be eligible to participate in and benefit from it?

5. *Changing Values and Belief Systems*. Yankelovich (1981) offers incisive information about how to cope with changing values and beliefs. It is important to be aware of and understand some of the value changes in society. One is the shift from long-term to more temporary commitments, both on personal and work levels. Another value shift that creates a dilemma involves whether to alter traditional ways of working and products to accommodate new inventions and creative experiments. System cultures are having to decide which practices, products, and services to keep and which to change. In addition, there are a variety of meanings

for "success" these days. Success may mean just having a job; it may mean having a job that is self-actualizing, interesting, challenging, and changing; or it may connote upward mobility.

6. *Inequities in Remuneration.* Such inequities may be differences in salaries paid to males versus those paid to females for the same or very similar work, in wages for technically skilled workers versus those for professional people, or in the pay for administrative workers versus direct-service people.

7. *Changing Philosophies and Practices of Personnel Departments.* These departments are focusing on human resource development—often changing the name of units responsible for the administration of salaries, benefit packages, job assessment, and educational experiences and offerings, as well as of those responsible for the development of employment and severance criteria and action plans.

CREATIVE INITIATIVES AND INTERVENTIONS

Several creative initiatives are being developed to address the previously discussed trends:

1. *Educational Opportunities.* Many educational, training, and employee-growth opportunities are being enhanced. Such opportunities may be available on or off site. It is clear that when top management participates in ongoing learning, the role modeling can be felt throughout the system. All levels of any system need opportunities to learn, to be updated, to be challenged, and to expand their knowledge, skills, and abilities. These educational opportunities must be tailored to the needs of the system and the various workers at various levels. Also, the designs chosen must be participative enough to use and build on the participants' resources.

2. *Transition Strategies.* Such strategies are critical to employee health, welfare, and effectiveness. Transitions for which strategies are being designed include entry into a new work place, change of work or jobs within the system, entry into new management positions and policies, and voluntary or involuntary severance from the system. A humane work place demonstrates caring for people who are experiencing changes. During any such transition, an individual needs support; orientations should be designed to help new workers enter the system and to help people ease into new work responsibilities in such a way that they feel supported rather than tense, fearful, alone, and unappreciated.

3. *Management or Leadership Profiles.* Establishing profiles of management or leadership can help to humanize the work place by giving decision makers feedback on how their subordinates perceive them. Such profiles are usually developed by interviewing individual employees and analyzing the results.

4. *Leadership and Influencing Skills.* Many working people want to become leaders or to be more skillful leaders. Organizations are realizing that both the system and the workers benefit from an effort to train people in these skills. Other desirable skills that are beginning to receive attention are those of influencing upward and empowerment strategies and techniques.

5. *Strategic Short-Term and Future Planning Skills.* These skills, which are important assets for many people in the work place, can be learned readily through on-the-job educational programs. Planning expertise is among the survival skills needed by today's supervisors and executives, yet many people in such positions are not well equipped in the planning arena. The area of strategic planning is burgeoning now, and companies are starting to recognize its importance.

6. *Opportunities That Enhance and Expand Right-Brain Functioning.* Such opportunities are being added to many training curricula. The purpose is to release the creative potential of people in the work place. Certainly educational opportunities must be expanded and increasingly

planned in conjunction with those to be included in the workshops, classes, forums, and seminars. Activities need to be varied in content and format and instructors selected who are knowledgeable in the subject matters involved as well as in teaching and meeting technologies.

EMPLOYEE-ASSISTANCE PROGRAMS

Increasingly systems are establishing employee-assistance programs focusing on advice, support, and help to employees from all levels of the system. Many of these programs began as substance-abuse counseling programs but are becoming broader as well as more pervasive.

Some programs offer as part of an employee-assistance program the services of an ombudsperson. This is someone who listens to problems and tries either to solve them or to make appropriate referrals so that they can be solved. Counseling is available for a number of problems other than substance abuse. For example, counseling can be obtained for child, family, or spouse abuse and for parenting. In the future, counseling for physical ailments and mental illness may be needed, particularly in relation to diseases such as Alzheimer's or AIDS. Sometimes counseling is conducted by an expert counselor who works with an individual or a group on particular problems, and sometimes it is conducted by trained peer counselors.

Some employee-assistance programs act as referral services. After diagnosing a concern or problem, such a service refers the employee to help either within the system or through an appropriate community agency. Child care, for example, can be arranged through employee-assistance programs; in fact, some companies provide child-care facilities on site.

Sometimes support groups are developed for handicapped employees or for employees who are about to retire. Under expert guidance, the members of such groups talk about common problems, concerns, and plans. In addition, there are groups that do wellness planning, helping employees to plan nutritionally balanced meals and to develop suitable exercise programs.

Other kinds of assistance that would be extremely valuable in the future include the following:

- Counseling services for employees who are newcomers to the country, who are taking early retirement, or who need to retire because of illness;
- Counseling services for employees who are experiencing stress as a result of feeling burned out, bored, or directionless;
- Assistance for employees who wish to connect with volunteer agencies in the community that would provide them with additional educational and recreational opportunities and that would provide the system with an opportunity to be recognized in the community in new and different ways;
- Counseling services for employees regarding their benefits, the costs involved, changes that are occurring, and any options they have with regard to their benefits; and
- Education about an organization's action-research programs so that its employees become more productive and effective in the areas of the company's research.

Because employee-assistance programs of these types exist in very few systems thus far, it would be advisable to have professional people trained in these specific areas to lead them. Such people would include industrial social workers, recreational therapists, administrators of volunteers, and social workers and psychologists whose training is as licensed counselors. If the action-research function were to become part of an employee-assistance program, an organization development specialist also would be helpful.

SOCIAL-RESPONSIBILITY PROGRAMS

Social-responsibility programs connect the business world to community activities. Corporate social responsibility was given a visible push when President Reagan asked corporations to take over some of the work of the voluntary sector. In some companies there are directors of volunteers who help employees find useful and interesting volunteer opportunities in the community. In other companies the volunteering is done in house, such as with an internal volunteer-trainer corps. Other programs have been experimented with and developed, such as the "loaned-executive" program affiliated with United Way and the "adopt-a-school" program connected with particular schools in various school districts.

Some companies have foundations through which employees make donations of money directly to nonprofit systems or programs in the community. Another emerging trend is the development of a technology-transfer volunteer corps through which people who have a particular expertise are "lent" to civic and nonprofit systems to help these systems with such activities as selecting and installing computers or developing particular technologies to address particular needs. Several research and development centers of the Federal government have technology-transfer volunteers. Union Carbide developed this kind of service corps made up largely of pre-retirees or retirees who had expertise in special areas. It is clear from the research that systems that offer employees the opportunity to volunteer have decreased turnover, less burnout, and higher morale than those in which such opportunities are not available.

MENTORING PROGRAMS

In some organizations a mentoring program is part and parcel of the training or human resource development department. Experienced employees are offered an opportunity to help orient and teach new and/or younger employees. In addition, mentors are often used to help people who come from other countries to adjust to their new situations. Sometimes mentors act as interpreters, and sometimes older women and/or supportive men help younger women become managers and leaders, particularly when the younger women involved have had no experience and no role models to use in their new ventures. Certainly experienced people can be effective mentors in career and professional-development programs and sometimes in leadership-development courses. Part of a mentoring program should be the opportunity for people to learn to be mentors. Often this status opportunity is a way of recognizing people when salary increases or other forms of recognition are not available.

CHALLENGES AND POSSIBLE INTERVENTIONS

The field of human resource development still faces several challenges with regard to humanizing the work place. It may be possible to help initiate and make change happen in the following ways:

1. *Invent New Ways to Form Groups of Workers.* It seems increasingly possible to determine outcomes that need to be achieved and then to form units of people who have the right variety of resources to realize those outcomes. It may well be possible to experiment with different combinations of people; to open groups to volunteer participation; to try a variety of leadership patterns, including co-leadership arrangements, temporary leaderships, a system of sequential leaders, or allowing leaders to emerge naturally from the group.

2. *Actively Involve Those to Be Affected by Planning and Decision Making in Those Processes.* It is important to find ways to decrease the distance between decision makers and those affected by planning and decision making. This may be possible through informal meetings; vertical groups; well-designed, participative, open meetings; and small consultative sessions. All of these

can include the administration of feedback devices that collect data on whether the employees feel involved and how they feel about their involvement.

3. *Recognize and Respond Actively to Inadequate Short-Term and Future Planning Efforts.* It is important to develop ways to involve the many, to do consequence analysis, to use a variety of planning methods, and to obtain input that visibly influences decisions that are made.

4. *Implement Transition Management.* This would include conducting diagnostic work about the kind of transitions people are experiencing and their feelings about the changes. Educational activities could be designed to help individuals and groups to proceed through transitions more smoothly.

5. *Acknowledge and Appreciate a Multicultural, Intergenerational Work Force.* This approach would include in-house training on how to work with people who are different from oneself, value dialogs and discussions, and support-group meetings aimed at using differences as resources instead of as inhibiting factors.

6. *Move Toward More Interdependence and Collaboration Within and Among Systems.* As Gardner (1984) has said, "Necessity is the mother of collaboration." Collaboration means finding projects and efforts of a joint nature with unions; with outside groups; and with various levels inside the system that can work on solving problems, developing projects, and mediating conflicts.

7. *Invigorate and Revive the Work Force.* This could be accomplished by introducing new and appropriate technologies and ways of working.

8. *Use Recent Research Findings to Change and Update Educational and Training Programs.* These programs could be made more useful and the people who are involved in them more effective.

9. *Celebrate Movement, Change, and Transitions in Explicit Ways.* Recognition of effort and progress is seriously needed in the work place.

These are exciting and challenging times. Humanizing the work place is not a choice; it is a mandate in which everyone must be willing to take risks, to creatively confront, to initiate, and to experiment so that it becomes possible to realize the potential of and provide opportunities for the whole person.

REFERENCES

Gardner, J. (1984, September). Remarks on leadership delivered at the National Association of Community Leadership Organizations, Dallas, TX.

Yankelovich, D. (1981). *New rules: Searching for self-fulfillment in a world turned upside down.* New York: Random House.

Eva Schindler-Rainman, Ph.D., is an adjunct professor in the School of Public Administration at the University of Southern California in Los Angeles. She also consults with voluntary, corporate, and governmental organizations throughout the United States and abroad. Dr. Schindler-Rainman has developed and conducted courses, seminars, and workshops in major universities in several states; and she has written or co-authored seven books and more than three hundred articles.

DIAGNOSING THE TRAINING SITUATION: MATCHING INSTRUCTIONAL TECHNIQUES WITH LEARNING OUTCOMES AND ENVIRONMENT

Carol Rocklin Kay, Sue Kruse Peyton, and Robert Pike

Professionals in training and development often ask about the "best" instructional techniques. Many experienced trainers realize that what is best is relative to the learners, the trainer, the outcomes desired, and environmental conditions. Numerous techniques are available, and each has its own characteristics and potentials for making an effective training program. Knox (1980) suggests that the major reason trainers need to use a variety of training techniques is to promote interest and encourage persistence among the participants until the desired outcomes are achieved. This article provides a framework to assist trainers in effectively matching instructional techniques with desired outcomes in the learning environment.

It is especially important for trainers to tailor the techniques to accomplish specified outcomes, because application of knowledge and skill is the justification for training. To enable learners to use the content of training programs in their jobs or personal lives, trainers must plan for higher levels of learning than can be achieved with certain instructional techniques. According to Watson (1980), many adult-education trainers use structured, learner-centered group methods. Such methods include consensus problem solving (Hall & Williams, 1970), nominal group techniques (Ford & Nemiroff, 1975), role play (Jones & Pfeiffer, 1979; Wohling, 1976), and simulation (Coppard, 1976; Horn, 1978). Additionally, many trainers adapt such methods to their own situations. They do not need extensive knowledge of group dynamics in order to be effective in the use of structured, learner-centered group techniques; however, a less directive, more consultative role is necessary (Watson, 1980). Time must be allowed for participants to develop their groups and adjust to more active roles in the learning process. Thus, these techniques have implications for both the learning environment and the desired outcomes.

Although lower-level learning may not be accomplished best in group processes (Raven, 1969; Middleman & Goldberg, 1972), there is evidence that planned discussion can support learners who are encountering difficulty acquiring basic knowledge and understanding from lectures, readings, and other information-receiving techniques (Watson, 1980). By specifying the outcomes desired from training experiences and by using a variety of techniques that can effectively and efficiently produce those results, trainers have a greater probability of successful programs.

Effective teaching is the heart of a training program. This article identifies important relationships among instructional techniques, learning outcomes, and the learning environment to assist trainers in increasing teaching effectiveness.

INSTRUCTIONAL TECHNIQUES

Trainers need a broad repertoire of teaching techniques to incorporate into training programs. They need to understand the advantages, disadvantages, and potentials of techniques in order to match them with desired outcomes and the learning environment. Instructional techniques often evolve naturally from specific content. For example, in an introductory computer workshop, an appropriate strategy for introducing the concept of "booting the disk" is the demonstration technique. In a management-development session, on the other hand, a role-play technique could help participants become more adept at performance-appraisal interviews.

An effective trainer generally uses a variety of strategies, depending on what is appropriate for the content, outcomes, environment, and available resources. This section outlines some popular training techniques or methods, and they are grouped under the primary categories of "information receiving," "discussion," "information finding," and "dramatization." For each technique, the sentence numbered "1" describes the method; the number "2" sentence relates some of the advantages; and sentence number "3" enumerates some of the limitations.

Information Receiving

The Lecture

1. One person systematically presents information.
2. Maximum information is presented in a limited time; diverse materials and ideas can be arranged in an orderly system.
3. This method uses one person's point of view, one channel of communication, and no group participation; it is strongly influenced by the personality of the speaker.

Figure 1 illustrates the pattern of interaction in the lecture method.

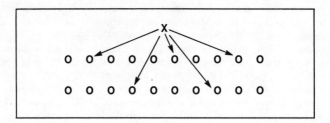

Figure 1. The Lecture

Demonstrations

1. A process is performed before an audience.
2. Processes that illustrate techniques and skills can be visually presented, and results of particular procedures can be shown.
3. This technique provides for limited participation by group members.

The Debate

1. Two sides of an issue are presented by speakers under the direction of a moderator.
2. Issues can be sharpened, questions can be clarified, and interest can reach a high level.
3. Debates can easily become too emotional, and a good moderator should be present to mediate differences.

Figure 2 illustrates the pattern of interaction in a debate.

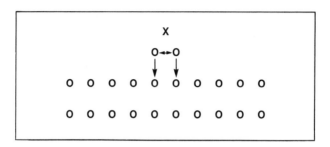

Figure 2. The Debate

Dialog

1. Two people informally discuss a topic before an audience.
2. Information is provided in an informal setting, which adds interest and emotional appeal and encourages discussion.
3. A dialog needs careful planning to keep it from becoming disorganized or dominated by the personalities of the participants.

Panel

1. Under the direction of a moderator, several people discuss an issue in front of an audience; frequently after all members of the panel have made their initial presentations, a full-panel discussion is held.
2. The different viewpoints stimulate thinking.
3. A skillful moderator is needed to keep the panel on the topic and to keep any of the members from monopolizing the discussion.

Discussion

Question-and-Answer Sessions

1. Responses are solicited by inquiries, which can come either from a leader to a member of the audience or from a member of the audience to either a leader or another member of the audience.
2. Clarification can be provided to answer specific needs, and this method is easily combined with other techniques.
3. A question-and-answer session can easily become threatening, embarrassing, dull, too formal, or too informal.

Figure 3 illustrates the pattern of interaction during question-and-answer sessions.

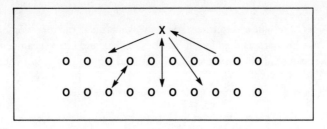

Figure 3. Question-and-Answer Sessions

Group Discussions

1. To reach an agreement or gain a better understanding, two or more people share knowledge, experiences, and opinions; build on ideas; clarify; evaluate; and coordinate.
2. Many needs of group members can be met with this method, because it provides a high degree of interaction, interest, and involvement.
3. Group discussions may not provide authoritative information, nor are they usually helpful when the group is large; they require time, patience, and capable leadership.

Figure 4 illustrates the pattern of interaction in group discussions.

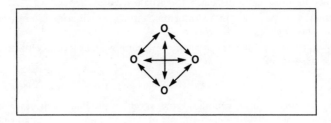

Figure 4. Group Discussions

Buzz Groups

1. Large groups are divided into smaller groups (frequently containing five to ten members) to discuss a particular topic and report back to the large group.
2. An opportunity is provided for a maximum discussion in a limited time, thereby promoting involvement and enthusiasm.
3. The discussion may be shallow, disorganized, or dominated by one or two people.

Brainstorming

1. Groups identify as many ideas related to a problem or topic as possible, without evaluating quality or practicality of the ideas.

2. This technique can produce excellent audience involvement and it encourages creativity; it can be done quickly; and a large group can be divided into small groups for the activity.
3. Creative thinking may be inhibited (and the method fail) unless participants adhere strictly to the guidelines and refrain from making evaluative comments.

Symposium

1. Several people with different points of view make presentations; often the presentations are followed by a question-and-answer session directed by a moderator.
2. This method presents several viewpoints on a topic.
3. To work effectively, this technique needs speakers with equal ability and a skillful moderator.

Listening Team

1. A team from the audience reacts to a presentation by a resource person in order to raise questions or clarify and summarize the presentation.
2. The audience becomes involved, helping the resource person to meet the needs of the group; this method can be helpful when the content is difficult.
3. This technique can be time consuming, and the quality depends on the team members.

Information Finding

A Field Trip or Tour

1. A visit to a place of interest is arranged for direct observation and study.
2. This method, which can be highly interesting to the participants, expands their understanding and broadens their interest; at least to a degree, it involves every member of the group.
3. This method is time consuming and requires a great deal of organization; without adequate discussion prior to and following the visit, the learning may be limited.

Group Project

1. Group members cooperatively work on a project.
2. This technique can provide first-hand information and practical experience; it can stimulate interest; and it can provide insights on teamwork.
3. Unless sufficient time is allowed for discussing the process, the project tends to become an end in itself.

Case Study

1. A description of a situation or an event is supplied, often supported by a handout, and participants are given instructions about dealing with the situation or finding a solution.
2. This technique requires participants to use higher learning processes and helps them to apply principles.

3. A case study may be difficult to develop, especially if adequate data are not available; and it is time consuming for groups to work through the case study and report their discussions.

Dramatization

Role Playing

1. Roles are assigned, and participants spontaneously act out a situation; usually the role play is followed by analysis and evaluation.
2. This method provides opportunities to "feel" human relations situations and to experiment with possible solutions or interactions.
3. Unless carefully handled, role playing can become merely entertaining or too artificial.

Skits

1. The skit is a short, planned, and usually rehearsed performance to convey a message or to present or interpret a situation.
2. This method is entertaining; it can be used to introduce a topic, or it can be interspersed to emphasize certain elements of a training session.
3. Effective skits require advance preparation and adequate processing.

Simulation Games

1. Games are fashioned from actual situations in order to explore concepts and to practice behavior.
2. These games provide a safe environment for practicing new behavior; they encourage active learning; and they can be fun and challenging.
3. Games may encourage a false sense of confidence in handling a real-life situation, and they may be expensive to develop.

INSTRUCTIONAL-DESIGN GRID

The Instructional-Design Grid (see Figure 5) was developed to help trainers and other program designers select instructional techniques that are appropriate for the desired learning outcomes in the learning environment. (Typical learning outcomes and environments are discussed in the following sections.) The grid provides an organized approach to planning a training program. To use the grid, the designer should first consider the desired outcomes and match the preferred outcomes with the appropriate techniques listed on the grid. Techniques with the greatest potential of producing a particular outcome are designated by a double "X" (i.e., "XX"), and those with less potential by a single "X." After those techniques are considered, they should be narrowed further by the constraints of the learning environment. The grid employs the same single-X and double-X system for the learning-environment section.

Learning Outcomes

As trainers design programs, a primary consideration must be the objectives or outcomes expected from the learning experiences. Learning outcomes suggest the end results of training activities and guide the selection of appropriate instructional techniques. Therefore, the

	Information Receiving					Discussion						Information Finding			Dramatization		
	Lecture	Demonstration	Debate	Dialog	Panel	Question-Answer	Group Discussion	Buzz Groups	Brainstorming	Symposium	Listening Team	Field Trip-Tour	Project-Experience	Case Study	Role Playing	Skit	Simulation-Games
Learning Outcomes																	
Clarification	XX	XX	XX	XX	XX	XX	XX	X	X	XX	X	XX	XX	XX	X	X	X
Problem Solving						X	X	X				X	XX	XX	X	X	X
Creativity									XX			X	XX	X	XX	XX	X
Consensus							X	XX				X	XX				
Enthusiasm							X	XX	XX			XX	XX	X	XX	XX	XX
Attitude Change		X	X			X	X	X	X			X	XX	X	X	X	X
Skill Change		X				X	X					X	XX	XX	X	X	X
Learning Environment																	
Communication One-Way	XX	XX	XX	XX	XX					X							
Two-Way						XX				X	XX	X	X	X			
Multiple						X	XX	XX	XX			XX	XX	XX	XX	XX	XX
Formal Setting	XX	XX	XX			XX				XX							
Informal Setting				X		XX	XX	XX	XX		X	XX	XX	XX	X	X	X
Learner Involvement					X	X	XX	XX	XX	X	X	XX	XX	XX	X	X	XX
Large Group	XX	X	XX	XX	XX	X				XX	XX					X	
Small Group		XX		XX		XX	XX	XX	XX			XX	XX	XX	XX	XX	XX
Time Efficiency	XX	XX	XX	X	XX	X	X	XX	XX	X	X		X		X	X	X

Figure 5. Instructional-Design Grid

trainer should be cognizant of the instructional techniques that can accomplish the desired outcomes. In addition to using the Instructional-Design Grid, trainers may be interested in studying the taxonomies of learning objectives in cognitive, affective, and psychomotor domains that were developed by Bloom (1956), Krathwohl (1964), and Simpson (1966).

Some typical learning outcomes, which are used in the grid, are briefly outlined in the following paragraphs.

Clarification

For clarification to occur, learners must understand the information and concepts presented and comprehend how they can be used outside the training situation.

Problem Solving

If learning to solve certain types of problems is the goal, then the learners need to be able to apply their training to other situations.

Creativity

If being creative is a desired outcome, learners should be encouraged and given the opportunity to use their own ideas and experiences in analyzing, synthesizing, and evaluating information.

Consensus

The term "consensus" is used in the grid to convey the concept that the learners are able to reach agreement on a decision or solution with peer input or support.

Enthusiasm

If learners receive and respond to ideas in a positive way, the objective of enthusiasm will be accomplished.

Attitude Change

Learners must become convinced that the ideas presented have merit in order to be motivated enough to change their attitudes.

Skill Change

After the training session, learners must be able to use the skills they acquired in order for skill change to occur.

Learning Environment

The learning environment must also be considered in the design stage. Factors such as communication patterns desired, the setting, and the type of audience affect the selection of instructional techniques.

Communication Patterns

Communication patterns in the training environment vary in the number of ways that messages can be sent or received, and the communication pattern has important implications for audience interactions. Instructional techniques that bring the learner and the trainer face to face vary in their communication patterns. One-way communication flows from trainer (or other speakers) to learners; two-way communication is an exchange between trainer and learners; and multiple communication includes exchanges among learners. A closely related factor is time efficiency, because generally time is more easily controlled with one-way communication. The time-efficiency factor refers to the degree to which a trainer can predict that the training can be completed and objectives met in a specified amount of time.

Leavitt (1951) contends that when communication moves from an open, unrestricted dialog to more restrictive one-way patterns, errors increase, less work is accomplished, and the learners are less satisfied with their participation. Leavitt's findings, however, do not mean that one-way communication is always bad and that two-way communication is always good. In a given setting, whether formal or informal, each has particular strengths and weaknesses that affect learner involvement. Table 1 identifies some of the advantages and disadvantages of both types of communication.

Table 1. Advantages and Disadvantages of Communication Patterns

Type of Communication	Advantages	Disadvantages
One-Way (from Trainer)	Trainer controls amount, pace, and flow of information. A lot of information can be transmitted in a short amount of time.	Learners have little or no opportunity for response. Since feedback is low, trainer makes assumptions about learners' skills. Learners take little initiative and may become apathetic.
Two-Way	Trainer's assumptions about learners' skills, prior training, and understanding of content are tested. Learners depend less on trainer and take more initiative and responsibility.	Information takes longer to be communicated. Amount, pace, and flow of information is not exclusively under the trainer's control.

Settings

Instructional techniques vary in the degree of formality required. Some call for an informal setting, whereas a formal learning environment is more suitable for others.

Audience

Some techniques require the audience to become actively involved during the learning process, whereas others allow the learners to be passive. Some techniques are appropriate for large groups, and others are more effective when used with small groups of learners.

CONCLUSION

Cross (1976) suggested that the selection and organization of instructional techniques reflect the trainer's style, preferences, and experience to a greater degree than do any other aspects of program planning. Planning an approach to the instructional design encourages trainers to consider the learners, outcomes, and environment as well as their own preferences for instructional techniques. Although the Instructional-Design Grid is expected to be helpful for emerging professionals, its greater strength may lie in stimulating experienced trainers to reconsider their habits, add some variety, and try to ascertain that selected techniques are compatible with desired outcomes and the learning environment.

REFERENCES

Bloom, B.S. (1956). *Taxonomy of educational objectives: Cognitive domain.* New York: Longmans, Green.

Coppard, L.C. (1976). Gaming simulation and the training process. In R. Craig (Ed.), *Training and development handbook.* New York: McGraw-Hill.

Cross, K.P. (1976). *Accent on learning: Improving instruction in reshaping the curriculum.* San Francisco: Jossey-Bass.

Ford, D.L., Jr., & Nemiroff, P.M. (1975). Applied group problem-solving: The nominal group technique. In J.E. Jones & J.W. Pfeiffer (Eds.), *The 1975 annual handbook for group facilitators.* San Diego, CA: University Associates.

Hall, J., & Williams, M.S. (1970). A comparison of decision making performances in established and ad hoc groups. *Journal of Personality and Social Psychology, 3*(2), 214-222.

Horn, R.E. (1978). *The guide to simulation games for education and training.* Lexington, MA: Information Sources.

Jones, J.E., & Pfeiffer, J.W. (1979). Role playing. In J.E. Jones & J.W. Pfeiffer (Eds.), *The 1979 annual handbook for group facilitators.* San Diego, CA: University Associates.

Knox, A.B. (1980). Helping teachers help adults learn. In A.B. Knox (Ed.), *New directions for continuing education: Teaching adults effectively.* San Francisco: Jossey-Bass.

Krathwohl, D. (1964). *Taxonomy of educational objectives: Affective domain.* New York: David McKay.

Leavitt, H.J. (1951). Some effects of certain communication patterns on group performance. *Journal of Abnormal and Social Psychology, 46,* 38-50.

Middleman, R.R., and Goldberg, G. (1972). The concept of structure in experiential learning. In J.W. Pfeiffer & J.E. Jones (Eds.), *The 1972 annual handbook for group facilitators.* San Diego, CA: University Associates.

Raven, B.H. (1969). *A bibliography of publications relating to the small group.* Washington, DC: Office of Naval Research, Group Psychology Branch.

Simpson, E. (1966). *The classification of objectives, psychomotor domain* (Research Project No. OE-5-85-104). Urbana, IL: University of Illinois.

Watson, E.R. (1980). Small group instruction. In A.B. Knox (Ed.), *New directions for continuing education: Teaching adults effectively.* San Francisco: Jossey-Bass.

Wohling, W. (1976). Role playing. In R. Craig (Ed.), *Training and development handbook.* New York: McGraw-Hill.

Carol Rocklin Kay, Ed.D., is an assistant professor of adult education and assistant to the vice president for student affairs at Iowa State University in Ames. Her specialties include teaching and learning styles, evaluation of training and development programs, and quality circles in educational settings. Dr. Kay is an active member of the American Society for Training and Development, the American Association for Adult and Continuing Education, and the American Educational Research Association.

Sue Kruse Peyton, Ph.D., is a consultant and designs workshops and seminars for groups and organizations. She has been a leader of staff development for Iowa State University in Ames since 1982 and has served on several committees of the American Society for Training and Development. Her areas of interest include teaching and learning, personal effectiveness, team building, and leadership development.

Robert Pike is president of Resources for Organizations in Eden Prairie, Minnesota. He has developed and implemented training programs for business, industry, government, and the professions since 1969. He served on the national board of the American Society for Training and Development and is on the 1987 ASTD design committee. He is also author of Creative Cost Effective Training Techniques.

FORECASTING THE ECONOMIC BENEFITS OF TRAINING

Richard A. Swanson and Gary D. Geroy

Although the concept of cost-benefit analysis has been around for decades, it is a concept that management continues to use selectively. When making capital outlays, one may find it relatively easy to forecast costs and benefits by using traditional methods. Furthermore, depreciation schedules and return-on-investment expectations are locked into the capital-investment perspective. Unfortunately, equivalent forecasting tools are not available when decision makers are faced with investments in employee training and development—or the human capital—of the organization. As a result, managers typically turn to a simple cost-based analysis when budgeting for employee training. They ask, "How much will it cost? How much did we spend last year? How much do we want to spend this year?"

With these simple cost questions, managers—in effect—avoid the realities of cost-benefit analysis and thus fail to realize the potential of large financial benefits to the organization. It is not surprising to find organizations of all sizes in almost all economic sectors making training decisions with no investment-forecasting information, as evidenced by the following examples.

- A medium-sized manufacturing company that produces electronic circuit boards has had a steady and profitable life. Even with high employee turnover and an unacceptable product rejection rate, they have been making money. The idea of investing in training had never entered management's mind. Consciously spending any money on training was a departure from normal practice. The twenty-thousand dollars proposed by an outside consultant for training ten assembly workers seemed extravagant. The company was not aware that in just forty days over $200,000 could be gained from the training.

- A Fortune-100 manufacturing firm—which had a stable and experienced work force that had been trained by trial-and-error job experience—recently learned a lesson. A closer look through a cost-benefit analysis revealed that there could be significant benefits from training. The actual results from four separate training efforts supported the forecasted benefits. As a result, the corporation is considering an orchestrated human-and-capital investment program throughout the organization.

- A manager of training in a corporation in a large metropolitan area found himself confronted with more training options than he expected. The engineering content could have been handled in-house by his staff, by three training vendors, or by two public institutions. The questions he faced included "Will any or all of the training options yield a benefit? Of those predicting a benefit, are there differences? How does a manager choose between rival training options?"

The authors wish to thank Brian P. Murphy and Onan Corporation of Minneapolis, Minnesota, for providing support to the Training and Development Research Center for the purpose of conducting inquiry related to financial assessment of human resource development programs and to thank Deane Gradous for her critical review of the manuscript.

SQUARE PEGS AND ROUND HOLES

Managers face a major problem: Their knowledge of the economics of training, a major tool for increasing the value of the human capital, is typically limited. Beyond a few studies (Cullen et al., 1976; Rosentreter, 1979; Thomas, Moxham, & Jones, 1969), attention to the microeconomic analysis of training has been minimal. Searches through the literature on the costs and benefits of training uncover large voids in the areas of economic descriptions of training efforts, forecasting of training costs and benefits, and experimental assessment of the economic factors of training. With few exceptions, cost-benefit analysis tools for capital investments continue to be applied to employee training. Because the idea of applying depreciation schedules to human learning is inappropriate, this practice is analogous to fitting square pegs in round holes.

FORECASTING TRAINING COSTS AND BENEFITS

Organizations exist to make gains. Decision makers establish goals to determine what gains will be pursued. They then allocate resources (financial or human) to attain the goals. In attempting to improve organizational performance, decision makers at the strategic planning level may choose to support training or nontraining performance improvement options. The training option includes both unstructured on-the-job training and structured training programs. Either of which incurs costs.

There are many alternative ways to view costs. Accountants perceive costs as the outlays necessary to achieve a given set of outcomes. Financial managers see costs as the value of the alternatives foregone in order to pursue a particular course of action. For example, by taking a worker off the job to receive training, the organization foregoes the worth of that worker's potential productivity had the worker remained on the job. Conversely, to retain an inadequately trained worker on the job eliminates expenditures for structured training while bearing the costs of less-than-acceptable productivity until the employee finally reaches competence.

Cost Considerations

The true costs of training—and, therefore, training budgets—are often inaccurately estimated by managers and trainers. All the costs that an organization can identify and associate with its structured or unstructured training must be counted. Employees who are performing at the level of their performance goals are not incurring training costs. Training costs do appear when any of the following situations exist:

1. A new employee arrives on the job.
2. An experienced employee is transferred or promoted to a job that requires the acquisition of additional skills or knowledge or a change in attitude.
3. The job of an experienced employee is modified and requires new skills and knowledge or different applications of expertise.
4. An experienced employee has a loss of knowledge or skill.

An accurate and complete analysis of training costs will include the measure of the value of production units *not* produced or performance *not* accomplished during the period of training. The costs of alternative training options may be measured by including comparisons of production lost during the time of training. Training costs also include expenses directly and indirectly associated with developing and delivering the structured training. The salaries and benefits paid to trainees and others involved with the training during the training period must also be considered in estimates of costs.

Measuring Training Costs

The managers, trainers, and accountants in a firm may not always agree on which specific items should be considered training costs. What is important is that they use identical criteria in costing each option under consideration. Furthermore, the period for measuring costs should be held constant in order to make valid comparisons among a set of training options.

The minimum measurable costs of on-the-job unstructured training is the value of employees' performance that remains below the performance goal during the training period. A Johns-Manville study (Cullen et al., 1976) provides evidence to support the position that the average performance per employee during the period of unstructured training is 50 percent of the performance goal.

The forecasting model proposed in this paper calls out generic categories of training costs for use in identifying those costs that are unique to the reader's organization. Categories have been included for costs incurred through losses of time, material, and production/performance. Examples of training cost categories are shown in Table 1.

Table 1. Categories of Training Costs

Cost Categories	Guidelines/Examples
Staff	Wages of clerical/secretarial, hourly or salaried subject-matter experts, trainers, or other employees involved in the training effort.
External Consultants	Fees and associated expenditures for externally hired subject-matter and training-design experts involved in the specific training effort.
Materials	Items that will either become a permanent part of the specific training effort or that will be consumed in the training-related effort.
External Support Costs	Professional, skilled, or semi-skilled labor or services required to support any or all aspects of the training effort.
Trainees	Wages, mileage, lodging, and meal expenses associated with trainee attendance of training effort.
Facilities	Expenses associated with room or equipment rental, utilities, or facility modification directly related to the specific training effort.
Tuition/Fees	Expenses directly related to school tuition, fees, books and materials, and laboratory costs associated with a given training effort.

Benefits Profiles

Positive returns on investments are called benefits. Investments are in the form of time, money, or material, and the benefits derived may be in the form of quality (effectiveness) or quantity (efficiency) of a product or service. Organizational or individual performance gains are benefits to which value may be assigned. For example, an increase in the quantity of production per unit of time has a measurable value when it is viewed as time gained and available for producing additional products or services at a given performance level. Likewise, when higher quality is achieved without decreasing the rate of production, it can be measured as a gain in the value of units produced (e.g., fewer rejects or lower warranty costs would be measured as a gain). The value of performance is an important part of the training benefit forecasting method. Determining the value of performance requires that the total performance, or performance units that make up the performance, be identified. Identifying these factors is not always as easy as one might think, and it remains the critical task of each analysis effort.

Performance value is the financial worth of all performance units produced in an organization. Performance units can be expressed in any manner specific to the organization. All performance units should be judged within a common time frame when training options are compared.

TRAINING BENEFIT FORECASTING METHOD

In its simplest form, the benefit forecasting method requires that all increases in performance values (minus the training costs) and the resulting benefits be determined for each training alternative under consideration. When the performance value exceeds the costs, the training yields a benefit. If the costs exceed the performance value, no benefit results. The highest projected benefit among training alternatives indicates the most desirable option from a financial perspective (see Figure 1).

Analysis of Costs

When costs are analyzed, care must be taken to include all the costs attributable to the specific training option being considered. Costs must be calculated for staff time, trainee time, consultants, materials, space, et cetera, needed to complete each step in the training process. Costs will be incurred for needs analysis, work-behavior analysis, designing the training, implementation, and evaluation. The final accounting for costs may be expressed as total dollar costs per training option or as costs per trainee in each option. Table 2 is a work sheet for recording the cost for each step of the training process.

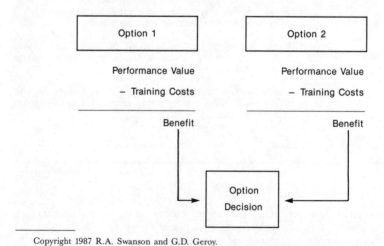

Copyright 1987 R.A. Swanson and G.D. Geroy.

Figure 1. Benefit Forecasting Model

Table 2. Work Sheet for Analyzing Training Costs

Training Phases	Training Options	
	Commerical	In-House
Analysis		
Needs Assessment	$ 0	$ 3,224
Work Analysis	0	510
Design		
Program	0	2,440
Instructional Aids	0	1,100
Development		
Pilot Testing	0	600
Formative Evaluation	0	100
Instructional Aids	0	1,020
Implementation		
Delivery	22,200	5,760
Management	0	2,294
Evaluation		
Summative Evaluation	0	208
Training Revision	0	600
Maintenance of Trainee Behavior	0	0
Total (A)	$ 22,200	$ 17,856
Number of Trainees (B)	10	10
Cost Per Trainee $\dfrac{(A)}{(B)}$	$ 2,220	$ 1,785

Table 2 also contains actual data used in the case study that appears later. When determining the appropriate figures to enter, the analyst should consult the comptroller and others who have financial-analysis responsibilities in the organization. The primary purpose of such consultation is to identify the costs that the organization considers relevant to the training programs being considered. The following list shows the items that are typically considered in costing each phase of the cost-analysis work sheet:

1. Salaries
   a. Participants
   b. Administrative support
   c. Training-staff professional
   d. Subject-matter experts
   e. Miscellaneous organizational support personnel
2. Fringe and Overhead
3. Logistics
   a. Travel
   b. Per diem
   c. Lodging
4. Facilities
5. Maintenance
6. Equipment
   a. Purchases
   b. Rentals
7. Materials
   a. Consumables
   b. Nonconsumables
8. Outside Services
   a. Fees
   b. Travel
   c. Direct Costs

Analysis of Performance Value

Performance value is defined as the worth of performance units produced in dollars. In analyzing performance values, one should identify those specific performance units that will result from the training options being considered and assess their dollar value to the organization. Several pieces of information are needed to carry out this step: the number of trainees, the desired performance level expressed in units, training time needed to reach the desired performance level, the performance accomplished during the period under consideration, the value of the units of performance, and the current level of the trainee's performance.

Some of this information, such as number of trainees and training time, is relatively easy to obtain. However, making valid comparisons among training options requires the analyst to determine a base period of time to be used in calculating performance values for each training option. This base period is the *longest* period of time required by any of the training options to bring the trainees' performance up to the desired level (see Figure 2).

On-the-job unstructured training, if this is one of the options, usually requires the longest period. Performance information may be obtained from a variety of sources; for example, the current level of worker performance and the desired level may be determined from the performance discrepancies cited in the original needs assessment, the performance standards set by production, or the stated training objectives for the particular training option. Information that aids in identifying the desired units of performance can be obtained from individual performance-review standards, production standards, and other records of productivity. Information needed to assess the value of the units of performance may be gathered by interviewing those responsible for budget development, production-cost analysis, or financial analysis.

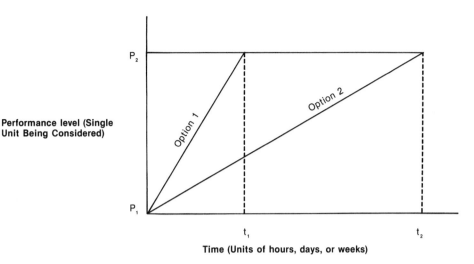

Performance level (Single Unit Being Considered)

P_2

P_1

t_1 t_2

Time (Units of hours, days, or weeks)

P_2 = Performance goal

P_1 = Existing performance level

t_2 = Time of comparison period
(longest time period among options)

t_1 = Time to performance goal for option 1

Figure 2. Performance-Level-Over-Time Comparison of Training Options

The Work Sheet

Once the information is obtained, a net-performance-value calculation work sheet can be used to organize it. Table 3 illustrates such a work sheet and contains data from the case study that appears later in this paper. When items g through m on the work sheet are completed, they provide specific figures to use in determining the value of the trainees' performance that results from the training.

A separate performance-value calculation is carried out for each training option. Frequently employees produce items or perform activities during the training that are valuable to the organization. This value is determined and calculated on the work sheet (items g through i) and is taken into consideration in the total performance value per individual (item j). Item j includes the employee performance during training plus the performance from the end of the training period for the option to the end of the period used for comparison. Determining the value of this total performance per option becomes a simple calculation in item k. In this value calculation, the option being considered should *not* be given credit for the value

Table 3. Performance-Value Calculation Work Sheet for Circuit-Board Training

	Option 1 Unstructured	Option 2 Commercial	Option 3 In-House
Data Required for Calculations			
a. What is the desired performance goal as a result of worker training?	1.5/day	1.5/day	1.5/day
b. What unit(s) of measure will be used to describe the performance?	Number of Boards	Number of Boards	Number of Boards
c. What is the dollar value that will be assigned to each unit of measure?	$600	$600	$600
d. What is the estimated training time to reach the goal?	40 days	10 days	8 days
e. What is the current level of worker performance?	0	0	0
f. How many workers will participate in the training?	10	10	10
Calculations to Determine Net Performance Value			
g. What is the estimated performance level during training? Will trainee produce during training? No $= 0$ Yes $= \dfrac{a+e}{2}$	.75/day	0	0
h. What is the length of the period being evaluated? (At a minimum, this will be the longest "d" of all options under consideration.)	40 days	40 days	40 days
i. What is the estimate of the total number of units (b) that will be achieved during training? (d × g)	30	0	0
j. What is the estimate of the total performance per individual for the evaluation period? [(h − d) × a] + i	30	45	48
k. What is the value for the total performance for the evaluation period? (c × j)	$ 18,000	$ 27,000	$ 28,800
l. What is the net performance value gain? [k − (e × c × h)]	$ 18,000	$ 27,000	$ 28,800
m. Do you want to calculate the total net performance value of all trainees? Yes ☐ No ☐ = Net performance value of one trainee which is calculated value of (l)	$ 180,000	$ 270,000	$ 288,800

Copyright 1987 R.A. Swanson and G.D. Geroy.

of the performance level at which the employee entered training. To insure that this value is subtracted from the calculation, item 1 accounts for the level of employee performance and its associated value prior to the training experience and substracts it from the total performance value for the comparison period. This calculation ensures that only the net performance gain due to training and its attendant economic value are used in determining the benefit from the particular training option.

A COST-BENEFIT FORECASTING CASE STUDY[1]

The employees of a manufacturer of specialized circuit boards for electronic equipment had previously been trained by an unstructured on-the-job method. The circuit-board assembly workers read at an average level of seventh grade, and all of them experienced difficulty in understanding the English language. Approximately forty working days were required for a new assembly worker to reach the acceptable performance level of three good circuit boards every two days. Each circuit board was valued at six hundred dollars, and assembly workers were paid nine dollars per hour. When workers reached the expected performance level, they generally produced rework at the rate of one circuit board in eighteen. The rejects were caused by poor soldering or incorrect positioning of one or two installed parts.

Management was considering designing or contracting for a training program to decrease the time in which new assembly workers achieved the desired level of performance. One option was a commercially available ten-day training course that cost $1,500 per trainee. This course would provide training in basic soldering techniques, component identification, blueprint reading, instrument calibration, basic circuitry design, theory and practice, and systems diagnostics.

To develop another option, management hired a training consultant to do a training needs assessment and propose the content for an in-house training course. The consultant submitted a report and a bill for $2,200. The consultant recommended that in order to meet the manufacturing skills needs of the company, the training should cover basic soldering techniques, identification of components for the circuit board, and electronic circuitry blueprint reading. He further recommended that the workers be provided with job aids to help them identify correct components and proper installation. The consultant recommended that the job aids be 8" x 10" color photographs of correctly built circuit boards. He believed that such a job aid would facilitate the workers' continued learning of the proper identification and placement of components. The consultant estimated that the total training time would be eight working days, at the conclusion of which the new assemblers would be able to produce at the rate of three boards every two days, the current quality level. Management believed that developing and delivering the in-house training course could be handled by the in-house training staff and the chief electronic engineer. Temporary clerical support could be hired to assist during the analysis, design, and development steps.

Management's role was to decide whether ten new employees would (option 1) be trained on the job as in the past, (option 2) attend the commercially available training course, or (option 3) receive the in-house training. A benefit analysis of the three options would lead

[1]This study, the first in a series of industry-based studies conducted by the Training and Development Research Center of the University of Minnesota, was funded by the Onan Corporation. Other studies in this series include forecasting the benefits of training for geometric tolerancing, welding training, grammar and punctuation for secretaries, and customer service for managers. All will use the benefit forecasting method.

the decision maker to the option with the highest project benefit: option 3, the in-house training (see Figure 3). The forecast benefit for that option was $270,144. Both Table 2 (the cost analysis) and Table 3 (the performance-value analysis) lead to the benefit analysis and option decision.

CONCLUSION

Analysis of the economics of training has become one of the important issues of the decade for business and industry. The quality of the analysis tools available to managers and training professionals will affect the quality of their training decisions. The benefit forecasting method described in this article demonstrates that training decisions can be made on the basis of rational thought and economic analysis.

Training benefit forecasting methods, such as the one presented here, are important decision-making tools in the work place. Managers and trainers who can discuss training activities in economic terms will be in a position to contribute to the strategic plans for the human capital in their firms. As top management thinks more seriously about human capital and about strategic planning for human resources, the training function will become more central to the firm.

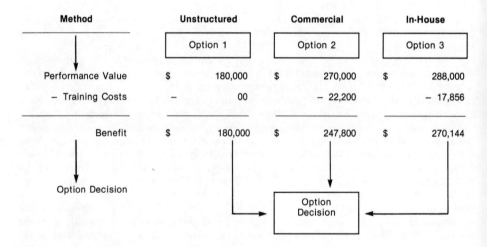

First Choice = Option 3: In-House Training.

Second Choice = Option 2: Commercially Available Training.

Third Choice = Option 1: Unstructured Training.

Figure 3: Benefit Analysis for Circuit-Board Training

REFERENCES

Cullen, J.G., Sawzin, S.A., Sisson, G.R., & Swanson, R.A. (1976). Training, what's it worth? *Training and Development Journal*, *30*(8), 12-20.

Rosentreter, G.E. (1979). Economic evaluation of a training program. In R.O. Peterson (Ed.), *Training and development: Research papers from the 1978 ASTD national conference* (pp. 164-182). Madison, WI: American Society for Training and Development.

Thomas, B., Moxham, J., & Jones, J.A.G. (1969). A cost benefit analysis of industrial training. *British Journal of Industrial Relations, 7*(2), 231-264.

Richard S. Swanson, Ed. D., *is a professor and director of the training and development research center at the University of Minnesota.* He co-authored Performance at Work: A Systematic Program for Analyzing Work Behavior *and* Training Technology System, *abridged edition. Dr. Swanson is the former editor of the* Performance and Instruction Journal *and the* Journal of Industrial Teacher Education.

Gary D. Geroy, Ed. D., is a faculty member of the Division of Counseling and Educational Psychology and Career Studies at The Pennsylvania State University. He is academic coordinator for the graduate and undergraduate training and development programs and teaches the program's professional development courses. Dr. Geroy is the recipient of the NSPI's first national research award. He has conducted domestic and international research on education for work and economic development and has presented several national and international papers related to economics of training.

CAREER STAGES AND LIFE STAGES: A CAREER-DEVELOPMENT PERSPECTIVE

Daniel C. Feldman

Implicit in the concept of a career is the idea of *change*, because a person's job skills and career aspirations change over time. In their twenties, people are more willing to do technical work assignments and take direction from others; in their fifties that type of career seems much less attractive. Moreover, the experiences in the early years of a career influence later career aspirations (Hall, Schneider, & Nygren, 1970). Early career success on highly specialized assignments might well influence individuals to pursue career paths in staff areas; for others, early success as project managers may convince them to pursue careers as general managers.

Careers are not the only aspects of people's lives that change as they grow older; people change biologically and emotionally as well. Freud's early work suggested that most of the major psychological development of individuals occurred before they reached fifteen. Since that time, psychologists and psychiatrists have grown much more aware of the extensive emotional development that takes place in adults (Kegan, 1982; Levinson, 1986). The boundless optimism that "you can have it all" gives way to the realization that tough choices have to be made and that many decisions (e.g., having or not having a child) are irreversible. Also the emotional reactions of single adults are frequently different from those of parents or grandparents.

This article examines the different career stages and life stages that people pass through as they mature and the interaction between life stages and career stages. The article also considers the implications of several developmental models for individual and organizational career planning.

CAREER STAGES

To understand career stages, one must look at the *commonalities* in job experiences of workers at the same point in their careers without regard to their occupations. Although the work of doctors is dramatically different from that of lawyers or engineers, research suggests that the types of challenges and frustrations these various workers face at the same stage in their careers are remarkably similar. Thus, what is discussed in this article is, in one sense, the ideal career— not ideal in the sense of perfection, but rather what a career would look like if it were pursued fully and successfully from beginning to end (Schein, 1978).

The Career Cone

Perhaps the earliest and most influential work on career stages was done by Edgar Schein at the Massachusetts Institute of Technology. To illustrate how individuals change jobs within an organization, Schein (1971) developed the concept of a career cone. Schein argues that individuals' careers in organizations can develop along three directions: vertically, horizontally, and "radially."

Vertical Moves

The most common type of career move is along the hierarchical or vertical dimension. People can obtain promotions and rise to levels of increasing leadership within the organization. In some occupations (e.g., general management) there are many steps between the bottom and top of the organizational hierarchy; in other occupations (e.g., doctor or lawyer) very few promotions are available.

Horizontal Moves

Although many people pursue the same job function or technical specialty throughout their careers, others switch their functions or specialties. For example, a person may move from accounting to marketing or from engineering to human resource management. Schein refers to such career moves as horizontal or lateral career growth. Individuals who move horizontally into second careers change their type of work but do not necessarily change the amount of their responsibilities.

Radial Moves

A more subtle dimension of career growth involves radial movement, that is, movement toward (or away from) the inner circle of the organization. People who move toward the core of an organization are given access to its special privileges and organizational secrets about future business decisions and personnel decisions. Although radial movement often follows vertical movement (promotion), these two types of movement are conceptually and practically distinct. Examples of radial movement toward the center without promotion are common, and there are also cases of simultaneous promotion and radial movement away from the core. For example, an employee may be "kicked upstairs," that is, the employee receives a promotion to a less critical work area.

Schein (1971, 1978) also uses the career cone to discuss the concept of aborted or ruined careers. When a person is unable to move as desired within an organization—or is forced to move in an undesired direction—then the person has evidently failed in some way to make a crucial transition from one position to another.

Stages of a Professional Career

Schein's work focused mainly on the series of jobs an employee would hold *within* an organization. Building on Schein's concepts, Dalton, Thompson, and Price (1977) developed a model (which will be referred to as the "Dalton model") of *professional* careers (see Table 1). They considered the question of how careers in the professions (e.g., medicine, law, engineering, accounting, and management) typically unfold. Because few people spend their entire work life in one firm, an important issue is how careers in professions develop when viewed independently from the organizations in which they are pursued. Dalton and his colleagues identify four stages of a professional career: apprentice, colleague, mentor, and sponsor. At each stage an individual has both important work activities to attend to and important psychological issues to resolve.

As Table 1 suggests, important issues in career development include dependence, independence, and control. At the earliest stage of the professional career, individuals are relatively dependent on their supervisors for training; their work is primarily technical and they are learning how to apply their knowledge from school to real-world situations. At the next stage, employees are expected to work more independently, to make contributions to the organization, and to work collegially with co-workers. At the third stage, employees are expected to

Table 1. Four Stages of Professional Careers[1]

	I	II	III	IV
Central Activity	Helping, learning, following directions	Independently contributing	Training and interfacing	Shaping the direction of the organization
Primary Relationship	Apprentice	Colleague	Mentor	Sponsor
Major Psychological Issue	Dependence	Independence	Assuming responsibility for others	Exercising power

take on more responsibility for others. At the fourth stage, they are expected to extend their controlling responsibilities from developing subordinates to managing the growth and development of the organization.

By drawing from childhood-development literature and extending the important ideas to adult development, Dalton and his colleagues made salient two facts about career stages. First, the Dalton model makes clear that career stages are defined not only by the main work activities, but also by critical psychological issues that need to be resolved. Individuals who master the learning and the day-to-day job duties of their early assignments are sometimes unable to obtain important promotions because they are emotionally unready to work independently. Only when a person has mastered both the work issues and the psychological issues at one career stage will he or she be able to advance to the next stage.

Second, the Dalton model suggests that organizations do not value very highly those individuals who fail to make the expected progress through these four career stages. Even a casual look at organizations indicates that very few of the older professionals are still in junior positions. Organizations expect professionals to take on increasing amounts of independence at work and, ultimately, responsibility for others. If individuals fail to grow professionally, organizations are likely to try to push them out of their jobs even if they are technically competent in their present positions. Organizations would rather fill these positions with new employees who are younger, more enthusiastic, more recently trained, and more likely to grow into responsible positions in the firm.

Age-Based Models

Whereas Dalton and his colleagues focused mainly on careers in the professions and on four broad stages of careers, a number of scholars (e.g., Arnold & Feldman, 1986; Schein, 1978) have developed a set of career-stage models (the age-based models) that are linked to the individual's age. Refining the Dalton model, these authors suggest that Dalton's four career stages can be broken down into smaller, more discrete stages and that career stages apply not only to professionals, but to most other occupations as well. Although different authors use slightly different terminology for the names of the stages in the age-based models and they differ on the exact age ranges, Table 2 represents a distillation of the major age-based models of career development.

[1]Source: Dalton, Thompson, & Price (1977, p.23).

Table 2. Career Stages and Career Concerns[2]

Age Group	Career Stage	Career Tasks	Psychological Issues
15-22	Pre-Career Exploration	1. Finding the right career. 2. Obtaining the appropriate education.	1. Discovering one's own needs and interests. 2. Developing a realistic self-assessment of one's abilities.
22-30	Early Career: Trial	1. Obtaining a viable first job. 2. Adjusting to daily work routines and supervisors.	1. Overcoming the insecurity of inexperience; developing self-confidence. 2. Learning to get along with others in a work setting.
30-38	Early Career: Establishment	1. Choosing a special area of competence. 2. Becoming an independent contributor to the organization.	1. Deciding on level of professional and organizational commitment. 2. Dealing with feelings of failure of first independent projects or challenges.
38-45	Middle Career: Transition	1. Reassessing one's true career abilities, talents, and interests. 2. Withdrawing from one's own mentor and preparing to become a mentor to others.	1. Reassessing one's progress relative to one's ambitions. 2. Resolving work-life personal-life conflicts.
45-55	Middle Career: Growth	1. Being a mentor. 2. Taking on more responsibilities of general management.	1. Dealing with the competitiveness and aggression of younger persons on the fast track up the organization. 2. Learning to substitute wisdom-based experience for immediate technical skills.

Like the Dalton model, the age-based models suggest that employees need both to master work activities and to resolve important psychological issues at each point in their careers. These models also suggest a repeating pattern of *career growth, stabilization,* and *transition.* In each stage of a person's career (early, middle, and late), the individual must first grow and develop new skills. Next comes a period of stabilization, in which the employee performs the

---

[2]Based on material from Arnold & Feldman (1986) and Schein (1978).

Table 2 (continued).

Age Group	Career Stage	Career Tasks	Psychological Issues
55-62	Late Career: Maintenance	1. Making strategic decisions about the future of the business. 2. Becoming concerned with the broader role of the organization in civic and political arenas.	1. Becoming primarily concerned with the organization's welfare rather than one's own career. 2. Handling highly political or important decisions without becoming emotionally upset.
62-70	Late Career: Withdrawal	1. Selecting and developing key subodinates for future leadership roles. 2. Accepting reduced levels of power and responsibility.	1. Finding new sources of life satisfaction outside the job. 2. Maintaining a sense of self-worth without a job.

new skills in a highly productive way. In the third period, the employee makes a transition between the demands of the present stage and the anticipated demands of the next stage. In general, the times of growth are marked by excitement and challenge; the times of stabilization, by outstanding performance; and the times of transition, by reassessment and anxiety.

LIFE STAGES

This section looks at the stages of the life cycle and the way a person's emotional needs change over time. Personal lives also go through cycles of growth, stability, and transition.

Increasing attention has been paid to identifying the life stages of adults (Gould, 1978; Lowenthal, Thurnher, and Chiriboga, 1975; Vaillant, 1977). Levinson (1978, 1986) called these stages the *seasons* of a person's life. Central to all these treatments of life stages is the idea that at each stage of life a person is faced with important psychological issues to resolve (e.g., how to deal with the death of a parent). How—or even whether—a person resolves such issues will determine whether or not that person can grow emotionally and lead a satisfying life. Models of life stages—like those of career stages—identify a series of stages based on age; and for each stage, they identify a set of psychological issues to be confronted.

Theories of life stages also examine the impact of family status on adult development (Arnold & Feldman, 1986; Levinson, 1978; Schein, 1978). Marriage and parenthood involve major commitments to other people; decisions about what type of family to have and about how to integrate family demands and work demands play a large role in a person's psychological development. Thus, most models of life stages include family status (e.g., married with no children or married with young children) and the psychological demands precipitated by each stage of family development. Table 3 summarizes the major theories of adult life stages. As with the career-stage models, the life-stage models represent the typical pattern of adult development and not necessarily what all adults experience at each point in life.

Table 3. Life and Family Stages[3]

Age Group	Life Stage	Family Stage	Psychological Issues
15-22	Adolescence	Single adult	1. Developing a self-identity separate from parents and teachers. 2. Balancing the need for total independence with need for emotional support from adults.
22-30	Young-Adulthood Transition	Married Adult	1. Balancing one's own needs with those of another person in an intimate relationship. 2. Making commitments to spouse about life style, family values, child-rearing.
30-38	Young Adulthood	Parent of young children	1. Adjusting to the emotional demands of parenthood. 2. Maintaining intimate relationship with spouse in light of children's demands.
38-45	Mid-Life Transition	Parent of adolescents	1. Reassessing current values and commitments; feeling this might be the last chance to make major changes in life. 2. Dealing with ambivalent feelings of love and anger toward adolescent children.
45-55	Middle Adulthood	Parent of grown children	1. Building a deeper relationship with spouse, not focused on children. 2 Dealing with feelings of loss when children leave home and parents age or die.
55-62	Late-Life Adulthood Transition	Grandparent of young children	1. Developing new hobbies, activities, and friendships that will be more appropriate with a declining work role. 2. Helping children cope financially and emotionally with their new family responsibilities.
62-70	Late Adulthood	Grandparent of adolescents; widow/widower	1. Dealing with increased awareness of death, perhaps brought on by illness or death of spouse. 2. Coming to terms with one's life choices.

[3]Based on material from Arnold & Feldman (1986), Levinson (1986), Schein (1978), and Super (1977).

The life-stage models have made salient the constraints that biological aging and family growth put on career development. When people are young, they have the physical and emotional energy to have an active career and a family with young children. As they grow older, the psychological demands of the career and the family become greater, and the trade-offs become more and more difficult to make. During their thirties, for example, most professional and managerial workers have to invest a great deal of energy in their careers if they are going to make it to the top of their professions. During this period, time is also running out for having children. At each stage, reverses or disappointments in either arena will spill over into the other, making choices in each arena even more difficult.

Life-stage models point out another important phenomenon about career development. In periods of transition (ages twenty-two to thirty; thirty-eight to forty-five; fifty-five to sixty-two) people are more self-centered. These periods are marked by introspection and ambivalence about intimate relationships. In the twenties, people have to balance their needs for independence with their desire for a spouse and stability; from ages thirty-eight to forty-five, people have to balance their desire for a new life with their attachments to their present life; from fifty-five to sixty-two, people have to start coping with a new life ahead that will be less focused on children and work friendships.

The periods of stability are more other-centered and are marked by whole-hearted investment in important social relationships. From ages thirty to thirty-eight, individuals are typically committed to the nuclear family with young children; from forty-five to fifty-five, they are typically committed to re-establishing an intimate relationship with the spouse; in late adulthood, they put energy into nurturing both spouse and friendship relationships.

Three issues are important about the research on life stages. First, much of the basic work on adult development has been conducted with middle-class white males. More recently, researchers on life stages have extended their analyses to the adult development of black men (Gooden, 1980) and women (Levinson, in press; Lowenthal, Thurnher, & Chiriboga, 1975; Stewart, 1976). Nevertheless, the models of adult development are weighted more heavily to the seasons of a man's life than to the season's of a woman's life.

Second—with only a few exceptions (e.g., Vaillant, 1977)—researchers have not watched a set of individuals grow and develop over a period of years. Instead, the research has been mainly cross-sectional; researchers have compared the emotional needs of twenty-, thirty-, forty-, fifty-, and sixty-year olds at one point in time. This is problematic, because some of the differences between the age groups may be due to changes in the environment rather than changes within the individuals. For example, sixty-year-old people may have a higher need for stability than do the thirty-year-old group because the older people grew up in a depression instead of prosperous economic times. The difference would not be due simply to a difference in age.

Third, implicit in several of these models is the notion of the stable nuclear family with children, with one spouse (typically the woman) not in the work force on a full-time basis. Today's high divorce rate, the large number of single parents and remarriages, the increasing frequency of the stepparent role, and the growing number of married couples (now over 50 percent) who work full-time outside the home make the "typical" family stage far less typical.

A CAREER-DEVELOPMENT PERSPECTIVE

By understanding the nature of career stages and life stages, people can cope more effectively with important transitions in their lives, and organizations can manage more smoothly the career transitions of their employees. The career-stage and life-stage models that have been discussed address four career-development issues: the integration of work life and home life, nontraditional career paths, the impact of career stage on job satisfaction, and critical choice points in career planning.

Integration of Work Life and Home Life

Kotter (1975) notes:

> People occasionally like to deny that [career and personal life] decisions are interdependent. They want to believe that what they do at work and what they do out of work can be totally separated. They want that "freedom." As they soon learn, the world as we experience it today is one big interdependent mass, and the interdependencies are growing, not shrinking. And those who do not understand that, or who refuse to accept it, are in for a tough time.

Parents have to make some conscious decisions about how to integrate career growth and family growth, and they must recognize that trying to wall off one arena from the other is fruitless. Schein (1978) and Bailyn (1977) suggest several strategies for work-family integration:

1. *Limiting the impact of family on work.* If the parents have only one or two children, they may subcontract the child rearing to day-care centers or household help.

2. *Taking turns.* Partners may trade career-growth opportunities and parenting responsibilities at different times.

3. *Participating in joint ventures.* Both partners may have the same career or different careers in the same organization.

4. *Choosing independent careers.* Both partners may pursue their respective careers to the fullest degree and cope with the consequences as they arise.

5. *Subordinating one career to the other.* One partner may be out of the work force or may have a job with a much lower investment.

One strategy is not necessarily better than another. Each places the burden on a different place in the family-work network. The joint-ventures strategy is likely to increase stress for both partners (Cooke & Rousseau, 1984), and subordinating one career or taking turns is likely to create stress for the less-dominant partner (Yogev & Brett, 1985). Limiting the family impact is likely to increase stress for the children (Bartolome & Evans, 1979), whereas independent careers often cause stress for the colleagues of the couple (Hall & Hall, 1978). However, without a conscious strategy, individuals will not be able to develop a career plan, a family plan, and a life style that mesh. Such a strategy would also help couples to evaluate important life and career decisions (e.g., whether to have another child or whether to accept a geographical transfer) in terms of overall goals to be attained and constraints to be considered.

Nontraditional Career Paths

The theories of life stages and career stages present an explanation for why employees who enter careers either early or late will experience unusual amounts of stress. For example, implicit in the Dalton model is the idea that employees are relatively young when they are apprentices, becoming middle-aged when they become mentors and relatively old when they are sponsors. However, people who enter a career late or start a second career may find that the work demands of the professional career stage are out of sync with their emotional demands.

At age twenty-two, an engineer may adjust well to being in a dependent psychological relationship with his or her manager, but a forty-year-old engineer who has just graduated from college would have much more difficulty with that type of relationship. On the other hand, a fast-track employee who reaches the mentor stage by the age of thirty-five may feel uncomfortable advising older subordinates. Organizations often expect employees in their forties or fifties to take on more responsibility and to be free to travel; therefore, an organization may not know how to handle a forty-year-old employee who has just started a second family.

Individuals who decide to start new careers or new families at an untraditional age need to recognize in advance the peculiar emotional demands of these roles. Decisions to take on these roles should be based not only on career growth factors, but also on willingness to experience some personal frustration. Organizations that employ individuals at an untraditional age should recognize that what may seem to be recalcitrance at work may not be as much disapproval of the job as it is discomfort at the lack of synchronism between job demands and personal needs. Some organizations are recognizing these factors and are providing support groups and extra training and orientation for employees who switch careers or enter a career at an untraditional age (Schein, 1985).

Impact of Career Stage on Job Satisfaction

Research on the impact that career stages have on job satisfaction (Alderfer & Guzzo, 1979; Gould & Hawkins, 1978; Veiga, 1983) suggests that workers in their twenties are somewhat dissatisfied with their wages and the dependent nature of their relationships with their supervisors but are very satisfied with their peer relationships and with opportunities to learn on the job. Workers in their thirties tend to be satisfied with their jobs in general. Workers in the mid-life transition notice a marked decrease in their satisfaction with most aspects of their jobs. After age forty-five, the employee's satisfaction with the job increases, but older workers tend to show lower professional commitment and job involvement.

Employees need to understand that their career stage has a major impact on their satisfaction with their occupation and organization. The tendencies discussed in the last paragraph are independent of the occupation or organization. Before changing careers or organizations, a person should determine which parts of the dissatisfaction are due to the particular career stage and which are due to the specific idiosyncrasies of the job situation. Otherwise, employees will make job changes that alleviate only the symptoms, but not the causes, of their unhappiness. Similarly, in dealing with employees' complaints about the organization, managers should separate the issues that are peculiar to the immediate situation and those that are generic to the occupation or career stage (Storey, 1986a, 1986b, 1986c).

Critical Choice Points in Career Planning

The models of career stages and life stages suggest three critical choice points in adult development and that the choices at these points will strongly influence how productive and content individuals will be in the years ahead.

The first critical choice point occurs around age thirty. At this time most individuals are faced with several irreversible—or hard-to-reverse—decisions; for example, whom to marry, whether to start a family, the extent to which the career or family will be the central life interest, and whether to go back to school and/or change careers. Another major decision at this stage is whether to pursue a primarily technical career or to switch to a broader managerial or administrative career.

The second critical choice point occurs in the early forties. At this time most people are faced with both major family decisions and career decisions; for example, whether to have a last (or first) child, whether to end a marriage or to substantially redefine the relationship, what—after coming to terms with how far one can go professionally—will have to be done to arrive at that point, and whether to remain with the same organization or, perhaps, start one's own business.

The third point occurs in the late fifties. At this time most people are faced with important decisions about how to lead the rest of their lives; for example, whether to move (perhaps from a house to an apartment or even to a different state), how involved to be with their children and grandchildren, and whether to remain active at work until retirement or withdraw gradually.

The decisions made at each of these points have a tremendous impact on the quality of life for years to come. At age thirty, a decision to pursue a primarily technical career commits the individual to remaining current in the literature and competing with younger, more recently trained graduates. A decision for a managerial career commits the person to more intense social and political involvements with subordinates and superiors. The decision about whether to have an additional child has implications for career growth, the intimacy of the spouse relationship, and family finances. The decision to take a low-career investment path after one reaches forty can mean less stress but more apathy or bitterness as younger colleagues climb the organizational ladder. The decision to strike out on one's own at this stage can mean freedom from certain constraints but less financial security, less social contact, and more anxiety about the future.

CONCLUSION

Career options constitute a double-edged sword. Many people believe that by delaying a decision or remaining in a holding pattern (e.g., remaining in a job but constantly hunting another one or living together for years without getting married) they are keeping their options open. However, keeping options open is more difficult than it seems, because the decision to delay a family or a job change is indeed a decision; it is a decision to remain at a lower level of psychological involvement. The trade-off is between a low-commitment, low-risk position and a high-commitment, high-risk position; the decision to delay is a decision in favor of the former.

Furthermore, many people try to make life-style and career decisions that will keep their options open without realizing that any decision may close more doors than it opens. For example, the decision to accept job A is the decision to reject all other offers. The models that have been discussed suggest that in making important career and life-style decisions, individuals should think as much about what they are eliminating from their lives as what they are including. An emotionally healthy resolution of these transitional periods should leave people focused on the road ahead and not regretting the path not taken.

REFERENCES

Alderfer, C.P., & Guzzo, R.A. (1979). Life experiences and adults' enduring strength of desires in organizations. *Administrative Science Quarterly, 24,* 347-361.

Arnold, H.J., & Feldman, D.C. (1986). *Organizational behavior.* New York: McGraw-Hill.

Bailyn, L. (1977). Involvement and accommodation in technical careers: An inquiry into the relation to work at mid-career. In J. Van Maanen (Ed.), *Organizational careers: Some new perspectives.* New York: John Wiley.

Bartolome, F., & Evans, P.A.L. (1979). Professional lives versus private lives: Shifting patterns of managerial commitment. *Organizational Dynamics, 7,* 2-29.

Cooke, R.A., & Rousseau, D.M. (1984). Stress and strain from family roles and work-role expectations. *Journal of Applied Psychology, 69,* 252-260.

Dalton, G.W., Thompson, P.H., & Price, R.L. (1977). The four stages of professional careers: A new look at performance by professionals. *Organizational Dynamics, 6,* 19-42.

Gooden, W.E. (1980). *The adult development of black men.* Unpublished doctoral dissertation, Yale University, New Haven, CT.

Gould, R. (1978). *Transformations: Growth and change in adult life.* New York: Simon & Schuster.

Gould, S., & Hawkins, B.L. (1978). Organizational career stage as a moderator of the satisfaction-performance relationship. *Academy of Management Journal, 21,* 434-450.

Hall, F.S., & Hall, D.T. (1978). Dual careers: How do couples and companies cope with the problem? *Organizational Dynamics, 6,* 57-77.

Hall, D.T., Schneider, B., & Nygren, H.T. (1970). Personal factors in organizational identification. *Administrative Science Quarterly, 15,* 176-190.

Kegan, R. (1982). *The evolving self: Problem and process in human development.* Cambridge, MA: Harvard University Press.

Kotter, J.P. (1975). *The first year out.* Unpublished manuscript, Harvard Business School, Boston, MA.

Levinson, D.J. (1978). *The seasons of a man's life.* New York: Alfred A. Knopf.

Levinson, D.J. (1986). A conception of adult development. *American Psychologist, 41,* 3-13.

Levinson, D.J. (in press). *The seasons of a woman's life.* New York: Alfred A. Knopf.

Lowenthal, M.F., Thurnher, M., & Chiriboga, D. (1975). *Four stages of life: A comparative study of women and men facing transitions.* San Francisco: Jossey-Bass.

Schein, E.H. (1971). The individual, the organization, and the career: A conceptual scheme. *Journal of Applied Behavioral Science, 7,* 401-426.

Schein, E.H. (1978). *Career dynamics: Matching individual and organizational needs.* Reading, MA: Addison-Wesley.

Schein, E.H. (1985). *Career anchors: Discovering your real values.* San Diego, CA: University Associates.

Stewart, W.A. (1976). *A psychological study of the formation of the early adult life structure in women.* Unpublished doctoral dissertation, Columbia University, New York.

Storey, W.D. (1986a). *Career dimensions I: Personal planning guide* (rev. ed.). San Diego, CA: University Associates.

Storey, W.D. (1986b). *Career dimensions II: Manager's guide* (rev. ed.). San Diego, CA: University Associates.

Storey, W.D. (1986c). *Career dimensions III: Trainer's guide* (rev. ed.). San Diego, CA: University Associates.

Super, D.E. (1977). *The psychology of careers.* New York: Harper & Row.

Vaillant, G. (1977). *Adaptation to life.* Boston, MA: Little, Brown.

Veiga, J.F. (1983). Mobility influences during managerial career stages. *Academy of Management Journal, 26,* 64-85.

Yogev, S., & Brett, J.M. (1985). Patterns of work and family involvement among single- and dual-career couples. *Journal of Applied Psychology, 70,* 754-768.

Daniel C. Feldman, Ph.D., is a professor of management at the University of Florida Graduate School of Business. He has also served on the faculties of Yale College, the University of Minnesota Industrial Relations Center, and Northwestern University's J.L. Kellogg Graduate School of Management. Dr. Feldman has published many articles in the areas of career development and group dynamics and is the author of Managing Careers in Organizations *and co-author of three other books. He serves on the editorial boards of the* Academy of Management Journal, *the* Journal of Management, *and* The Industrial Psychologist.

THE LOST ART OF FEEDBACK

Hank Karp

The ability and willingness to communicate effectively is the key to supervisory success. Although communication effectiveness is based on the ability to make and maintain effective contact, regardless of the situation, specific areas of communications require some additional thought and planning.

One of the most important tools for maintaining control and developing people is the proper use of feedback. Although feedback has been categorized as positive and negative, another way of viewing it is to classify it into *supportive* feedback (which reinforces an ongoing behavior) and *corrective* feedback (which indicates that a change in behavior is appropriate). In this sense, all feedback is positive. The purpose of all feedback should be to assist an individual in maintaining or enhancing his or her present level of effectiveness or appropriateness.

Some feedback, by definition, is better than no feedback. There are, however, ways to do it well and ways to do it superbly. This article presents some guidelines that can help to sharpen the process. The most important function of feedback is to help the individual who is receiving the feedback to keep in touch with what is going on in the environment.

SUPPORTIVE FEEDBACK

Supportive feedback is used to reinforce behavior that is effective and desirable. An axiom of effective supervision is "Catch them doing something right and let them know it " (Blanchard & Johnson, 1982). One of the most damaging and erroneous assumptions that many supervisors make is that good performance and appropriate behavior are to be expected from the employee and that the only time feedback is needed is when the employee does something wrong. Therefore, these supervisors never give supportive feedback. If a supervisor, however, were determined to give only one kind of feedback, he or she would be ahead to choose supportive feedback and let corrective feedback go. In other words, if a supervisor stresses errors only, the end result would be—at most—an attempt by employees to do standard, error-free work. This accomplishment would not be *bad,* but there is a better way.

If a supervisor concentrated on what the employees were doing well, then superior work is what the employees would become aware of. They would begin to view their work in terms of performing as well and as creatively as possible. What is reinforced has a tendency to become stronger. What is not reinforced has a tendency to fade away. If excellence is actively reinforced and errors are simply mentioned, employees will focus on excellence and tend to diminish errors. The following example of the two types of feedback illustrates the difference.

Focus on errors: "The last three pieces in that batch contained wrong figures. We cannot have that kind of sloppy work in this department."

Focus on good work: "This batch looks good, except for the last three pieces, which contain wrong figures. You probably used the wrong formula. Take them back and check them out, just the way you did the first group."

Fortunately, however, no one has to make a choice between using only supportive or only corrective feedback. Both are essential and valuable, and it is important to understand how each works so that the maximum gain can be received from the process.

CORRECTIVE FEEDBACK

Corrective feedback is used to alter a behavior that is ineffective or inappropriate. It is as essential to the growth process as supportive feedback. A corrective feedback session, although never hurtful if done properly, is not a particularly pleasant experience. Under the best of circumstances, the subordinate will probably feel a little defensive or embarrassed.

In giving corrective feedback, the manager should have an option ready to present. When the employee is made aware of the inappropriate behavior, having an immediate alternative can be effective and powerful in shaping behavior. By presenting the alternative immediately after the corrective feedback, the manager is helping the subordinate to come out of a personally uncomfortable situation in the shortest possible time. This protects the dignity of the subordinate. The manager would also be establishing himself or herself as a supporter of good work and good workers, which would go a long way in developing strong, productive, and supportive working relationships. Also very important, the manager would be presenting an alternative that the employee might never have considered—or that was considered and rejected. This provides for immediate learning. Most important, however, is the fact that the manager would make the employee aware that an alternative was available at the time the employee chose to act otherwise. This awareness can facilitate the employee in taking responsibility for his or her own choices. That is, the employee would realize, "That's right, I could have done it that way." The following example shows how an alternative can be effectively added to the feedback.

"When you snapped at Ann in front of the group, she appeared to be very embarrassed and angry. *When you must remind an employee to be on time, it's less embarrassing for everyone to discuss it with the employee privately after the meeting.*"

GUIDELINES FOR EFFECTIVE FEEDBACK

The following guidelines are helpful for managers who are trying to improve their feedback skills, and they may also be used as a review prior to giving feedback.

1. Deal in Specifics

Being specific is the most important rule in giving feedback, whether it is supportive or corrective. Unless the feedback is specific, very little learning or reinforcement is possible. The following examples illustrate the difference in general and specific statements.

General: "I'm glad to see that your work is improving."
Specific: "I'm pleased that you met every deadline in the last three weeks.

General: "You're a very supportive person."
Specific: "I appreciate your taking time to explain the contract to our new employee."

General: "You're falling down on the job again."
Specific: "Last month most of your cost reports were completely accurate, but last week four of your profit/loss figures were wrong."

The last set is, of course, an example of corrective feedback. General statements in corrective feedback frequently result in hostile or defensive confrontations, whereas specific statements set the stage for problem-solving interaction. Carrying the last illustration one step farther, the manager could add an alternative: "Start checking the typed report against the computer printouts. Some of the errors may be typos, not miscalculations."

If the employee is to learn from feedback and respond to it, then he or she must see it in terms of *observable* effects. That is, the employee must be able to see clearly how his or her behavior had a direct impact on the group's performance, morale, etc. When the employee sees the point of the feedback objectively, the issue will be depersonalized, and the employee will be more willing to continue with appropriate behaviors or to modify inappropriate behaviors. Although the manager's personal approval ("I'm glad to see. . .") or disapproval ("I'm disappointed that. . .") can give emphasis to feedback, it must be supported by specific data in order to effect a change in behavior.

2. Focus on Actions, Not Attitudes

Just as feedback must be specific and observable in order to be effective, it must be nonthreatening in order to be acceptable. Although subordinates—like supervisors—are always accountable for their *behavior*, they are never accountable for their attitudes or feelings. Attitudes and feelings cannot be measured, nor can a manager determine if or when an employee's feelings have changed. For feedback to be acceptable, it must respect the dignity of the person receiving the feedback.

No one can attack attitudes without dealing in generalities, and frequently attacks on attitudes result in defensive reactions. The following example illustrates the difference in giving feedback on behavior and giving feedback on attitudes.

Feedback on attitude: "You have been acting hostile toward Jim."

Feedback on behavior: "You threw the papers down on Jim's desk and used profanity."

An attitude that managers often try to measure is loyalty. Certain actions that *seem* to indicate loyalty or disloyalty can be observed, but loyalty is a *result*, not an action. It cannot be demanded; it must be earned. Whereas people have total control over their own behavior, they often exercise little control over their feelings and attitudes. They feel what they feel. If a manager keeps this in mind and focuses more energy on things that can be influenced (i.e., employee behavior), changes are more likely to occur.

The more that corrective feedback is cast in specific behavioral terms, the more it supports problem solving and the easier it is to control. The more that corrective feedback is cast in attitudinal terms, the more it will be perceived as a personal attack and the more difficult it will be to deal with. The more that supportive feedback is cast in terms of specific behaviors, the higher the probability that those behaviors will be repeated and eventually become part of the person's natural way of doing things.

3. Determine the Appropriate Time and Place

Feedback of either type works best if it is given as soon as feasible after the behavior occurs. Waiting decreases the impact that the feedback will have on the behavior. The passage of time may make the behavior seem less important to the manager; other important events begin to drain the energy of the manager and some of the details of the behavior might be forgotten. On the other hand, dwelling on it for a long period could blow it out of proportion. From the subordinates viewpoint, the longer the wait for the feedback, the less important it must be. The following example illustrates this point.

Tardy feedback: "Several times last month you fell below your quota."

Immediate feedback: "There are only ten products here; your quota for today was fourteen."

Enough time should be allotted to deal with the issues in their entirety. A manager can undercut the effectiveness by looking at the clock and speeding up the input so that an appointment can be met. Answering the telephone or allowing visitors to interrupt the conversation can have the same effect. The manager can also cause unnecessary stress by telling an employee at ten o'clock in the morning "I want to see you at three this afternoon." A more appropriate procedure would be to say, "Would you please come to my office now" or "When you reach a stopping point, drop by my office. I have something good to tell you."

In addition to an appropriate time, the setting for the feedback is important. The old proverb, "Praise in public, censure in private," is partially correct. Almost without exception, corrective feedback is more appropriately given in private. In the case of supportive feedback, however, discretion is needed. In many instances, praise in public is appropriate and will be appreciated by the subordinate. In other instances, privacy is needed to keep the positive effect from being short-circuited. For example, some people make a virtue out of humility; any feedback that reinforces their sense of worth is embarrassing. Rather than appreciating an audience, this type of employee would find it painful and perhaps resent it.

Sometimes a norm arises in a work group that prevents anyone from making a big deal out of good work. This does not mean that the group does not value good work, but supportive feedback in private might prevent the employee from feeling he or she was responsible for breaking the norm. In other instances, public praise can cause jealousy, hostility, or tense working relationships. Therefore, a conscious decision should be made about whether or not to give the supportive feedback publicly.

Another important consideration is the actual location selected for giving the feedback. The delivery of the feedback should match its importance. If the feedback concerns an important action, the manager's office would be better than an accidental encounter in the hall. On the other hand, the manager might convey a quick observation by telling someone at the water fountain, "Say, that was beautiful artwork on the Madison report." Choosing the time and place is a matter of mixing a little common sense with an awareness of what is going on.

4. Refrain from Inappropriately Including Other Issues

Frequently when feedback is given, other issues are salient. When supportive feedback is given, any topic that does not relate to the specific feedback point should not be discussed if it would undercut the supportive feedback. For example, the manager could destroy the good just accomplished by adding, "And by the way, as long as you are here, I want to ask you to try to keep your files a little neater. While you were away, I couldn't find a thing."

When corrective feedback is given, however, the situation is different. The manager will want the feedback to be absorbed as quickly and as easily as possible, with the employee's negative feelings lasting no longer than necessary. Therefore, as soon as the feedback has been understood and acknowledged, the manager is free to change the subject. The manager may want to add, "I'm glad that you see where the error occurred. Now, as long as you are here, I'd like to ask your opinion about. . . ." This type of statement, when used appropriately, lets the subordinate know that he or she is still valued. Obviously, the manager should not contrive a situation just to add this type of statement, but when the situation is naturally there, the manager is free to take advantage of it.

In certain situations, it is appropriate to give supportive and corrective feedback simultaneously. Training periods of new employees, performance-appraisal sessions, and times when experienced employees are tackling new and challenging tasks are all good examples of times when both types of feedback are appropriate. Nevertheless, some cautions are necessary:

Never follow the feedback with the word "but." It will negate everything that was said before it. If it is appropriate to give supportive and corrective feedback within the same sentence, the clauses should be connected with "and." This method allows both parts of the sentence to be heard clearly and sets the stage for a positive suggestion. The following examples illustrate the difference.

Connected with but: "Your first report was accurate, but your others should have measured up to it."

Connected with and: "Your first report was accurate, and your others should have measured up to it."

Connected with but: "You were late this morning, but Anderson called to tell you what a great job you did on the Miller account."

Connected with and: "You were late this morning, and Anderson called to tell you what a great job you did on the Miller account."

Alternate the supportive and corrective feedback. When a great deal of feedback must be given, it is frequently better to mix the supportive feedback with the corrective feedback than to give all of one type and then all of the other. Regardless of which type comes first, the latter will be remembered the most clearly. If a chronic self-doubter is first given supportive feedback and then only corrective feedback, he or she is likely to believe the supportive feedback was given just to soften the blow of the other type. Alternating between the two types will make all the feedback seem more genuine.

Where feasible, use the supportive feedback to cushion the corrective feedback. When both types of feedback are appropriate, there is usually no reason to start with corrective feedback. However, this does not mean that corrective feedback should be quickly sandwiched in between supportive feedback statements. Each type is important, but frequently supportive feedback can be used as an excellent teaching device for areas that need correcting. This is especially true if the employee has done a good job previously and then failed later under similar circumstances. For example, the manager might say, "The way you helped Fred to learn the codes when he was transferred to this department would be appropriate in training the new employees."

PRINCIPLES OF FEEDBACK

Two major principles govern the use of feedback. The first principle, which relates to how feedback is conducted, can be paraphrased "I can't tell you how you are, and you can't tell me what I see." In other words, the person giving the feedback is responsible to relate the situation as he or she observes it, and the person receiving the feedback is responsible for relating what he or she meant, felt, or thought. The second principle is that feedback supports growth.

Giving Feedback:
"You Can't Tell Me What I See"

The object of giving feedback is not to judge the other person, but to report what was seen and heard and what the effects of the behavior were. Personal approval or disapproval, even if important, is secondary.

Feedback should be given directly to the person for whom it is intended. When others are present, the manager sometimes addresses them almost to the exclusive of the intended recipient, who sits quietly and gathers information by eavesdropping. Good contact with the recipient is an essential element in giving feedback.

It is never necessary to apologize for giving corrective feedback. Corrective or otherwise, feedback is a gift; apologies will discount its importance and lessen its impact. Nevertheless, corrective feedback must be given in a way that does not jeopardize the recipient's dignity and sense of self-worth.

It is sometimes helpful to offer an interpretation of the behavior or a hunch about what the behavior might indicate. What is of paramount importance is that the interpretation be offered as a suggestion and *never* as a judgment or clinical evaluation of the person. Only the recipient is capable of putting it into a meaningful context. For example, the manager might say, "When Pete showed you the error you made, you told him it was none of his concern. I wonder if you were mad at Pete for some other reason." This statement shows the recipient the behavior and allows him or her to consider a possible cause for that behavior.

Receiving Feedback:
"You Can't Tell Me How I Am"

From the recipient's viewpoint, the first principle is "You can't tell me how I am, and I can't tell you what I see." Although most people realize that giving feedback correctly requires skill and awareness, they are less aware of the importance of knowing how to receive feedback. When receiving feedback, many people tend to argue about, disown, or attempt to justify the information. Statements like "I didn't say that," "That's not what I meant," and "You don't understand what I was trying to do" are attempts to convince the person giving the feedback that he or she didn't see or observe what he or she claims. However, the recipient needs to understand that the observer—whether manager, peer, or subordinate—is relating what he or she experienced as a result of the recipient's behavior. There is nothing wrong with the giver and receiver having different viewpoints. The purpose of feedback is to give a new view or to increase awareness. If an argument ensues and the observer backs down, the recipient is the loser.

The appropriate response, as a rule of thumb, is to say "thank you" when either type of feedback is received. It is also appropriate, of course, to ask for clarity or more detail on any issue.

The purpose of feedback is to help the recipient. Feedback can be thought of as food. It is very nourishing. When people are hungry, food is what they need; but when they are full, food is the last thing they want or need. The same applies to ingesting feedback. When people have had enough, they should call a halt. Attempting to absorb all the feedback that might be available, or that various people would like to give, is like forcing food into a full stomach just because someone says, "Please have some more."

The recipient is responsible for demanding specificity in feedback. No feedback should be accepted as legitimate if it cannot be clearly demonstrated by an observable behavior. For example, if someone says, "You're very arrogant," an appropriate response would be "What specifically have I said or done to cause you to think that?" If that response is countered with "I don't know; I just experience you that way," then the accusation should be immediately forgotten. People cannot afford to change just to meet everyone's personal likes or expectations.

In fact, it is impossible to change to meet *everyone's* expectations, and the situation becomes compounded as more and more people give the feedback. A single act can generate disparate feedback from different people who observe the behavior. For example, a loud exclamation could be viewed as appropriately angry by one person; overly harsh, by another; and merely uncouth, by a third. Each person will see it from his or her unique perspective. Therefore feedback requires action from both the giver and the receiver. Only the giver can tell what he or she observed or experienced, and only the recipient can use the information in deciding whether or not to change the behavior.

For feedback to be effective, the receiver must hear what the giver is saying, weigh it, and then determine whether or not the information is relevant. The following example illustrates how this can be done.

Department manager: "Waste in your unit is up by 4 percent. Are you having any problems with your employees?"

Supervisor: "I was not aware of the waste increase. No, I am not having trouble with my employees. I suppose I have been focusing on the quality so much that I lost sight of the waste figures. Thanks for bringing this to my attention."

Feedback Supports Growth

The second major principle, "feedback supports growth," is important, because we cannot always see ourselves as others see us. Although an individual may be the world's foremost authority on himself or herself, there are still parts of the individual that are more obvious to other people. Although people may be more aware of their own needs and capabilities and more concerned about their own welfare than other people are, they are able to stretch themselves and grow if they pay attention to feedback from others. Although feedback may be extremely uncomfortable at the time, the individual can look back later and realize the feedback was the spark that inspired the change that turned his or her career or personal life in a different direction. If the feedback is not rejected or avoided, recipients can discover and develop ways to work that they did not think were available.

FEEDBACK STRATEGIES

The strategies suggested here are not step-by-step procedures to be blindly followed. Their purpose is to help in planning and organizing an approach to dealing with an issue. They offer a logical and effective sequence of events for the feedback session. The person planning the session must decide on the desired future objective. (The "future," however, could be five minutes after the session or two years later.) During the feedback session, attention must be focused on what is happening in terms of the outcome. That is, the focus must be on obtaining the goal, not on sticking to the strategy. This focus allows the giver to change tactics or even modify the original strategy if conditions change or unforeseen events occur. After the strategy is selected, the following three rules should be kept in mind:

1. Be clear about what you want in terms of specific, identifiable outcomes for yourself, your subordinate, and the organization.
2. Plan what you intend to say and how you intend to conduct the meeting, according to the particular strategy you will use.
3. Have the strategy in mind as you engage the individual, but keep it in the background.

Supportive Feedback Strategy

The following steps are suggested as a strategy for supportive feedback:

1. *Acknowledge the specific action and result to be reinforced.* Immediately let the subordinate know that you are pleased about something he or she did. Be specific and describe the event in behavioral terms. "You finished the project (*action*) on time (*result*)."

2. *Explain the effects of the accomplishment and state your appreciation.* For the behavior to be reinforced, the person must be able to see the effects of that behavior in specific, observable ways. Your appreciation is important but as an additional reinforcing element. The main reinforcement is the effect. "It was a major factor in getting the contract (*effect*), and I am pleased with your outstanding work (*appreciation*)."

3. *Help the subordinate to take full responsibility for the success.* If the employee acknowledges the feedback, this step is accomplished. If the employee seems overly modest, more work

is needed. Unless he or she can, to some degree, internalize the success and receive satisfaction from it, very little growth will occur. One approach would be to ask how the success was accomplished or if any problems were encountered and how they were overcome. In talking about what happened, the employee is likely to realize how much he or she was really responsible for. It is important for both you and the employee to hear how the success was accomplished.

4. *Ask if the subordinate wants to talk about anything else.* While the employee is feeling positive and knows that you are appreciative and receptive, he or she may be willing to open up about other issues. The positive energy created by this meeting can be directed toward other work-related issues, so take advantage of the opportunity.

5. *Thank the subordinate for the good performance.* The final step, again thanking the subordinate for the accomplishment, assures that your appreciation will be uppermost in his or her mind as he or she leaves and returns to the work setting.

Corrective Feedback Strategy

The following steps are suggested as a strategy for corrective feedback:

1. *Immediately describe the event in behavioral terms and explain the effect.* Relate clearly in specific, observable, and behavioral terms the nature of the failure or behavior and the effect of the failure or behavior or the work group or organization. If you can appropriately say something to reduce the employee's embarrassment, the employee is more likely to accept the feedback nondefensively.

2. *Ask what happened.* Before assuming that the subordinate is at fault, ask what happened. In many instances, the subordinate is not at fault or is only partially responsible. At the worst, the employee is given an opportunity to explain before you proceed; at the best, you may receive information that would prevent you from censuring the employee.

3. *Help the subordinate to take full responsibility for the actions.* The more time spent in step 2 (finding out what happened), the easier step 3 will be. The subordinate needs to learn from the experience in order to reduce the probability of a reoccurrence. Unless this step is handled effectively, the subordinate will see himself or herself as a victim, rather than as someone who made a mistake and is willing to correct it.

4. *Develop a plan to deal with the issues.* Once the subordinate has accepted responsibility, the next step is to help rectify the situation. Now that the employee is willing to be accountable for errors, you can jointly devise a plan that will help eliminate them. That is, both of you must agree to take action. If you both want the same thing (i.e., better performance from the subordinate), then both of you are obligated to do something about it. This is also an excellent opportunity to build on the subordinate's strengths (e.g., "I'd like for you to show the same fine attention to safety regulations that you show to job specifications").

5. *State your confidence in the subordinate's ability.* Once the issue is resolved, end the session by stating your confidence in the ability of the employee to handle the situation. The object is to allow the subordinate to re-enter the work setting feeling as optimistic about himself as the situation permits. The subordinate must also understand that you will follow up and give additional feedback when the situation warrants it.

REFERENCE

Blanchard, K., & Johnson, S. (1982). *One minute manager.* New York: Morrow.

Hank Karp, Ph.D., *provides training and consulting services, public seminars, and in-house programs through his organization, Personal Growth Systems, in Norfolk, Virginia. His specialties are team building, supervisory/leadership development, motivation, conflict management, and dealing with resistance. Dr. Karp's background is in organizational psychology, organization development, human motivation, and Gestalt applications to individual and organizational growth. He is the author of* Personal Power: An Unorthodox Guide to Success.

IMPROVING CLIENT-CONSULTANT RELATIONSHIPS: RESEARCH-BASED SUGGESTIONS

Diane McKinney Kellogg

A study to identify the factors that contribute to developing successful client-consultant relationships has revealed some information that can be useful to consultants who want to improve their working relationships with clients.

Twenty organization development consultants were interviewed for two to three hours each; each described two consultation relationships that he or she had experienced, one positive and one negative, tracing the development of the client-consultant relationship. The cases were then analyzed to identify the variables that affected the quality of these relationships. Characteristics associated with relationships considered to be most successful were isolated by contrasting the twenty positive cases with the twenty negative ones.

Many of the consultants interviewed were well-known, long-established OD consultants selected for their expertise in dealing with clients. However, for balance, several recently trained consultants also were interviewed. They described their working relationship with the person(s) they considered their primary client(s) or contact within the client organization.

The most pertinent findings of the study that will be discussed here relate to three processes that are pivotal to the success of the consultation relationship: the matching process, the contracting process, and the ongoing communication process. The consultant is involved in and has an impact on all of these.

Some of the factors that distinguished the positive cases from the negative ones were not ones in which the consultant was involved or could make a difference. These seemed to be related to the amount of influence or power that the contact person had within his or her own organization. These factors will be discussed also, even though the consultant may not be able to influence them, because understanding the need for the client to have sufficient organizational power may help consultants to determine the potential for the project's success and whether to undertake it at all.

THE MATCHING PROCESS

This study indicated that good client-consultant relationships result from a good match or "fit" between:

- The client's and consultant's personalities;
- The client's and consultant's goals for the project; and
- The consultant's skills and the client's needs.

Personalities

One consultant described a very positive experience he had had with a client who hired him "on the spot" at their first meeting. The consultant had felt as enthusiastic about working with the client as the client had about hiring the consultant. The "fit" simply was right.

In contrast were reports of numerous experiences in which consultants accepted contracts because the projects were challenging, even though the personality match was absent. Steve told of being invited by the president of a very large, multinational corporation to help assess "why middle managers were quitting or proving themselves incompetent and having to be fired." Steve wanted to work with a multinational corporation and overlooked the fact that he did not trust or like the president.

The more Steve saw of the president's management techniques, the less respect he had for the man. Steve's extensive data-collection efforts led him to conclude that the president and his close-knit group of executives (friends of twenty to thirty years) did not really want to see the young, up-and-coming managers succeed, and that they actually engaged in efforts to prove that they were more qualified to lead the company than the new generation of managers. Interviews revealed that top management set up unrealistic hurdles for middle managers and had actually blocked their success in a number of projects. As a result, some of the new managers quit, others hung on until they were fired or resigned themselves to a permanent slot in a middle position. Two months before Steve began the project, the president had fired three middle managers while they were offsite at a training program to which the president himself had sent them with the words, "We want to groom you guys for the executive committee...."

In the end, Steve said, "The project became pointless; my relationship with the president became increasingly acrimonious." After one heated discussion, Steve concluded his contract.

One might easily infer that, to the president, Steve looked just like one of the up-and-coming new managers that he wanted to prove incompetent. It was important to the president to dismiss this younger person's inputs about his own management style. Perhaps a consultant whose age and style were closer to the president's would have had more influence with him and could have developed a more positive relationship.

Goals for the Project

In the case described above, the client's expressed goal turned out to be quite different from his real objectives. When a consultant begins to work toward such an expressed goal, but the client actually is working toward a different one, they almost always will come to conflict.

Jane was fired for not succeeding in improving the management skills of a director. Initially, the president of a company called her in and told her "the problem": the director of public relations had not been able to manage his staff effectively and would be fired unless things changed quickly. Jane suspected that she had been hired to prove the president's perception that the director was incompetent rather than to improve the director's management skills. However, she and the director got along very well, and he seemed grateful for the help. He was an open, receptive manager whose staff was productive and seemed to enjoy working together. Jane felt that his most serious problem was a bad relationship with the president. After analyzing the problem, she and the director decided to proceed on this hypothesis and to work on improving his relationship with the president. Not surprisingly, the president discovered Jane's analysis of the situation and fired her for being incompetent in dealing with the problem she was hired to solve. The director was fired two months later.

Jane could have managed the client-consultant relationship better by going to the president and sharing the dilemma with him: her view of what the project's goal should be versus the problem that he had identified initially. The conflict here could be diagnosed as Jane's confusion about whether the president or the director was her client. The research seems to indicate that consultants are wise to consider anyone a client who has either been involved in the hiring process or who is paying the bill out of his or her budget. In Jane's case, the president had hired her and held her accountable for results, even though the director's budget covered her fees.

The depth of commitment to project goals also surfaced during the study as a significant issue. Positive client-consultant relationships developed where there was genuine interest in the consulting project on the part of the client. In negative relationships, consultants felt that their contact persons had hired them for reasons other than personal commitment to the project (e.g., at the directive of a superior, to look impressive to their colleagues, or simply to pass on a project in which they had little interest but which someone else thought should be done). In one case, a personnel director persuaded a company president to persuade a vice president to hire a particular consultant (using the vice president's budget) because the personnel director wanted to have the experience of working with that particular consultant. The project never "got off the ground," and the consultant realized that his primary contact person—the vice president—did not have enough interest in the project to invest any time in it.

In most cases, "persuaded managers" are reluctant clients. However, in two cases in which managers were persuaded to hire consultants, they did develop genuine interest in the projects. Genuine interest, more than even self-initiated use of the consultant, seems to be the critical variable.

Consultant Skills and Client Needs

In each positive case reported, the client had confidence in the consultant's competence. Comments such as "He respected the need for more attention to process, and he knew I made a difference at his staff meetings" and "I knew he was more confident of my approach than of his own" affirmed that consultants value working relationships in which the clients respect them. This confidence was not perceived in the negative consultations, e.g., "He never quite believed that I knew what I was doing"; "He didn't trust anybody who talked about worker satisfaction"; and "I always had the impression that he wished I were more experienced."

The amount of time that a client spent in choosing a consultant did not prove to be related to success in matching skills to needs. In fact, especially quick decisions had both good and bad outcomes, as did especially slow decisions. In some positive cases, the client's confidence in the consultant was based on "gut feelings." In others, clients interviewed extensively before hiring anyone. Whatever the process, having the client begin with feelings of confidence that he or she has found the "right" consultant seems to be very important. The principle of the self-fulfilling prophecy may be at work here; predicting positive outcomes may contribute greatly to obtaining positive outcomes.

The reverse also holds true: with self-fulfilling prophecy at work, a client's negative first impression could lead to his or her finding even more reasons for concern as time passes. In many cases reported, questions about the consultant's skills hindered the consultant's ability to work freely within a client organization. A consultant who senses uncertainty or reticence on the part of the client would be wise to raise the issue or even to reconsider accepting the assignment. Trying to discover the source of the concern may or may not succeed; clients may deny their concerns rather than admit to having reservations. However, if they are invited to discuss concerns at the beginning of the relationship, they may feel more free to do so and may raise questions that could become more serious if left unaddressed.

The matching process is the responsibility of both the client and the consultant. Both can work to assure a good match of personalities, of project goals, and of consultant skills with client needs.

THE CONTRACTING PROCESS

Having a clear contract includes agreeing on project goals but goes beyond that to include clear definitions of expectations, roles, and tasks. The contract should state who will do what, when, and how, and these things should be discussed thoroughly before the project begins and throughout the project as new or unanticipated situations arise.

In each positive case reported, by the end of the contracting phase, the client and consultant had reached specific agreements about what each person's involvement would be at various points in the consultation. In many of the negative cases, however, the consultant described an uncertain conclusion to the contracting phase, e.g., "We eventually decided just to get started and see if things became more clear as we got into the project." In two cases, the consultants knew at the time that they and their clients did not fully understand how much time and energy their projects would involve, but these consultants chose to proceed with their projects rather than to prolong the discussions and risk discouragement on the part of their clients. Both of these situations had negative results. Being eager to begin the work or simply being tired of negotiating can preclude creating a contract that has sufficient clarity.

Role clarity is another basic need. It is important that clients know what is expected of them and what they can expect from the consultant. Of the consultants interviewed for this study, 80 percent discussed the importance of role clarity to the success of the relationship. The other 20 percent would likely have discussed the need for it if the question had been put to them directly.

Many of the negative cases involved examples in which much time was spent regrouping because either the client or consultant became involved in some area or at some time when the other party had not expected it. These "violations" of expectations put a strain on the client-consultant relationship. Allowing expectations to be assumed rather than articulated (or never examined at all) is sure to lead to violations of them. Because conflict almost always is a result of unmet expectations, one can assume that lack of role clarity inevitably will lead to conflict.

The tasks to be completed should be defined as clearly as possible at the beginning of the project. However, as new information is accumulated, other events occur, or people in the organization change, the terms of the contract and the roles should be renegotiated or reclarified. The best consulting relationships are characterized by a continuing commitment to the contracting process.

It may be the consultant's role (only because he or she probably has had more experience in consulting relationships and appreciates the need) to articulate why it is important to establish a clear contract in the beginning and to re-examine the contract at various points in time. Taking the initiative and suggesting the need for more contracting as the project continues can strengthen the client-consultant relationship.

Jeremy's work at a chemical company is a good example of a consultant's sensitivity to the need for a clear contract and clear client expectations about what will be done. The client hired Jeremy on the recommendation of a friend who had used him a few years before. As far as Jeremy knew, the client had not done an extensive search for a consultant but had liked him from the start.

The client was not sure what the problem was in the company, but turnover seemed unusually high, and there seemed to be a lot of complaints about supervisors being too strict ("too many rules"). Jeremy and the client agreed on a contract after a three-hour discussion. The agreement included the fact that the client would complete an extensive diagnosis of the organization, utilizing an attitude survey, interviews, and observation. The client was convinced that the consultant needed such extensive research in order to be able to present reliable information about the problems to the management team. Jeremy also agreed to conduct a discussion of what could be done about the problems that were identified, but he was careful not to agree to independently recommend solutions or to become involved in the implementation phase. He saw himself as a diagnostic specialist. This was agreeable to the client because he was not sure how the other managers would react to the data and he did not want to attempt to lock them into a plan for solving problems that they did not necessarily agree on.

The data-collection phase involved the usual slow-downs because questionnaires were not returned on time and it was difficult to schedule follow-up interviews with busy managers, but Jeremy was careful to keep the client aware of his progress and to renegotiate completion dates when necessary. The interviews gave Jeremy a chance to meet the managers who would be in the data-reporting meeting. It also let them know what questions were being asked of their employees.

The data-feedback session was not all good news, and some managers seemed a little uncomfortable, but they were as open as could be expected and probed for the reasoning behind Jeremy's conclusions. Eventually they began to discuss which solutions would not work in the organization. A continuation of the meeting was suggested and scheduled.

However, Jeremy's contract had been completed. He had a final session with the client the next day, during which he requested that the client let him know what the managers decided to do, just to satisfy his own curiosity. The client agreed to do this and, in fact, called Jeremy later to ask him to recommend consultants to help in designing some new programs.

Obviously, this case had many strengths: the match between Jeremy's skills and the client's needs; a clearly defined goal for the project (diagnosing organizational problems); and a well-defined, specific contract. However, behind the well-defined contract was some other consultant widsom. Jeremy knew what his strengths were (he felt that he was a better diagnostician than program designer) and he would not commit to do something that he was not highly qualified to do. Secondly, it was a short-term contract. The successful relationships described for the study tended to occur over short periods of time (from one to six months). In some cases, the consultant was hired to do additional work beyond the original contract, but this was only the happy result of the success of the first project, not the course intended all along.

The realization that the successful relationships were, in general, of short duration suggests that consultants may be wise to structure consulting contracts accordingly. Long-term projects can be broken down into a series of shorter contracts, with each subsequent contract contingent on the success of the previous one. Subsequent contracts could be re-evaluated as each new phase of the project begins. Periodically scheduled meetings to evaluate progress, including the strengths/successes and weaknesses/failures of the project to date, also can enhance the communication process between the client and the consultant.

Another benefit of working on projects with short time frames is that it gives both the client and the consultant a chance to experience success. With long-term projects, one can become discouraged, bored, or begin to take things for granted. The success of reaching one goal can add momentum to the effort to achieve the next one and can help to create positive feelings about the consulting effort.

THE COMMUNICATION PROCESS

A surprising aspect of the interviews in this study appeared in the area of communication. The word "defensive" appeared so frequently that it emerged as a specific focus of concern in the communication process between clients and consultants.

The consulting relationship inevitably involves change, and change inevitably creates anxiety in clients. Thus, consultants must be conscious of their clients' level of defensiveness. It is a fact of organizational consulting that a manager at some level (it may or may not be the one who hired the consultant) often is either responsible for much of the problem or must change his or her way of doing things to solve the problem. Positive relationships are characterized by clients who are willing—and sometimes eager—to receive information about themselves or their organization in order to make improvements. Consultants appreciate and admire clients who are willing to hear about and seriously consider the negative impact of their own behavior. As one consultant noted, "Good clients usually know that they must be part of the problem, and one of the things they hire you to tell them is how much a part of the problem they are."

Just as often, however, consultants reported that their clients' defensiveness blocked further progress. They also expressed dismay about clients who adamantly defend their own approach and discount the consultant's observations. The range of defensive tactics employed by such clients included "not hearing" things that would cause them to re-evaluate their own positions.

Reducing Defensiveness

Because defensiveness can result simply from the presence of an outside consultant, it is important for consultants to examine carefully their own styles of giving and receiving negative feedback. A change in the consultant's approach might reduce the client's defensiveness and increase his or her willingness to receive new information. Another strategy for approaching the problem of client defensiveness is to openly discuss the fears that are generated when consultants are used. This conversation could be built appropriately and effectively into the contracting discussions. The client and consultant also could discuss the importance of nondefensive communication to the overall success of the consultation.

Inviting Feedback

It is equally important that the consultant invite the client to provide feedback freely. In the positive relationships reported, consultants were willing to receive negative information about themselves and found it helpful to hear more, rather than less, from the client. One consultant described such a relationship: "I was honest with him, and he could take it; but he also was honest with me and let me know when he thought I had botched it." This kind of exchange provides the consultant with an opportunity to model nondefensive behavior for the client.

Some consultants reporting negative relationships said that their clients were reluctant to express their opinions and reluctant to pass on informal information about how others in the client organization were perceiving or responding to the consultant or the project. This reluctance obviously had a negative effect on the communication process and, thus, on the consulting relationship.

Exchanging Information Often

A frequent exchange of objective information and facts relevant to the project also is important. A common source of frustration for the consultants studied was that their clients did not share information freely, particularly information about organizational politics. In some cases, the consultants felt that their clients simply did not recognize relevant information when they saw it and so did not pass it on. In other cases, the consultants felt that their clients were unwilling or unable to take the initiative to contact the consultant when the need arose. Although the consultants acknowledged their responsibility to "ask the right questions," they also felt that there was a limit to how thorough they could be and they felt more comfortable in the relationship if they could rely on their clients to initiate contact to exchange relevant information.

Similarly, the consultants believed that one of their own serious mistakes was to forge ahead with a project without providing frequent updates to the client. In one case, the client and the consultant had a serious falling out when the consultant had a questionnaire printed and distributed without informing the client of his intent. Although it was done according to the timetable in the original contract, it was a mistake to rely on the contract in the place of face-to-face communication.

Because consultants are not always accessible to managers for the exchange of information (and managers are used to their subordinates and peers being accessible), communication must be planned deliberately. When informal contact is unlikely, it is important that formal plans for communication be made. The remedy for infrequent contact with the client is obvious: schedule more appointments, make more telephone calls, drop in more often. These contacts are within the consultant's control, provided that the client is available. If the client is extremely busy or frequently absent, the problem may be more difficult to resolve. However, the consultants interviewed for this study felt that "attempts to get in touch" might be worth a great deal to the client even if they did not succeed. Many clients seemed to be assuaged by messages or notes when a conversation was not possible. Such substitute communication at least establishes the consultant's intent to keep the client well-informed.

SUMMARY OF THE PROCESS VARIABLES

In general, consultants can improve the quality of their relationships with clients by paying more attention to three important processes:

1. *The Matching Process.* Is there a personal fit between the consultant and the client? Do the two have the same goals for the project? Are the consultant's skills well-matched to the client's needs?

2. *The Contracting Process.* Does the contract contain sufficient detail about what the consultant will do and what is expected of the client? Can the project be broken down into stages, so that a shorter-term project is contracted for first?

3. *The Communication Process.* What can the consultant do to reduce the client's defensiveness? How can the consultant and the client schedule more opportunities to talk with each other and to share information?

ORGANIZATIONAL POWER

There are limits to what a consultant can do to improve the consulting experience. The power of the client within his or her own organization is a critically important variable in the success of the project. An illustration of this is Matthew's report of his experience as a consultant to a packaging company, in which the client's lack of organizational power hampered the potential for a successful consulting relationship.

The primary client had been promoted from assistant personnel director to line manager and relocated to another city. Six months later, he became dissatisfied with what he had been able to accomplish and hired Matthew to help him to assess why morale was low and absenteeism was high.

Matthew found it difficult to obtain reliable information from any level within the plant, and the relationship between Matthew and the client became increasingly tense. Eventually, the client's superior told Matthew that he believed that the workers were resentful because the client had been brought in to fill the management position that they felt their long-time supervisor should have received. Obviously, this superior had been grooming the local man for the position and, feeling coerced by the home office, had failed to support the client from the beginning. This had allowed the workers to demonstrate their resistance to the "outsider."

As a consultant, Matthew had no more power than his primary client, and his client had, according to some theories (Kanter, 1977), taken the wrong route to a position that otherwise might have entailed some power. Without the support of either his subordinates or his direct superior, the client had little power to function effectively.

The conclusion is that in order for a consulting project to succeed, the contact person must possess at least a minimum amount of organizational power, enough to effect the change called for by the project. The measure of organizational power repeatedly mentioned by consultants include: (a) budgetary control; (b) respect from superiors; (c) access to political information; and (d) some independence in decision making.

Budgetary control tends to be an indicator of discretionary power in general, the ability of the client to exercise his or her own judgment in a wide range of decisions. It also may be an indicator of the organization's confidence or trust in an individual, relating this factor to "respect from superiors."

It is important to have higher management's support if either the client or the consultant is to be able to function effectively. If a superior respects the client, he or she is more likely to support the client's judgments and provide help and encouragement rather than roadblocks.

A number of consultants reported placing a strong value on clients who made decisions independently, as is evidenced by statements such as "Even though I made the recommendations, he was very clear that he was responsible for making the final decision." It may be that the client who lacks organizational power or is on shaky ground within the organization is more likely to defer to the consultant, perhaps because he or she is not used to making important decisions independently or is unwilling to risk taking responsibility for the outcome of the project. Consultants would be wise to attend to clues that this situation exists.

The importance of having accurate political information about the organization is illustrated by a negative case in which the consultant felt that the contact person's naivete about certain political realities had caused serious problems in implementing an OD project. If more information had been available to him, the consultant never would have made the recommendation he did for the approach to the project. It is clear that it is crucial for the consultant who is a newcomer to an organization to be able to rely on the quality and completeness of the information with which he or she is provided.

Consultants should, therefore, attempt to assess, before beginning a project, whether the potential client has the ability to command enough influence or power to win the support of others for the project. If the client does not have the necessary organizational power to obtain the resources and commitment to support the project, the consultant may choose not to accept the assignment or to set more modest goals that are realistic in terms of the client's situation within the organization.

REFERENCE

Kanter, R.M. (1977). *Men and women of the corporation.* New York: Basic Books.

Diane McKinney Kellogg, Ed.D., is an associate professor of management at Bentley College. In addition to consulting, she is expanding her research on client-consultant relationships to include small businesses and is conducting a longitudinal study on senior managers' careers in the high-tech industry. Dr. Kellogg serves on the executive boards of the Institute for Women and Organizations and the Women in Management Division of the Academy of Management.

A NEW MODEL OF TEAM BUILDING: A TECHNOLOGY FOR TODAY AND TOMORROW

Chuck Kormanski and Andrew Mozenter

In this age of rapidly changing technology, market-driven decision making, customer sophistication, and employee restlessness, leaders and managers are faced with new challenges. For corporations, small companies, educational institutions, and service organizations to become competitive and to survive, new structures must be built and new skills must be mastered.

As our work settings become more complex and involve increased numbers of interpersonal interactions, individual effort has less and less impact. In order to gain control over change by increasing efficiency and effectiveness, a group effort is required. The creation of teams to accomplish tasks and effect desired change has become a key strategy in many organizations. Team building has become necessary as a process to control organizational change by a group whose members are joined together in pursuit of a common purpose.

Although much has been written about the management of change (Ferguson, 1980; Kanter, 1983) and the new leadership required to inspire excellence (Bennis & Nanus, 1985; Burns, 1978; Maccoby, 1976; Peters & Waterman, 1982), surprisingly little has been written about the elements of effective team building. As teams rapidly replace individuals as the primary unit of focus in innovative companies and organizations, learning how to build, nurture, lead, and dismantle teams becomes a critical management skill.

Hellriegel, Slocum, & Woodman (1986) state that team building is used to improve the effectiveness of work groups by focusing on any of the following four purposes: setting goals and priorities, deciding on means and methods, examining the way in which the group works, and exploring the quality of working relationships. A cycle then develops; it begins with the awareness or perception of a problem and is followed sequentially by data collection, data sharing, diagnosis, action planning, action implementation, and behavioral evaluation. This cycle is repeated as new problems are identified.

TEAM ELEMENTS

Some work groups technically are not teams. Reilly and Jones (1974) note four essential elements of team behavior: the team members must have mutual goals or a reason to work together; team members must perceive a need for an interdependent working relationship; individuals must be committed to the group effort; and the group must be accountable to a higher level within the organization. Karp (1980) cites the example of an athletic team. A reason to work together is defined by team goals and overall purpose. Individual players have specific assignments for which each is independently responsible, but each player also must depend on other team members to complete their assignments. Lack of commitment to team efforts creates dissension and reduces overall effectiveness. Finally, the team usually operates within the framework of a higher organization such as a league.

Teams are differentiated from groups in that they possess the four essential elements of goals, interdependence, commitment, and accountability. Groups that are not teams include the following: a group of workers who meet daily for their coffee break but who have no defined goals and no accountability for what happened during the break; a monthly coin club composed of individual collectors who are not accountable to a higher organization; a group of pageant contestants who are working independently to win and who have little commitment to the group if it lessens their chances of winning; and an office staff that does not volunteer for but is assigned to a training program.

Team Objectives

The overall objective of a team is to exercise control over organizational change (functionally, this involves increased decision-making and problem-solving efforts), although a side effect may be to increase the productivity of individual members. Solomon (1977) stresses the need in contemporary work settings to provide for increased organizational democracy. From a structural perspective, new work groups may be created that will differ in terms of composition, time span, and assigned tasks. A primary objective will be to increase awareness of group process. In essence, the group members will learn how to control change externally by experimenting internally. The team-building effort will concentrate on barriers to effective functioning and the selection of strategies to overcome these barriers.

Peters and Waterman (1982) discuss breaking things into manageable "chunks" as a means of facilitating organizational fluidity and encouraging action and note that the small group is the most visible of the chunking devices. They also state that the small group is critical to effective organizational functioning and that the task force is a key strategy in creating a bias for action. Gibb and Gibb (1969) identify the group experience as being more powerful and more permanent if it is embedded in significant organizational life. Team building is an essential element in improving the effectiveness of small groups and task forces and must be a key part of a total program of organizational change.

Values

As the cultural values of our society change from the "selfish seventies" to the "concerned eighties," with emphasis on personal fulfillment, increased concern for others is required of each individual (Schnall, 1981). New criteria are emerging for success. More attention is paid to job-related creativity, interdependence, and freedom as well as to more intangible factors such as health, education, family, and leisure time. Individuals are not afraid of hard work but they also seek increased appreciation for their efforts and more involvement in the decision-making process. The growth of quality circles is an example of values translated into action in the workplace. Employee volunteers meet on a regular basis to analyze work-related problems and suggest solutions. Quality circles are valuable team efforts that can improve both production and quality of work life (Lawler & Mohrman, 1985).

Solomon (1977) identifies five values that represent implicit assumptions about human nature and organizational life. The values underlie the strategies used in team-building efforts. They include a belief in and advocacy of democratic society, freedom of choice, scientific inquiry, a healthy organization, and interpersonal knowledge. Peters and Waterman (1982) cite the values of quality, innovativeness, informality, customer service, and people. As a team operates within an organization, the role of leadership is to instill and protect the values of the organization (Burns, 1978). The role of the team is to act on those values.

Team Characteristics

Organizational failures often are not a result of poor leadership but of poor followership. Numerous training programs have been developed to teach leadership theories and skills, but few teach how to be an effective follower. More importantly, few teach how to be an effective member of a democratic group. A team member is one of a group of mutual followers. Observation of individuals functioning within teams leads to the following list of characteristics of an effective team member. Such a person:

- Understands and is committed to group goals;
- Is friendly, concerned, and interested in others;
- Acknowledges and confronts conflict openly;
- Listens to others with understanding;
- Includes others in the decision-making process;
- Recognizes and respects individual differences;
- Contributes ideas and solutions;
- Values the ideas and contributions of others;
- Recognizes and rewards team efforts; and
- Encourages and appreciates comments about team performance.

These characteristics are in a sequential pattern, alternating task and relationship behaviors. This pattern of behaviors is the starting point for the development of a model of team building.

A NEW MODEL OF TEAM BUILDING

The following model is in accord with current theories of group development (e.g., Bennis & Shepard, 1956; Bion, 1961; Gibb, 1964; Schutz, 1958, 1982; Tuckman, 1965; Tuckman & Jensen, 1977; and Yalom, 1970). A summary of selected theories is presented in Table 1. Because Tuckman's work is a summarization of numerous studies and is expressed in short, descriptive terms, it will be used as a generic model. Tuckman's (1977) stages of group development are forming, storming, norming, performing, and adjourning.

The model presented here is sequential, developmental, and thematic, as are most theories of group development. The model is sequential in that there are five stages that occur in order; each stage has a general theme that describes group activity. The developmental nature of the model requires that the theme activities be accomplished and problems resolved at each

Table 1. Models of Group Development

Models	Stages				
	One	Two	Three	Four	Five
Tuckman (1965, 1977)	Forming	Storming	Norming	Performing	Adjourning
Bennis and Shepard (1956)	Dependence	Counter dependence	Resolution	Interde- pendence	
Schutz (1958, 1982)	Inclusion	Control	Openness/ affection	Control	Inclusion
Bion (1961)	Dependency	Fight/flight	Pairing	Work	
Gibb (1964)	Acceptance	Data flow	Goals and norms	Control	
Yalom (1970)	Orientation and hesitant participation	Conflict, dominance, and rebellion	Intimacy, closeness, and cohe- siveness		Termination

stage before movement to the next stage. The model includes behaviors that are task oriented and relationship oriented and it reflects the elements and characteristics of teams presented earlier in this paper. Table 2 is a presentation of the model.

Table 2. A Model of Team Building

Stage	Theme	Task Outcome	Relationship Outcome
One	Awareness	Commitment	Acceptance
Two	Conflict	Clarification	Belonging
Three	Cooperation	Involvement	Support
Four	Productivity	Achievement	Pride
Five	Separation	Recognition	Satisfaction

To summarize the model, the five themes and their respective task and relationship outcomes are as follows: awareness (commitment and acceptance); conflict (clarification and belonging); cooperation (involvement and support); productivity (achievement and pride); and separation (recognition and satisfaction).

Stage One: Awareness

The forming stage of group development involves the task objective of *becoming oriented* and the relationship objective of *resolving dependencies*. Awareness is an overall theme. In team building, team members need to understand and become committed to group goals as a task behavior and to be friendly, concerned, and interested in others from a relationship perspective. The desired outcomes for the first stage are *commitment and acceptance*. These outcomes are critical to team development and are prerequisites to movement to the next stage.

In team building, individuals must begin by getting acquainted with one another. The unique identities and personal skills of individuals are important resources to be shared in order to create feelings of acceptance. However, getting acquainted is not enough; there are many groups in which the members feel comfortable with one another and know one another's strengths and weaknesses yet accomplish nothing. Therefore, the initial task activity is *setting goals*. This gives meaning to the team's existence. Not only do individuals need to understand how the team fits within the organization, they also need to understand how they are related to the team's goals.

Stage Two: Conflict

The storming stage of group development involves the task objective of *resistance* and the relationship objective of *resolving feelings of hostility*. Conflict emerges naturally as a general theme. Team building behaviors at this stage include acknowledging and confronting conflict openly at the task level and listening with understanding to others at the relationship level. Desired outcomes in this stage are *clarification and belonging*.

It is important that individuals listen attentively and actively to all viewpoints at this stage. The diversity of opinions shared provides the team with a vital source of group energy. Team members become responsible for developing an atmosphere that encourages and supports the expression of opinions. This opportunity for individuals to contribute to the group effort fosters a sense of belonging. As opinions are shared, there undoubtedly will be both expressed and unexpressed disagreement. By openly confronting and managing disagreements, a team further clarifies its purpose and begins to define its most effective means for working together. Thus, effective conflict-management strategies contribute to a deeper understanding and a more accurate clarification of the team's purpose.

Stage Three: Cooperation

The norming stage of group development involves the task objective of *promoting open communication* and the relationship objective of *increasing cohesion*. The overall theme is one of cooperation. Appropriate behaviors for team members are including others in the decision-making process, to meet task needs, and recognizing and respecting individual differences, to meet relationship needs. The desired outcomes for teams in the third stage are *involvement and support*.

Effective team members recognize and respect individual differences. They see that opportunities for group success increase as they share power and resources. Collaboration becomes a team norm, and a feeling of genuine support develops. Members realize that if they are to work effectively together, they must learn to give and receive feedback. As the giving and receiving of feedback increase within the team, members have a better understanding of where they stand and become more involved in decision making.

Stage Four: Productivity

The performing stage of group development involves the task objective of *solving problems* and the relationship objective of *promoting interdependence*. The general theme is productivity. Team building behaviors encourage team members to contribute ideas and problem solutions and to value the contributions and ideas of others. Desired outcomes for this stage are *achievement* and *pride*.

In team building, members work collaboratively to achieve desired goals and objectives. In successful teams, members are challenged to work to their greatest potential in order to do this. A major concern at this stage is sustaining momentum and enthusiasm. Teams are faced with complex goals and objectives that require the creation of incremental steps and subgoals. The establishment of milestones or benchmarks for success at such points and the celebration when these points are reached contribute both to motivation and team revitalization.

Stage Five: Separation

The adjourning stage of group development may occur for groups that have a specified lifetime. It also may occur when a major task is completed or when a number of new team members are added. Some ongoing teams do not conclude at the fifth stage but recycle from stage five to stage one without adjourning.

During stage five, the task objective involves *recognizing and rewarding team efforts* while the relationship objective stresses *encouraging and appreciating comments on team performance*. The desired outcomes of the final stage of team building are *recognition and satisfaction*.

For those groups that are adjourning, an evaluation of team accomplishments provides important feedback regarding job performance and working relationships. This documentation of team history can be used to plan future ventures involving other teams. This also provides a sense of closure for the group and allows individuals to either say goodbye or commit to a future of further collaboration. This stage is, in essence, a final celebration that includes both recognition and satisfaction.

Table 3 presents an integration of group-development theory and the team-building model described here. For each of the five stages of Tuckman's model, a task and relationship behavior is noted, a general theme is identified, and both task and relationship team-building outcomes are listed.

Table 3. Integration of Group Development Theory and a Model of Team Building

Group Development				Team Building	
Tuckman Stage	Task Behavior	Relationship Behavior	General Theme	Task Outcome	Relationship Outcome
1. Forming	Orientation	Dependency	Awareness	Commitment	Acceptance
2. Storming	Resistance	Hostility	Conflict	Clarification	Belonging
3. Norming	Communication	Cohesion	Cooperation	Involvement	Support
4. Performing	Problem Solving	Inter-dependence	Productivity	Achievement	Pride
5. Adjourning	Termination	Disengage-ment	Separation	Recognition	Satisfaction

OTHER MODELS

Three team-building models have appeared in the literature. Francis and Young (1979) describe a four-stage model by noting participant reactions. Sequentially, the stages are testing, in-fighting, getting organized, and mature closeness. In this model, the first three stages appear to be behaviors while the forth is an outcome. Francis and Young also provide an activity to rate stages of team development; it is composed of adjectives (polite, open), a noun (difficulties), specific behaviors (developing skills, giving feedback), and an emotion (feeling stuck). However, the stages do, in a general way, resemble the themes suggested in this paper.

Woodcock (1979) also presents a four-stage model. The sequential stages describe team performance and are: the undeveloped team, the experimenting team, the consolidated team, and the mature team. The initial stage is described as a floundering stage full of negative characteristics and behaviors. Stage two is a set of positive behaviors focused on listening and experimenting. Stage three sees the addition of some work methods and procedures to the behaviors listed in the second stage. Finally, stage four adds another set of behaviors, which describe work outcomes, to those of the preceding two stages.

Woodcock and Francis (1981) propose a model consisting of five stages and based on a revision and combination of their earlier efforts. The first stage is called ritual sniffing, but the behavioral description of team members continues to be one of negative floundering. In-fighting is the second stage; it appears more positive, and the focus is on beginning to develop relationships. Experimentation is moved from stage two to stage three and continues to involve improved relationships. However, task functions are described negatively at this stage. The forth stage is a renamed version of the third stages of the two earlier theories. It is called effectiveness and highlights working relationships and task functions. The fifth stage resembles the fourth stages of the two earlier models and is called maturity. It includes the description of stages three and four plus a description of ideal team functioning in both the task and relationship spheres.

TEAM-DEVELOPMENT RATING SCALE

All three of the models described in the previous section are presented in terms of team-member behaviors, with the final stage representing a desired outcome. The new model presented in this paper identifies specific outcomes at each stage. This permits an assessment by team members of the effectiveness of the team's functioning. Figure 1 presents a Team Development Rating Scale to be used for such a purpose.

INSTRUCTIONS: Provide a rating from one (low) to ten (high) by circling the appropriate number that you think is most descriptive of your team.

1. **Commitment**

Team members understand group goals and are committed to them.

| 10 | 9 | 8 | 7 | 6 | 5 | 4 | 3 | 2 | 1 |

2. **Acceptance**

Team members are friendly, concerned, and interested in each other.

| 10 | 9 | 8 | 7 | 6 | 5 | 4 | 3 | 2 | 1 |

3. **Clarification**

Team members acknowledge and confront conflict openly.

| 10 | 9 | 8 | 7 | 6 | 5 | 4 | 3 | 2 | 1 |

4. **Belonging**

Team members listen with understanding to others.

| 10 | 9 | 8 | 7 | 6 | 5 | 4 | 3 | 2 | 1 |

5. **Involvement**

Team members include others in the decision-making process.

| 10 | 9 | 8 | 7 | 6 | 5 | 4 | 3 | 2 | 1 |

6. **Support**

Team members recognize and respect individual differences.

| 10 | 9 | 8 | 7 | 6 | 5 | 4 | 3 | 2 | 1 |

7. **Achievement**

Team members contribute ideas and solutions to problems.

| 10 | 9 | 8 | 7 | 6 | 5 | 4 | 3 | 2 | 1 |

8. **Pride**

Team members value the contributions and ideas of others.

| 10 | 9 | 8 | 7 | 6 | 5 | 4 | 3 | 2 | 1 |

9. **Recognition**

Team members recognize and reward team performance.

| 10 | 9 | 8 | 7 | 6 | 5 | 4 | 3 | 2 | 1 |

10. **Satisfaction**

Team members encourage and appreciate comments about team efforts.

| 10 | 9 | 8 | 7 | 6 | 5 | 4 | 3 | 2 | 1 |

Figure 1. Team-Development Rating Scale

LEADERSHIP

Although team development is presented as a process in which the members are mutual followers, the context in which team building occurs requires the facilitator or team leader to have a thorough understanding of the process of leadership. The two are mutually reciprocal. Effectiveness in one improves performance outcomes as well as working relationships; effectiveness in both creates a synergistic effect.

Kormanski (1985) describes the relationship between group development and leadership style. Using the Situational Leadership® theory of Hersey and Blanchard (1982), he matches leader behavior with follower readiness and pairs them with stages of group development. A high-task, low-relationship leadership style (S1: Telling) is used with a group in stage one (awareness), which implies a low level of readiness. Relationship behavior by the leader is increased as performance and level of readiness improve. This results in a high-task, high-relationship style (S2: Selling) as the group moves into stage two (conflict). The leader's task behavior is reduced as the readiness level increases and the group enters stage three (cooperation). The leadership style involves low-task, high-relationship behaviors (S3: Participating), with the followers assuming more task responsibilities. Relationship behavior by the leader is reduced as stage four (productivity) evolves. Readiness is at its highest level, and the appropriate leader style is a low-task, low-relationship one (S4: Delegating). Finally, when the group enters stage five (separation) and concludes a particular task or its own existence, a crisis occurs. This requires the leader to increase relationship behaviors in order to support the team members (followers) as events move toward a close. This results in a low-task, high-relationship (S3: Participating) style that matches the decreasing readiness level of the members brought on by the crisis of separation. Table 4 presents a summary of the stages of group and team development, along with the appropriate leadership styles.

Hersey and Blanchard (1982) describe leadership as influence. Burns (1978) says that outcomes ought to reflect the aspirations and expectations of both leaders and followers. He also defines two fundamentally different forms of leadership: transactional leadership involves

Table 4. Stages of Group and Team Development and Leadership Style

Stage of Group Development	Group/Team Development Theme	Situational Leadership® Style	Group/Team Leader Behavior	Follower-Readiness Behavior
1	Awareness	Telling	High task, low relationship	Inexperienced and hesitant
2	Conflict	Selling	High task, high relationship	Inexperienced and willing
3	Cooperation	Participating	Low task, high relationship	Experienced and hesitant or unconfident
4	Productivity	Delegating	Low task, low relationship	Experienced and willing
5	Separation	Participating	Low task, high relationship	Experienced and hesitant

the exchange of valued things as the major purpose, and transforming leadership increases awareness and acceptance of higher levels of motivation and morality.

Bennis and Nanus (1985) suggest that the difference between transacting and transforming is the difference between managing and leading. Leaders, they say, influence and inspire others through value-driven vision; persuasive, anecdotal communication; and the development of a strong, predictable self. Managers, on the other hand, lead by employing the skills necessary to get the job done. The truly successful teams are both managed and led. While managing skills enable teams to successfully advance through each stage of team development, leading skills inspire individual team members to realize their full potential at each stage.

Both forms of leadership are critical if outcomes of both a task and relationship nature are desired. However, team members require more transactional leadership during the early stages of group life (and low levels of follower-readiness) in order to achieve the team-building outcomes of commitment, acceptance, clarification, and belonging. Increased transformational leadership is required as the team develops and matures. The team-building outcomes of involvement and support require equal amounts of transactional and transformational leadership. Finally, in the advanced stages of group development and readiness, more transformational leadership is required to bring about the team-building outcomes of achievement, pride, recognition, and satisfaction. Figure 2 presents a summary of team-development outcomes and Burns' (1978) forms of leadership.

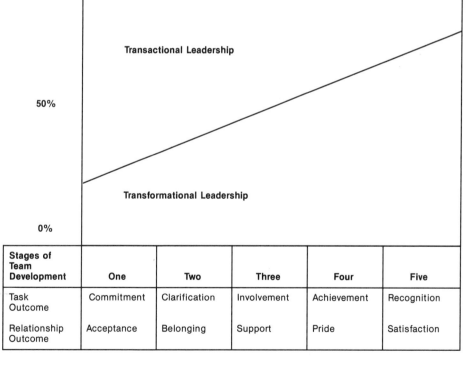

Stages of Team Development	One	Two	Three	Four	Five
Task Outcome	Commitment	Clarification	Involvement	Achievement	Recognition
Relationship Outcome	Acceptance	Belonging	Support	Pride	Satisfaction

Figure 2. Forms of Leadership and Team-Development Outcomes

Skills

In order to bring about the desired outcomes of the team-development process, the team leader needs to master specific skills and teach them to the team members. Although all of these skills may be needed and used all the time, a special group of skills is especially needed at each stage of team development. As has been stated, both transactional and transformational skills are required during the early stages of team development, while more transformational skills are needed during the latter stages. Team leaders will discover more opportunities to use transformational skills, and team members will find more situations in which transactional skills are required.

Transactional Skills

The literature describes a number of transactional skills useful in team building (Alexander, 1985; Francis & Young, 1979; Karp, 1980; Reilly & Jones, 1974; Shonk, 1982; Solomon, 1977; Woodcock, 1979; and Woodcock & Francis, 1981). The skills used extensively during stage one (awareness) to bring about commitment and acceptance are getting acquainted, goal setting, and organizing. The skills that bring resolution to stage two (conflict) and develop clarification and belonging are active listening, assertiveness, and conflict management. During the third stage (cooperation), the skills used most frequently to promote involvement and support are communication, feedback, and affirmation. The forth stage (productivity) requires the skills of problem solving, decision making, and rewarding to develop achievement and pride. Finally, during the fifth stage (separation), the skills needed to create recognition and satisfaction are evaluating and reviewing.

Transformational Skills

Transformational skills have received attention only recently. Although Selznick (1957) was one of the first to suggest the importance of these skills as critical components of dynamic leadership, it was Burns (1978) who provided a thorough introduction to them. The current literature continues to offer insight into the importance and development of transformational skills (Ackerman, 1984; Bass, 1985; Bennis & Nanus, 1985; Ferguson, 1980; Kanter, 1983; Peters & Waterman, 1982).

In the awareness stage of the team-development model, the transformational skills needed to encourage commitment and acceptance are value clarification, visioning (identifying mission and purpose), and communicating through myth and metaphor (using stories and anecdotes to describe philosophy and define culture). During the conflict stage, the skills of flexibility (developing openness and versatility), creativity, and kaleidoscopic thinking (discovering new ways of viewing old problems) will assist with the development of clarification and belonging. The cooperation stage requires the skills of playfulness and humor, entrepreneurship, and networking (building coalitions of support). At the productivity stage, the skills of multicultural awareness, mentoring, and futuring (forecasting outcomes through trend analysis) help to create achievement and pride. The last stage, separation, requires the skills of celebrating (using ceremony to acknowledge accomplishment) and closure to promote recognition and satisfaction.

The skills essential for successful team development are both simple and complex. They are used by both team leaders and team members. One set (transactional) provides for efficient management, and the other (transformational) promotes effective leadership. Table 5 depicts the team-building skills that are used predominantly in each stage of team development.

Table 5. Team-Building Skills

Stage of Team Development	Task and Relationship Outcomes	Transactional Skills (Management)	Transformational Skills (Leadership)
1. Awareness	Commitment and acceptance	Getting acquainted, goal setting, organizing	Value clarification, visioning, communication through myth and metaphor
2. Conflict	Clarification and belonging	Active listening, assertiveness, conflict management	Flexibility, creativity, kaleidoscopic thinking
3. Cooperation	Involvement and support	Communicating, feedback, affirmation	Playfulness and humor, entrepreneuring, networking
4. Productivity	Achievement and pride	Decision making, problem solving, rewarding	Multicultural awareness, mentoring, futuring
5. Separation	Recognition and satisfaction	Evaluating, reviewing	Celebrating, bringing closure

PRACTICAL APPLICATIONS OF THE MODEL

The team-building model and its relationship to group development provides a sound basis for organizational use in the formation, growth, and conclusion of groups who might function best as teams in order to accomplish specific goals. With the identification of both task and relationship outcomes at each stage of development, progress can be assessed and interventions can be made when time is critical or when barriers to development occur. Skills for both team leaders and team members can be identified at each stage, and appropriate leadership styles can be determined.

This model also is an excellent starting point for the design of team-building programs. In addition to teaching new groups about the team-building process and skills, it can be used to enhance and/or remedy groups in all stages of the developmental sequence. Groups that have mastered the transactional skills can be encouraged to acquire the transformational skills or vice versa.

The Team-Development Rating Scale (see Figure 1) can be used to monitor progress on all ten outcomes. Both task and relationship functions can be assessed, along with the two related outcomes, to determine each stage of development. A total score also can be obtained. Data from the rating scale currently is being collected in business, industrial, educational, volunteer, and sports settings. Initial data suggest that new teams usually rate themselves relatively high on each outcome (from 7 to 9.5 on the ten-point scale). Overall scores also tend to be high (between 75 and 90) and suggest a somewhat positive expectation of success. As the team members spend more time working together, the ratings decrease until the stage-two outcomes are achieved. Following this critical point, effective teams gradually show increasingly higher ratings until they reach the approximate level of the initial scores. Figure 3 presents a graphic interpretation of the general sequence of team development in relation to the scores from the Team-Development Rating Scale for twenty-three teams, each consisting of five to seven members, who worked on a planning/implementing task for five weeks. (These initial findings are tentative, and data is continuing to be collected and analyzed.)

The team-building model and rating scale provide an internal measurement of the effectiveness of the team to accompany external assessments of goal accomplishment. Both are important, but too often little attention is paid to how the group members work as a team. Essential outcomes can be measured by team members and used to enhance team development.

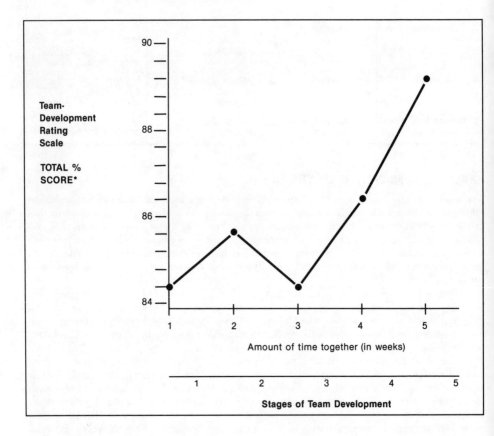

*N=23 teams

Figure 3. Team-Development Rating Scale and Stages of Team Development

SUMMARY

The model of team building presented in this paper is compatible with major theories of group development. It emphasizes the role of the team members as mutual followers. Using specific elements, objectives, and values as a starting point, it identifies a group of observable behaviors that characterize effective teamwork. Descriptive outcomes representing both the task dimension and the relationship dimension for each stage of group development are identified. The team-building model is integrated with group-development theory using the five major themes of awareness, conflict, cooperation, productivity, and separation.

This paper also discusses other models of team building and presents a Team-Development Rating Scale. The role of team leader is discussed in relation to appropriate leadership style for each stage of team development. Specific skills for both team leaders and team members are outlined for each stage of team-building, including both transactional and transformational skills. Finally, some practical suggestions are offered for the use of the model, and tentative research data is presented.

REFERENCES

Ackerman, L.S. (1984). The transformational manager: Facilitating the flow state. In J.W. Pfeiffer & L.D. Goodstein (Eds.), *The 1984 annual: Developing human resources.* San Diego, CA: University Associates.

Alexander, M. (1985). The team-effectiveness critique. In L.D. Goodstein & J.W. Pfeiffer (Eds.), *The 1985 annual: Developing human resources.* San Diego, CA: University Associates.

Bass, B.M. (1985) *Leadership and performance beyond expectations.* New York: Free Press.

Bennis, W., & Nanus, B. (1985). *Leaders: The strategies for taking charge.* New York: Harper & Row.

Bennis, W.G., & Shepard, H.A. (1956). A theory of group development. *Human Relations, 9,* 415-437.

Bion, W.R. (1961). *Experiences in groups.* New York: Basic Books.

Burns, J.M. (1978). *Leadership.* New York: Harper & Row.

Ferguson, M. (1980). *The aquarian conspiracy: Personal and social transformation in the 1980s.* Los Angeles: Tarcher.

Francis, D., & Young, D. (1979). *Improving work groups: A practical manual for team building.* San Diego, CA: University Associates.

Gibb, J.R. (1964). Climate for trust. In L.P. Bradford, J.R. Gibb, & K.D. Benne (Eds.), *T-group theory and laboratory method: Innovation in re-education.* New York: John Wiley.

Gibb, J.R., & Gibb, L.M. (1969). Role freedom in a TORI group. In A. Burton (Ed.), *Encounter.* San Francisco: Jossey-Bass.

Hellriegel, D., Slocum, J.W., & Woodman, R.W. (1986). *Organizational behavior.* St. Paul, MN: West.

Hersey, P., & Blanchard, K.H. (1982). *Management of organizational behavior: Utilizing human resources* (4th ed.). Englewood Cliffs, NJ: Prentice-Hall.

Kanter, R.M. (1983). *The change masters.* New York: Simon & Schuster.

Karp, H.B. (1980). Team building from a Gestalt perspective. In J. W. Pfeiffer & J.E. Jones (Eds.), *The 1980 annual handbook for group facilitators.* San Diego, CA: University Associates.

Kormanski, C.L. (1985). A Situational Leadership® approach to groups using the Tuckman model of group development. In L.D. Goodstein & J.W. Pfeiffer (Eds.), *The 1985 annual: Developing human resources.* San Diego, CA: University Associates.

Lawler, E.E., & Mohrman, S.A. (1985, January-February). Quality circles after the fad. *Harvard Business Review,* pp. 65-71.

Maccoby, M. (1976). *The gamesman, the new corporate leaders.* New York: Simon & Schuster.

Peters, T.J., & Waterman, R.H. (1982). *In search of excellence: Lessons from America's best-run companies.* New York: Harper & Row.

Reilly, A.J., & Jones, J.E. (1974). Team-building. In J.W. Pfeiffer & J.E. Jones (Eds.), *The 1974 annual handbook for group facilitators.* San Diego, CA: University Associates.

Schnall, M. (1981). *Limits: A search for new values.* New York: Potter.

Selznick, P. (1957). *Leadership in administration: A sociological interpretation.* New York: Harper & Row.

Shonk, J.H. (1982). *Working in teams: A practical manual for improving work groups.* New York: AMACOM.

Schutz, W.D. (1958). *FIRO: A three-dimensional theory of interpersonal behavior.* New York: Rinehart.

Schutz, W.D. (1982). *The Schutz measures: An integrated system for assessing elements of awareness.* San Diego, CA: University Associates.

Solomon, L.N. (1977). Team development: A training approach. In J.E. Jones & J.W. Pfeiffer (Eds.), *The 1977 annual handbook for group facilitators*. San Diego, CA: University Associates.

Tuckman, B.W. (1965). Developmental sequence in small groups. *Psychological Bulletin, 63*, 384-399.

Tuckman, B.W., & Jensen, M.A. (1977). Stages of small group development revisited. *Group & Organization Studies, 2* (4), 419-427.

Yalom, I.D. (1970). *The theory and practice of group psychotherapy*. New York: Basic Books.

Woodcock, M. (1979). *Team development manual*. New York: John Wiley.

Woodcock, M., & Francis, D. (1981). *Organization development through team building: Planning a cost effective strategy*. New York: John Wiley.

Chuck Kormanski, Ed.D., is a counselor for the Career Development and Placement Center at the Altoona, Pennsylvania, campus of The Pennsylvania State University. He counsels and teaches college students and is involved in organizational training and development and research in leadership. Dr. Kormanski is past president of the Pennsylvania Association of Specialists in Group Work and the Pennsylvania Association of Counselor Educators and Supervisors.

Andrew Mozenter is the acting director of the Office of Student Organizations and Program Development at The Pennsylvania State University. He is also a trainer and consultant with Playfair, Inc., for whom he does workshops on leadership development and team building for businesses, social-services agencies, and universities. His other areas of training experience include cross-cultural communications, race relations, and intergroup relations.

THIRTY YEARS OF HUMAN SERVICE EDUCATION AND TRAINING—ONE PERSPECTIVE

Hedley G. Dimock

In 1947, the Taylor Statten Camps, Algonquin Park, Ontario in cooperation with the University of Toronto established the National Camp Training Institute. Charles E. Hendry, director of the school of social work, led the ten-day residential program given that summer. During the program he made extensive use of role playing, case studies, and small group discussions. This was my first exposure to methods of education and training other than the traditional lecture and discussion methods. This article is an attempt to put my thirty odd years experience with trends in training since then into perspective. In closing I'll attempt to summarize the present "state-of-the-art" and make some hunches about future directions.

THE EARLY YEARS

The 1947 Training Institute provides a useful example of training methods and educational philosophies for that time. Hendry, the Institute leader, had pioneered the application of Dewey's educational theories (Dewey, 1915, 1939, 1940), the University of Toronto's Dr. Blatz's radical ideas about child rearing (Blatz & Bott, 1928), and current social sciences in the camping field. His book, *Camping and Character* (Dimock & Hendry, 1929) set the standards for modern camping and became the springboard for a series of Camping Institutes (Dimock, 1930-42) which dealt at length with leadership training and provided early forums for Carl Rogers and Goodwin Watson and others who were to have a great influence on human service workers' training and their later practices in the field. During the 1930's the social sciences were in vogue: progressive education; mental hygiene; the application of sociology to group and community processes; and new personnel developments, with emphasis on educational supervision. Hendry brought this background to the National Institute as well as additional experience in Boys Clubs of America and Boy Scouts' training which also involved Ron Lippitt and Alvin Zander (who were soon to start the National Training Institute in Bethel, Maine and revolutionize education and training).

The three innovations in training that were presented at the National Institute (Role Playing, The Case Method, and The Small Group or Workshop Method) had been developed earlier but were not well known.

Role playing was an adaption of Moreno's psychodrama and sociodrama (Moreno, 1934, 1946) for educational purposes. Hendry called it reality practice as educational method (Hendry, Lippitt & Zander, 1944) as learners were encouraged to try out different ways of handling situations and assess their outcomes. It was a powerful educational method and one of the first to add affective (feeling) dimensions to the traditional cognitive (thinking) approaches. It also represented a major shift in learning theory for in role playing the learner participates

---

Reprinted with permission. Abridged from "Thirty Years of Human Service Education and Training in Canada—One Perspective" by Hedley G. Dimock (1984). Published in *Canadian Journal of Community Mental Health, 3*(2), 15-41.

in the teaching-learning process and shares responsibility for what is learned. Role playing concepts were quickly expanded to include skits where specific roles were assigned the players, demonstrations which the watchers could critique, complacency shock approaches that would alert the trainees to the importance and emotional dynamics of a problem, and simulations or reenactments of actual or possible situations that would involve the learners in working through the situations presented (Lippitt, 1943; Bavelas, 1947; Argyris, 1951). Maier (1952) popularized role playing methods in problem solving and decision making, introduced multiple role playing which could involve scores of trainees as players simultaneously, and integrated role playing with the case method in several creative ways.

The case method was in use by the 1930's (Fraser, 1931) but did not gain much acceptance until it was adopted as the Harvard Case Method for business training some years later (Andrews, 1951, 1953). The camping area again reflects the acceptance and use of the case method in the human services with some attention given to their use in the 1947 National Institute based on Ure's (1935) *Fifty Cases for Camp Counselors*. The development of interest in the case method for training in the camping field is reflected in the later publication of Becker's *Human Relations in Camping* (1960). Case studies were often used by traditional educator/trainers simply as examples to round out or illustrate their lectures. More often students were asked to figure out what they would do in the situation presented in the case and after a couple of student comments the teacher delivered the usual lecture. In the process, the students were told the correct answer to the case. However, even when used as an extension of the lecture method it did add a new dimension to learning theory as it shifted the learner from a passive listening role to being challenged to think through a personal course of action which could later be compared to the teacher's answer. This was an important shift and its significance increased during the next few years with the introduction of the incident process (Pigors & Pigors, 1954, 1955) where the students were responsible for collecting the relevant data about the case and had to figure out what they would need to know in order to handle the case in an effective way. This shifted responsibility for much of the process of learning to the students and made it more appropriate for the teacher to accept a position that there was not one "correct" answer to the case study, just informed choices.

The workshop method or use of small groups in the learning process had even more impact on educational method and theory than role playing or the case method. The major components of the workshop method were: the learners worked in small groups, on interests or problems they had helped to identify, and using the teacher as a coordinator of the workshop activities and resource person. In the camping field the workshop method had been in use for many years (Dimock & Hendry, 1929; Dimock, 1930-1942), but was not widely used.

The audio-visual innovation stem in training is an important one to identify at this point because of its pervasive influence during the next thirty years and its potential for the future. Compared to the traditional lecture model it adds the seeing to the listening dimension and the probability of some affective response through an identification with the characters in the film. This response may be similar to watching a role playing demonstration, yet unlikely as powerful as participating in a role play.

Traditional educators tend to use a film as a recreational activity or diversion to lighten up the intensity of their lectures. Yet the real, relatively undiscovered, value of motion picture films is in their integration with the lecture, small group, case study, and role playing approaches. This integration of methods was accomplished by Maier (1952) when he integrated the case method with role playing and the small group/workshop approach, built on by Malamud (1955) who added and integrated educational films plus interpersonal sharing and feedback, and was summarized in my first monograph on designing and conducting training programs (Dimock, 1959, Dimock, 1973).

Summary of Human Service Education and Training Moving into the 1950's

Traditional education methods dominated the human services in the early 1950's. These methods tended to see learning as a passive—essentially reading, listening and memorizing—activity. The teacher designed the education activities and was responsible for covering the material and evaluating the students' progress. The student-teacher relationship was authoritarian in focus and based on the assumption that teachers knew what students should learn. The teaching process had those who did know telling the students what they should know, drilling them in the knowledge, and then testing them to see how much they remembered.

In each of the human services, education, health services, recreation, and community work, there is a body of knowledge and professional competencies that relate to technical skills and another that relates to the human dimension (human relations, leadership or helping, and interpersonal relations). In recreation the technical skills may be how to play ten group games or make pottery; in nursing the technical skills range from giving an injection to cardiac resuscitation. However, nursing has been defined as the practice of interpersonal relations and recreation talks about its programs as leisure time education. As the camping illustration demonstrated, most of the technical skills were taught with learning-by-doing methods. The knowledge, attitudes, understandings, self-insights and skills related to working more effectively with people were more likely taught by the lecture method with appropriate related readings.

The camping illustration suggested that by the close of the 1940's four trends in educational method had emerged that started moving the human services away from the traditional model. These in order of importance were the workshop method, role playing, the case method, and educational films. Two other major influences on education and training had also emerged at this time. They were the group dynamics-human relations training combination that started the National Training laboratories in 1947 (Bradford, 1974), and the publication in 1942 of Carl Rogers' first book on a new approach to helping people called client-centered therapy. Both of these innovations were to have a powerful, pervasive influence during the next decade.

Three major components of an educational system can help to focus a summary of it and compare and contrast it with other systems. The three major components of a system are its goals, its assumptions about how learning takes place (and the educational methods used to implement these assumptions), and who is responsible for what in the learning process.

Education's goals during this period were to transmit the culture and teach mental discipline, and learning them was assumed to be a cognitive activity. Responsibility for curriculum rested with experts in the field of study and teachers were responsible for the learning process. Only when students failed were they seen as responsible for their learning.

The orientation to teaching and training in the human services at the close of the 1940's era can be summarized as knowledgeable teachers giving the important understandings and know-how in that field to receptive students.

CHANGES DURING THE 1950's

The important innovations in educational theory and practice of the 1950's had all surfaced previously but became well known and accepted during this decade. These included the progressive education movement started by John Dewey (1915, 1930) in the United States and represented in Canada by the University of Toronto's Institute of Child Studies, and St. Georges School in Montreal; the client-centered, non-directive counseling approach to helping people (Rogers, 1942; Axline, 1947); the various approaches to using the learners' interests as the curriculum for educational programs (Kelley, 1951; Maier, 1952); and the social-psychological concepts of education and change which led to the group dynamics and progressive management movements, and culminated in the human relations training revolution. No one or two innovative stems stood out in the 1950's, rather it was the accumulation and integration of these several areas that accounted for the most significant impact.

Progressive Education

Progressive education is most closely associated with John Dewey and is based on the twin assumptions that people "learn-by-doing" and the role of the teacher is one of guiding and facilitating the learning process. The initiative and responsibility for learning was moved from the teacher to the student, and "learning-by-doing" was seen to involve perceptual, motor, and emotional dimensions in addition to the traditional cognitive one.

Progressive education stressed working with the whole person in teaching situations and this focused attention of educators on previous experiences, home and social environment, ethnic and religious mores, nutrition and physical health, goals and motivations, and personality and personal abilities. Above all it stressed that how people were taught could be as important as what they were taught. Expertise in subject content was no longer a basis for qualifying as a teacher. These concepts developed during the 1950's, made their major impact in the next decade as part of the humanistic education thrust. Growth and development concepts, mental hygiene, and classroom methods became standard components in the one year training programs required for teacher certification programs in most provinces, and as their importance was more fully recognized and accepted, they became part of the background in requiring a full bachelors degree for teacher certification many years later.

Field Theory and Group Dynamics

While Kurt Lewin is best known as the founder of the group dynamics school of thought he also conceived field theory or topological and vector psychology theories of learning. Field theory assumes that a person and that person's environment are interdependent factors in a learning situation. To understand, influence, and predict behavior requires knowing the person; the person's physical condition, needs, and abilities; and the environmental, social, and cultural forces which compose the person's life space. Learning, or the development of insights, is seen as changes in the structure of a person's life space. Lewinian learning has little to do with knowledge and the ability to verbalize concepts but is based on awareness of relationships or patterns in one's life space. Popular offshoots of field theory have been the powerful force field analysis concept (forces sustaining and forces restraining a particular action), and the unfreezing-learning-refreezing model of adult learning.

Lewin's students at the University of Iowa's Child Welfare Research Station in the late 1930's and early 1940's carried out many now classical studies on autocratic-democratic leadership (Lewin, Lippitt & White, 1939; White & Lippitt, 1960); and the use of small groups with group discussion and decision as a training method of behavior change (Lewin & Grabbe, 1945). Field theory and the applications of the leadership and small group insights gained considerable acceptance in the 1950's with their inclusion in the standard texts in child psychology (Carmichael, 1954), social psychology (Swanson, Newcomb & Hartley, 1952), group dynamics (Cartwright & Zander, 1953) and management training (Maier, 1952). All the related concepts and techniques in group dynamics, field theory, leadership, action research, and the management of change were pulled together as a book which had a huge impact on the education field (Benne & Muntyan, 1951).

Human Relations Training

Kurt Lewin established the Research Center for Group Dynamics at M.I.T. in 1945 and the following summer the Center staff led a workshop on interracial problems (Lippitt, 1949). After each day's sessions, the workshop staff met to review the day and hear observer reports from each work group. The observers reported on "here and now" group process concerns such as leadership, decision-making, interaction, and individual member roles. The participants asked to attend these sessions and soon everyone was analyzing and reflecting on what had happened during the day. This discussion of group process became the focus of training groups (T-groups for short) that were the basic training component the following summer of programs held at the newly established National Training Laboratory in Group Development at Bethel, Maine.

Bethel, the Mecca of the human relations training movement and the Research Center for Group Dynamics (which moved to the University of Michigan in 1947), became the academic associate and leader in group dynamics theory and practice. Human relations training became very popular rather quickly and spread to Canada in the early 1950's. A grass roots group from Saskatchewan attended Bethel and set up a similar summer residential program in Saskatchewan which continued into the mid 1960's. The Canadian YMCA experimented with a residential laboratory training program, and in 1957 the first academic human relations training course was established at Sir George Williams University in Montreal. During the same year, the Registered Nurses Association of Ontario established a laboratory training program at Honey Harbour that ran for the next twenty years.

The basic element of human relations training is a T-group activity where participants in a group observe and analyze their own experiences in the group as the major part of their learnings. This reflexive, group analysis process fitted in well with the workshop method, and the work conference method which also used small group activity as the training method. During this decade there were numerous human service conferences and professional training programs that used these methods, often to the surprise of the participants who came with their pens and notebooks and were expecting to, once again, be told what they should be doing and how they should be doing it.

Nothing has influenced the education and training of human service workers during the past thirty years as much as the integration of progressive education, field theory and group dynamics, role playing (psychodrama) and the workshop method into this new ideology of human relations training.

THE REVOLUTION OF THE 1960's

The humanistic trends identified in the preceding sections, reached the apex of their acceptance and influence during the sixties. Social, political, and economic developments were all interwoven with the human service revolutions. The growth rate in the economy was bounding ahead and huge sums of money were put into all human service programs. In the U.S. Johnson's "Just Society" paid for all kinds of individual and community development programs, increased welfare and subsidies to the disadvantaged, and established health care programs—protection from the cradle to the grave.

Group Dynamics and Action Research

During the Sixties several universities introduced a course in group dynamics and a large number of group oriented continuing education programs were offered in the human service field. The small group and workshop methods became well established and many traditional programs were enlarged to include a small group or "buzz" group component. By the mid-Sixties much of the group dynamics tradition had been incorporated by Human Relations Training and what was left reverted to group development and leadership training (Miles, 1959).

Action research moved in two different directions during these years. Many psychologists did not understand that Lewin's concept of action research was that it integrated personal reeducation and social change into the same process (Benne, 1976). But they knew it was popular and called any research they were doing that related to people "action research." The other, and appropriate, direction was into the emerging field of organization development where action research became the major intervention strategy under the name of survey feedback, self-analysis, or some kind of utilization focused research.

Human Relations Training

During this decade human relations training permeated most human service training programs and scores of training centres sprang up across the country. . . . Small group courses were added in several universities and many community colleges such that the training of most human service workers included some small group experience. Others related to the human services were also effected as human relations training was incorporated by universities in training student leaders, YMCA's and Boy Scouts in training volunteer leaders, and churches and other community organizations in training board members. . . .

Human relations training was the most visible and preferred training fad during the decade. And during this time, it developed a very solid body of theory and clearly described training methods (Bradford, Gibb & Benne, 1964; Schein & Bennis, 1965). Consistent research was also being carried out and reported on to professionals and training staff (Schutz, 1960; Durham & Gibb, 1960, 1967; Dimock, 1965, 1970). This research and theory building did a lot to integrate progressive education, emerging management concepts in business and industry (McGregor, 1960) field theory and group dynamics, and the more psychoanalytic orientations developing at the Tavistock Institute in England (Thelen, 1954; Bion, 1961). The theory and practice consolidated during the decade of the Sixties has been pervasive in explaining personal and organizational change in the human services, and it became the springboard from which the new field of organization development was launched. It has been my experience in the last five years or so that many people in the field who are using these concepts—professors, students and practitioners—are not aware of the legacy that came from the human relations training movement.

The Human Growth Thrust

Human relations training was based on field theory and group dynamics research and theory. Its basic elements were a reflexive, self-analytic focus on group process with a goal of understanding more about helping groups become more effective. The trainer's role or leadership style was clearly positioned in the democratic or participative stance and the small group/workshop method provided much of the content for training. In time, the study of the group's process was expected to become the major content.

All well and good, but during the Sixties the approach became so popular that the demand for training exceeded the cadre of people who had the skills required in participative leadership, group analysis, and group development theory. The people who had these skills were usually social psychologists or adult educators who had considerable experience in working with community groups and in conducting action research.

As the popularity of human relations or T-group training peaked, many professionals rushed in to help cover the demand. Most of the first new group to arrive were clinical psychologists and as they used the new training method they modified it to use their skills and understandings. Where T-groups focused on understanding how groups set goals and worked toward them, the new psychologists who called their groups sensitivity training, focused on individual behavior in the group setting. This used their individual diagnostic skills and shifted the T-group to more of a modified group therapy approach. Thus, the human growth movement came into being and quickly expanded as it encouraged people with all kinds of backgrounds and skills to use them to facilitate the personal growth of participants in these new group experiences.

The first group to develop their own version of human relations training were from the University of California at Los Angeles (Weschler & Reisel, 1959; Tennenbaub, Weschler & Massarik, 1961) and most of the developments of the human potential movement were California-based. By the end of the decade, Eselen was operational, as well as the Western Behavioral Sciences Institute, and the Centre for Studies of the Person—all in southern California. And people with skills in music, dance, arts and crafts, audio-visual techniques (especially film and video/TV), poetry, psychodrama, individual therapy (gestalt, rational-emotive, Rogerian, transactional, reality, etc.) dream analysis, drug use, sensory relaxation, non-verbal communication, out of body travel, rolfing, yoga, altered states of consciousness, bioenergetics, hypnosis, and so on (as the list is almost endless), added their expertise to this rapidly growing human potential movement.

While human relations training reflected the democratic (interdependent) organization and community change interests of the Forties and Fifties, human potential reflected the mood of the Sixties. This was the me-now era, independence and counter-dependence reflected in the hippie fad, the "do your own thing" approach, and the rise of protests and group activism. While the two training methods were very different and represented very different eras, they are frequently coupled as if they were one. The human growth trainers had doctrines which they taught in directive ways to the learners. They were often gurus who had the answers. While learners were free to participate or not, the teaching style was likely traditional in that it was directive with the process determined by the teacher, yet the progressive spin-off was present as the teaching method was always experiential—learning-by-doing. And it was almost totally affective (feeling) oriented with a goal of freeing up creative potential in participants and helping them become more authentic and self-actualizing.

These innovative methods also had a profound effect on the content and administration of human service education. The role of the human service helper moved along the continuum from telling and directing clients based on expert information to facilitating the learning and decision making of the service recipient. The medical model with the workers responsible for the service participant's improvement moved to a collaborative, consulting model joining worker and client in a common goal. At the same time, the importance of the worker's knowledge and skills in the technical area gave way to the worker's self-understanding, interpersonal sensitivity and ability to use himself as part of the helping process. Patients became clients and collaborators in their developmental program.

Degree requirements and professional certification crumbled in many areas as it was found that sensitive, authentic people were as successful as professionally trained workers. This shift to the personal qualities of workers, and the concept of using oneself as the major tool of helping was especially common in the new areas of human service that sprang up in the Sixties—community development, street work, day care, emergency health and counseling services, free schools, and minority group advocacy and consumer protection. But other traditional areas were affected: the YMCA dismantled its university-based certification program for staff; schools hired people who were not certified teachers; and social service agencies that had restricted new staff to those with a degree in social work actively sought others who could do the new jobs.

Interwoven with the changes in selecting and training human service workers described above were significant program developments. And they continued to affect and be affected by the changes in training.

All areas of human service tried to humanize their programs and were involved in some kind of outreach activity in an attempt to reach people they had been missing. Human service programs became proactive rather than reactive, and prevention rather than treatment oriented. For example, street clinics and hot line services were set up for youth involved in drug and sex issues. Community workers headed these programs with doctors and nurses assisting. Informal education and counseling programs were held at the clinic and in local schools as part of the prevention program. School boards established alternative schools and programs to get at hard-to-reach youth while individual schools targeted potential dropouts for group guidance and other remedial programs. YMCA's and community organizations fielded teams of street workers and set up drop-in centres to get in touch with disadvantaged or alienated youth. Counselors in schools and universities started working with teachers and school-wide programs rather than just seeing individual students. And most community services that had only responded to needs with treatment—a handicapped child, a broken home, a distressed person, an unwanted pregnancy, or unemployment—added an outreach education/counseling component and usually an advocacy, networking, community relations program.

With the monies available for the rapid expansion of human service programs, there was a chronic shortage of trained workers and students flooded into the professional programs in colleges and universities. They in turn responded by enlarging old programs and creating new ones. Often people with fewer years of training took over some areas of work previously done by more "senior" people. Paramedics assisted doctors, nursing aides and nursing assistants took over some jobs previously done by registered nurses, counselors did the therapy previously handled by psychologists and psychiatrists, case aids helped out professional social workers, and so on down the list of human services.

But likely just as important and pervasive in its influence was the move to using peers and indigenous leaders in place of professional helpers. Carkhuff was a major experimenter, researcher and writer about peer helping and started with training parents to act as helpers (therapists) with their disturbed children (Carkhuff & Bierman, 1969). He also used lay helpers with hospitalized mental patients (Carkhuff, 1969) and then expanded into general areas of helping with a broad focus. His former student Bierman set up a community-wide peer helper program in Guelph, Ontario, a few years later. The indigenous leader concept was used extensively in the community development projects that proliferated in the 1960's. And the peer counseling method was especially popular in disadvantaged and "hard-to-reach" youth programs and soon became an acceptable way of providing help within the school system.

The impact of the lay helper movement on human service education and training was twofold. First, the well documented evidence that peers could be just as helpful as trained professionals broke down some of the rigid barriers defining who was allowed to do what. And second, many of the professionals who had previously been providing the helping services directly were now expected to do the selection and training of the lay helpers. Education programs in colleges and universities picked up this new expectation from the field and shifted their focus from the knowledge and skills needed for providing direct service to those required for training other people to do the work. Human service professionals were no longer just "doers," they were trainers and consultants. And books and programs for developing trainers leaped in popularity (Dimock, 1973).

THE REASSESSMENT OF THE 1970's

Newton's third law of motion is that to every action there is an equal and opposite reaction. Or, as Galton and others illustrated, there is always a regression toward the mean. Certainly this was the case in the decade of the Seventies as the excesses, fads and silliness of the Sixties were reexamined and put into a new and more pragmatic framework. The fun, excitement and spontaneity of the previous decade gave way to more thoughtful activities that tended to reflect more traditional approaches. But even the traditional approaches were never to be the same after the revolutions of the Sixties. There is no way "you can keep them down on the farm after they have seen Paris."

Let's look first at the excesses of the "me-now" decade and the failures of humanistic education and the human relations training movement. Then we can explore the awesome contributions and long-term legacies of the decade and see how these provided the springboard for the solid integrated advances that were forthcoming.

Etzioni (1983) in reviewing the 1960's argues that the individually oriented and self-fulfillment trends distanced people from one another and put heavy pressures on families, schools and other social systems that were based on interdependence and cooperation. He cites pollster Yankelovich's study showing eighty percent of the American population embracing in varying degrees a self-fulfillment orientation—ego needs, sensation and excitement take priority over work and needs of others including spouse and children.

The stress placed on independence and self-sufficiency not only broke down the structure of many human service group programs (school interest groups, YM-YWCA clubs, Scout troops, and social/recreational groups) but it put considerable pressure on young couples making them reluctant to seek help with problems of family relations and child rearing. As a result, human service programs had to shift their focus from strong, cohesive groups fulfilling members' needs through the give and take of interdependent relations to an individual development focus where the needs of others was a secondary consideration. And social workers and psychologists working with family problems had to develop integrated techniques for countering these attitudes.

During the Sixties, the independent style of relating (as contrasted with the interdependent style of the Fifties) and the disenchantment with the way things were, led to an increase of people who did not hold regular jobs. This trendy, anti-Establishment life style was very popular during the economic bonanza of the 1960's when people could regularly quit jobs knowing there were several more readily available. But as jobs became scarce in the next decade and the temporary workers could not find jobs, the whole ego satisfaction from quitting jobs and turning down new jobs, which was the fun of the anti-Establishment life style, came to an abrupt end. Young people once again wanted education and training that would give them job security.

This trend would ordinarily have been expected to reduce the number of students seeking human service professional training, yet the number stayed the same, or increased. Part of this was due to the rapid expansion of human service jobs in the early 1970's and part was due to some human service professional groups tightening certification requirements backed by provincial legislation to practice in their field. Education, social work, psychology and nursing all strengthened their control of their field with increased certification requirements backed by "laws." Probably much of this was a direct reaction to the looseness of the lay helper thrust of the 1960's.

The Failure of Humanistic Education

Humanistic education as a dominant movement failed. Free schools, open classrooms, confluent education and self-directed learning are hard to find these days. Part of the failure was related to the problem of changing an entrenched, bureaucratic system where seniority determines salary and performance or merit pay proposals are routinely rejected by teachers' unions. A review of thirty years of research on leadership training (Stogdill, 1974) indicates that attempts to change the way workers deal with other people have not been successful. Other research (APA Monitor, April, 1983) has shown that teacher training in new behaviors does not persist once the teacher gets back to the classroom.

In brief, humanistic educators operated on the mistaken assumption that their success in increasing the learning of their students and their satisfaction with the learning process, would ensure their acceptance and future role in education. But their inability to consider others in the educational system (teachers, administrators, school board, and parents), typical of the "me-now" independent oriented 1960's, contributed to their failure. In the process, however, they made a lasting contribution to the education and training of human service professionals. Self-directed learning, though under fire, is still alive and well today (Tough, 1982) and there is an increased readiness to consider a variety of ways in which individuals typically learn (Kolb, 1975) which is one of the true fulfillments of the humanistic education movement. And the acceptance of experiential learning paved the way for the almost immediate utilization of micro-computers in educational programs at all levels.

While most of the insights and methods of humanistic education were not integrated into on-going educational programs the learnings from these failures were recognized by the new field of organization development and became one of the underpinnings of their new theory and technology.

New Developments During the 1970's

After the unstructured, participant-directed training focus popular in the Sixties, the next decade saw a sharp move in the opposite direction as structured activities, simulations, and packaged programs increased in popularity. Structured activities were extensions of the skill training exercises used by the National Training Laboratory at Bethel, Maine and updated by Pfeiffer and Jones (1969 to-date) who built the University Associates training and consulting organization around them. For many people these leader-led, highly focused experiences were a welcome relief from the unstructured introspection and high emotional confrontations of T-groups and encounter groups. And they were particularly suited to short-term training timetables. The availability of handbooks and "hip pocket guides" made it possible for a new wave of trainers to get into the training business.

The popularity of packaged programs was also partially due to the ease with which they could be administered. The Blake Grid Program (Blake & Mouton, 1964) was one of the early prototypes that packaged a series of activities that were almost self-operating and that relatively inexperienced trainers (usually on the staff of the organization using the program) could handle. The Grid program became widely used world-wide and is still in use. Sensitivity training and encounter groups contained an element of risk and were usually led by highly trained professionals (whose presence also escalated training costs). Betty Berzon (Soloman & Berzon, 1972) put together a series of audio tape recordings which therapy and encounter groups used as a self-directed program. These were developed in such a way that a group could use the first session as a program by itself or add on the following sessions, in sequence, for up to eighteen sessions on some of her tapes. Information booklets for participants could accompany the program. This format became very popular for a variety of programs during the Seventies when audio cassettes became commonplace and videotape equipment was practical to use and affordable.

A large variety of preplanned, structured activities and programs emerged that could be led without a great deal of technical training. As these programs became big business they were taken over by major training organizations and book publishers and merchandised as any other product. High quality films, video recordings, cassette tapes, participants' workbooks, and trainers' kits for the leaders emerged. By the mid-Seventies many of these programs included a computer use component—an extension of the teaching machine approach of the previous decade.

The improved technology available for training at this time played a significant role in shifting training in the human services to a cafeteria assortment of training events lasting from a day to three days, each with a specific focus. These programs ranged from all day simulations such as Starpower, to Situational Leadership in a three-day format, to stress training by the hour or day. Even the in-house training programs put together by organizations tended to be composed of a series of these modules. While these programs appeared to be job related they were often described by participants as more entertainment than education. In any case, the era of the flexible, open-ended, participant focused workshop was over.

This decade was also characterized by the general acceptance of the organization development (OD) movement that started in the early Sixties. This field was pioneered by many of the same social scientists who had been heavily involved in the action research and T-group side (as contrasted with the personal growth and encounter group side) of human relations training. It is likely that the OD movement evolved out of the natural extension of the T-group approach to include more organizational aspects and concerns—especially when research (Dimock, 1971) suggested that this training method had little impact on organizational effectiveness. And, it is likely, that as the popularity of T-groups waned in the Seventies, more of the former trainers moved into OD as the place where the action was.

Organization development popularized survey feedback, team building, intergroup collaboration, conflict management, organizational goal setting, and role clarification/negotiating. In the mid-seventies it blended into the more social-technical approach of Quality of Work Life proponents. And as the interest in Japanese management increased, training for quality circles became the fad. While the Japanese version had a statistical quality control function, the North American model was more a worker participation group and this made a complete circle back to the action research activities (Coch & French, 1948) that led to the start of the human relations training movement.

While quality circles have not been picked up by human service organizations, the whole OD movement has been well accepted and in some cases led by the human services. The national councils of YMCA's in Canada and the U.S. started their first organization development program in 1961, and school systems saw OD and Quality of Work Life as useful to their interests (Schmuck et al., 1972, 1977).

A LOOK AT THE 1980's AND THE FUTURE

A major influence on the education and training of human service workers at this time is thought to be the economic recession in which we have been involved. The recession is described as instigating a "back to basics" approach based on a return to traditional methods of teaching/training and reality based feedback for learners. The above description of the 1970's however suggests that most of the present trends were well established by the middle of that decade. It is also likely that they became more relevant and acceptable as the recession deepened. A more important aspect of the recession is the large pool of well trained people looking for jobs. The availability of people practically begging for jobs has meant that human service organizations can deal with their staff in rather impersonal ways as a technique to handle the emotional stress of separation (firing) and reorganization as funding decreases and downsizing becomes necessary.

My prediction of trends for the future includes second generation type human relations training for human service workers who have been in the field for less than fifteen years. The focus of this human relations training will, I believe, be both interpersonal awareness and group leadership skills.

My second prediction for the future is a reflection of the present enthusiasm for hi-tech packaged programs and their development with a few wrinkles in the future. A case in point is the newest and probably most important program to surface called "Towards Excellence." It is based on the all time non-fiction best seller, *In Search of Excellence* (Peters & Waterman, 1982). The program includes a series of structured experiences for participants (about 20-25 hours) backed up by video recordings of the senior author, and individual cassettes and workbooks for each program participant.

The third major trend I see for this decade is not an easy one to document or substantiate. It suggests that more education and training will take place on-the-job with intact work groups. While this has some commonality with the apprenticeship system, it also includes the learnings from the Quality Circle approach of the past few years.

The historical perspective of this article suggests that education and training in the human services have gone through cycles in which old philosophies and methods are rediscovered and given new names, and that educational advances or fads tend to fade out in a few years following a regression toward the mean pattern. While these themes are present, the "state-of-the-art" has been clearly influenced by advances and developments during these years. New understandings about the needs of learners, how youth and adults learn, factors affecting the climate for learning, and methods to facilitate learner involvement and self-direction in the learning process have forged a new era in education. The information explosion coupled with the obliquitous micro computer will bring additional changes which will alter our educational programs to an extent comparable to the printing press and the availability of inexpensive, mass produced reading materials.

B.F. Skinner, the father of behavior modification and the teaching machine, recently went on record (Skinner, 1983) saying that the use of computers could cut in half the time and effort needed to teach what is now being taught in American schools. There will be humanistic counterforces to the universal use of computers as a major educational method and this tension sets the stage for a good deal of excitement and creativity in education for the second half of this decade.

REFERENCES[1]

Andrews, K.R. (Ed.) (1951). *Human relations and administration.* Cambridge, MA: Harvard University Press.

Andrews, K.R. (Ed.) (1953). *The case method of teaching human relations and administration.* Cambridge, MA: Harvard University Press.

Argyris, C. (1951). *Role-playing in action.* Bulletin No. 16. Ithaca, NY: New York School of Industrial and Labor Relations Cornell University.

Bavelas, A. (1947). Role-playing and management training. *Sociatry, 1,* 183-192.

Benne, K. & Sheats, P. (1948). Functional roles of group members. *Journal of Social Issues, 4,* 41-49.

Benne, K.D. & Muntyan, B. (1951). *Human relations in curriculum change.* New York: Dryden.

Benne, K. (1976). The process of re-education: An assessment of Kurt Lewin's views. In W.G. Bennis, K.D. Benne & R. Chin (Eds.), *The planning of change.* New York: Holt, Rinehart & Winston.

Bion, W.R. (1951). *Experience in groups.* New York: Basic Books.

Blake, R.R. & Mouton, J. (1964). *The Blake grid.* Houston, TX: Gulf Publishing.

Blatz, W.E. & Bott, H.M. (1928). *Parents and the pre-school child.* Toronto: Morrow.

Bradford, L., Gibb, T. & Benne, K. (1964). *T-group theory and laboratory method.* New York: Wiley.

---

[1]The reference section has not been abridged, because it also serves as a bibliography.

Bradford, L.P. (1974). *National training laboratories its history: 1947-1970.* Bethel, ME: NTL Institute.

Cantor, N. (1946). *Dynamics of learning.* Buffalo: Foster and Stewart.

Cantor, N. (1953). *The teaching-learning process.* New York: Dryden.

Carmichael, L. (Ed.) (1954). *Manual of child psychology* (2nd Ed.). New York: Wiley.

Cartwright, D. & Zander, A. (Eds.) (1983). *Group dynamics.* Evanston, IL: Row Peterson.

Carkhuff, R.R. (1969). *Helping and human relations.* New York: Holt, Rinehart & Winston.

Carkhuff, R. & Bierman, R. (1969). Filial therapy: the effects of training parents to help their children. *Journal of Counseling Psychology.*

Corey, S.M. (1953). *Action research to improve school practices.* New York: Teachers College, Columbia University.

Dewey, J. (1915). *Schools of tomorrow.* New York: E.P. Dutton & Co.

Dewey, J. (1930). *Democracy and education.* New York: Macmillan.

Dewey, J. (1939). *Experience and education.* New York: Macmillan.

Dewey, J. (1939). *Intelligence in the modern world (John Dewey's philosophy).* New York: Modern Library.

Dewey, J. (1940). *Education today.* New York: G.P. Putnam's Sons.

Dimock, H.G. (1956). Role-playing: An aid to learning and developing leadership skills. *Camping Magazine, 28* (7), 33-36.

Dimock, H.G. (1956). The group at work. *Adult Leadership, 5,* 80-82.

Dimock, H.G. (1956). Process notes on a pediatric work conference. *Canadian Nurse, 52,* 951-954.

Dimock, H.G. (1958). The case method in teaching and supervision. *Nursing Outlook, 6,* 46-47.

Dimock, H.G. (1958). Improving patient care through group procedures. *Hospital Topics, 36,* 33-35.

Dimock, H.G. (1959). How to design, conduct and evaluate a training program. Montreal: Montreal YMCA.

Dimock, H.G. (1960). Increasing our effectiveness in designing training activities. *Forum Magazine, 41,* 4-6.

Dimock, H.G. (1961). Improving communication skills through training. *Journal of Communication, 11,* 149-156.

Dimock, H.G. (1961). Staff care and the needs of the hospitalized child. *The Osteopathic Profession, 28,* 66-71.

Dimock, H.G. (1962). *A measurement project on Hi-Y clubs and advisors.* Montreal: Metropolitan YMCA.

Dimock, H.G. (1963). *A human relation training program for teen-age youth.* Montreal: Metropolitan YMCA.

Dimock, H.G. (1964). *Intergroup relations training: An experiment in citizenship education.* Montreal: Sir George Williams University.

Dimock, H.G. (1966). *Training for work with volunteers in community serving organizations.* Vancouver: Canadian Association of Adult Education National Conference.

Dimock, H.G. (1965). *Group development.* Montreal: Sir George Williams University.

Dimock, H.G. (1967, November). Training people to work with volunteers in community serving organizations. *Forum, 48,* 9-10.

Dimock, H.G. (1970). Selecting and training group leaders (Revised Edition) Report No. 13. Montreal: Centre for Human Relations and Community Studies, Sir George Williams University.

Dimock, H.G. (1971). Sensitivity training as a method of increasing on-the-job effectiveness. *Sociological Inquiry, 41,* 227-231.

Dimock, H.G. (1971, Fall). Sensitivity training in Canada: Perspective and comment. *Canada's Mental Health* (Special Supplement).

Dimock, H.G. (1973). *How to plan staff training programs.* Montreal: Sir George Williams University.

Dimock, H.G. (1975). Organization development—an experience report in dealing with change. *Ontario Council for Leadership in Educational Administration Journal, 5,* 6-8.

Dimock, H.G. (1975). Canada's experience with human relations training. In *Annual Handbooks for Group Facilitators.* San Diego, CA: University Associates.

Dimock, H.G. (1975). How to train successful camp leaders—Part One. *Social Agency Management, 1,* 26-32.

Dimock, H.G. (1976). *A study of process oriented, qualitative research using community collaboration as a social action and assessment method of community development.* Montreal: Centre for Human Relations and Community Studies, Concordia University.

Dimock, H.G. (1976). *Social intervention in the helping professions.* Montreal: Concordia University.

Dimock, H.G. (1978). Scout leadership: A national perspective and some implications. Unpublished article.

Dimock, H.G. (1978). The use of systems improvement research in developing a change strategy for human service organizations. *Group and Organization Studies, 3,* 365-375.

Dimock, H.G. (1978). Principles for group organization: Aspects of leadership and participation. In Kidd, J.R. & Selman, G. (Eds.), *Coming of age: Canadian adult education in the 1960's.* Toronto: Canadian Association for Adult Education, 100-108.

Dimock, H.G. (1979). Systems improvement strategies for community development. In *Community development: Theory and method of planned change.* New Delhi, India: VIKAS, 121-136.

Dimock, H.G. (1980). *Designing and facilitating training programs.* Guelph: University of Guelph.

Dimock, H.S. (Ed.) (1930-1942). *Character education in the summer camp.* New York: Association Press.

Dimock, H.G., Abeles, J., Carleton, E. & Thetford, K. (1975). Report of the Halton Region Applied Leadership Project. Burlington, Ontario: Halton County Board of Education.

Dimock, H.G. & Caplan, H. (1956). The student nurse in a pediatric setting. *Canadian Nurse, 52,* 959-962.

Dimock, H.G. & Gray, G. (1965). *Measurement and evaluation of an executive training laboratory on participants' organizational and interpersonal effectiveness.* Montreal: Centre for Human Relations and Community Services, Sir George Williams University.

Dimock, H.S. & Hendry, C.E. (1929). *Camping and character.* New York: Association Press.

Durham, L. & Gibb, J. (1967). *A bibliography of research.* Washington: NTL Institute.

Fraser, C.E. (1931). *The case method of instruction.* New York: McGraw-Hill.

Hendry, C.E., Lippitt, R. & Zander, A. (1944). Reality practice as educational method. In *Psychodrama Monograph* (No. 9). New York: Beacon.

Kelley, E.C. (1947). *Education for what is real.* New York: Harper.

Kelley, E.C. (1951). *Workshop way of learning.* New York: Harper & Bros.

Kolb, D. & Fry, K.V. (1975). Toward an applied theory of experiential learning. In *Theories of Group Processes.* London: Wiley.

Lewin, K. & Grabbe, P. (Eds.) (1945). Problems of re-education. *Journal of Social Issues, 1,* 3.

Lippitt, R. (1943). Psychodrama in leadership training. *Sociometry, 6,* 5-14.

Lippitt, R. (1949). *Training in community relations.* New York: Harper.

Maier, N.R.F. (1952). *Principles of human relations.* New York: Wiley.

McGregor, D. (1960). *The human side of enterprise.* New York: McGraw-Hill.

Miles, M.B. (1959). *Learning to work in groups.* New York: Teachers College, Columbia University.

Moreno, J.L. (1946). *Psychodrama and sociodrama.* New York: Beacon.

Moreno, J.L. (1953). *Who shall survive* (2nd Ed.). New York: Beacon House.

Neill, A.S. (1960). *Summerhill: A radical approach to child rearing.* New York: Hart.

Peters, T.J. & Waterman, R.H. (1982). *In search of excellence: Lessons from America's best-run companies.* New York: Harper & Row.

Pfeiffer, J.W. & Jones, J. (1969 to date). *A handbook for structured experiences: Volumes I-X.* San Diego, CA: University Associates.

Pigors, P. & Pigors, F. (1954, December; 1955, January). The case method by the incident process. *Adult Leadership, 3* (6 & 7), 7.

Schein, E. & Bennis, W. (1965). *Personal and organizational change through group methods.* New York: Wiley.

Skinner, B.F. (1983, October). Skinner: Use computer as teacher. Washington: *APA Monitor,* 5.

Soloman, L. & Berzon, B.B. (Eds.) (1972). *New perspectives on encounter groups.* San Francisco: Jossey-Bass.

Stogdill, R.M. (1974). *Handbook of leadership.* Glencoe: The Free Press.

Swanson, G., Newcomb, T. & Hartley, E. (Eds.) (1952). *Readings in social psychology* (2nd Ed.). New York: Holt.

Tannenbaum, R., Weschler, I. & Massarik, F. (1961). *Leadership and organization.* New York: McGraw-Hill.

Thelen, H.A. (1954). *Dynamics of groups at work.* Chicago: University of Chicago Press.

Tough, A. (1982). *Intentional changes.* Chicago: Follett.

Ure, R.W. (1935). *Fifty cases for camp counselors.* New York: Association Press.

Weschler, I. & Reisel, J. (1959). *Inside a sensitivity training group.* Los Angeles: Institute of Industrial Relations, University of California.

White, R.K. & Lippitt, R.O. (1960). *Autocracy and democracy.* New York: Harper.

Hedley G. Dimock, Ed.D., *is the director of the Centre for Human Resource Development, publishers and consultants, in Puslinch, Ontario, Canada. He is an adjunct professor at the University of Guelph and has served on the staffs at McGill, Columbia, Toronto, and Concordia universities. His writings appear in over one hundred books, magazines, journals, and reports. Five of his books on groups have been published in Japanese.*

GUIDELINES FOR CONTRIBUTORS TO UNIVERSITY ASSOCIATES PUBLICATIONS

In 1986 our guidelines for contributors were revised and expanded to include more helpful information to authors who are interested in submitting manuscripts to University Associates. Although these guidelines are available upon request from our Editorial Department, we wanted to disseminate this information as soon as possible. Therefore we are reprinting the guidelines here for our readers.

GENERAL STATEMENT OF PUBLISHING POLICIES AND INTERESTS OF UNIVERSITY ASSOCIATES

Copyright Policy

Authors submitting material to University Associates should be aware of our copyright policy for the *Annuals* and certain other books. These publications are copyrighted, but any materials published in them that is not copyrighted by others may be freely reproduced for *educational or training activities* (up to a maximum of one hundred copies per year) with no special written permission. University Associates does, however, require that appropriate credit appear on all reproductions (i.e., title of piece, author, name of source publication, editor/author of source, publisher, and date of publication).

This permission is limited to the reproduction of materials for educational or training events. Systematic or large-scale reproduction or distribution (more than one hundred copies)—or inclusion of items in publications for sale—may be done only with *prior written permission*.

The *Annual* Series

We are interested in receiving structured experiences; instruments (paper-and-pencil inventories, rating scales, and other feedback tools); professional development papers (theory along with practical application); lecturettes; and resource papers (bibliographies, lists of sources, etc.) for possible publication in the *Annual* series. These materials should be immediately useful to practicing professionals in the field of human resource development (HRD). (The *Annual* is not designed to accommodate statistical research; we recommend that such papers be sent to the many excellent journals in the field.)

Before undertaking a writing project intended for this publication, authors are advised to study recent *Annuals* and to inquire about the current need for materials on a particular topic. Materials intended for the *Annuals* should be sent to the Managing Editor, University Associates.

Book Manuscripts

We are interested in reviewing book-length manuscripts, complete training or instrumentation packages, and other publications that are practical, useful, and appropriate to University Associates' broadly based, HRD market. Authors of such manuscripts should enclose a specific proposal that includes a table of contents, two sample chapters, and a statement of the intended use, intended audience and market, and unique strengths or aspects of the proposed publication. Manuscripts for book-length publications should be sent to Acquisitions, University Associates.

SPECIFICATIONS FOR SUBMITTING BOOK PROPOSALS

Book proposals, in general, should include the following items, in the order shown.

- A letter or statement that includes the following:
  1. A description of the book (topics covered, length, etc.)
  2. The intended audience
     a. Specific characteristics
     b. Level of expertise
     c. Focus (training, organization development, management development, etc.)
  3. Special features or aspects of the manuscript
  4. Similar or competing publications
  5. The author's background in the subject
  6. The completion date for the manuscript

- Plus the following:
  1. A table of contents
  2. The introduction to the book
  3. A minimum of two sample chapters

For style considerations, consult the *Publications Manual of the American Psychological Association,* third edition, 1983, which may be purchased from the Order Department, American Psychological Association, 1200 Seventeenth Street, N.W., Washington, DC 20036.

SPECIFICATIONS FOR THE *ANNUAL* SERIES

Structured Experiences

Structured experiences are intended to be specific, practical tools for the HRD practitioner, describing complete experiential learning experiences. The following major divisions should be included, in order:

Goals (one or several—the objectives of the activity, which will be met by means of the process and discussions).

Group Size (total group or number of subgroups, if any, and minimum and maximum size of subgroups).

Time Required (actual time needed for the entire experience, including introduction, activity, and processing discussions).

Materials (a listing of any forms or work sheets needed— with exact titles indicated—and any special equipment or materials such as blank paper and pencils, scissors, lap boards, newsprint flip charts, etc.).

Physical Setting (size and number of rooms, arrangement of chairs and tables, if any, seating requirements, etc.).

Process (the step-by-step sequence that is necessary to complete the experience successfully, indicating what the facilitator *does* and what the participants *do* and ending with a discussion to help the participants to process and integrate their learnings. See "The Experiential Learning Cycle" in the *Reference Guide to Handbooks and Annuals* (pages 4-8 in the 1985 edition) or the "Introduction to the Structured Experiences Section" in *The 1983 Annual for Facilitators, Trainers, and Consultants*.

Variations (possible alterations or adaptations of the process).

All work sheets, role-play instructions, and other materials to be handed out to participants *must* be included with the structured experience. Work sheets and other handouts should be typed on separate sheets of paper following the description of the activity (as listed above).

If a structured experience calls for the use of a lecturette, the content of that lecturette must be provided in the form of a handout.

A detailed discussion of developing and preparing a structured experience can be found in the "Introduction to the Structured Experiences Section" of the 1974 *Annual* and in the "Introduction to Structured Experiences" of the *Reference Guide to Handbooks and Annuals* (1985 edition).

Contributors to structured experiences in the *Annuals* should bear in mind that these materials may be reproduced for training purposes by users of the *Annual*.

Instruments

The Instrumentation section of the *Annuals* contains paper-and-pencil survey-feedback devices—such as inventories, rating scales, and questionnaires—that are designed to be used for training purposes by group facilitators and may be reproduced for such uses. Thus, University Associates is looking for instruments that provide immediate, practical feedback to participants to help further their learning in a particular area. We do not publish instruments for research, psychodiagnostic, or therapeutic purposes, although many of those we do publish have been used for research in previous versions and have solid reliability and validity statistics to back up their usefulness.

Instruments submitted for the *Annuals* should not be overly complex and should be easy to score (preferably by the respondents themselves).

All instruments should contain the following elements:

1. An *introduction* containing the theoretical and technical rationale for the instrument and the background necessary to use it effectively.

2. A *description* of the instrument form, scoring sheet, and interpretation sheet, if any.

3. Discussion of how to *administer* the instrument, including general introduction, instructions, and time expectations.

4. Brief discussion of how best to *present* to the participants the theory behind the instrument. (Note that the theory is not presented until *after* the respondents have completed the instrument form.)

5. The best way to have the participants *predict* their scores in terms of the instrument's dimensions.

6. A description of the *scoring process* (i.e., how to fill out the scoring sheet).

7. Ways to help the participants *interpret* their scores, including an explanation of how to fill out the interpretation or profile sheet, if one exists.

8. Which data generated by the instrument is likely to be appropriate for *posting* (if posting individual scores is not appropriate, group or subgroup data frequently can be posted) and how best to facilitate a *discussion* to process and integrate the participants' learnings. This may include forming subgroups to compare scores, legitimizing differences, and integrating the feedback derived from the instrument with the participants' self-images, jobs, etc.

9. Other *suggested uses* for the instrument.

10. Data about *reliability, validity, etc.,* of the instrument.

11. Starting on a separate page, the *instrument form,* beginning with instructions to the respondent.

12. On a separate page, the *scoring sheet,* including instructions for completing it.

13. On a separate page, the *interpretation or profile sheet,* including instructions for completing it and interpreting the data.

For further information about devising and presenting instruments, see the "Introduction to the Instrumentation Section" of each of the *Annuals,* particularly the 1980, 1981, and 1983 volumes, and the "Introduction to Instruments" in the *Reference Guide to Handbooks and Annuals,* 1985 edition.

Professional Development Section

Professional Development Papers

Professional development papers (called "theory and practice papers" in the older *Annuals*) are intended to provide theoretical background as well as information about new techniques, models, and research applications for HRD professionals. They should be directed toward the further professional development of the trainer or consultant and should have a *practical, applicable* focus.

The length of a professional development paper generally is from fifteen to forty-five typed pages (double-spaced), which will appear as five to fifteen printed pages. Frequent headings and subheadings are recommended to indicate the paper's divisions and content.

As for all submissions, the best guide to subjects appropriate for this section is a survey of the current HRD literature and the contents of recent *Annuals.*

Specifications for typing manuscripts for the *Annual* are the same as those for all University Associates publications and can be found under the "General Specifications for Typing Manuscripts" section at the end of these guidelines. Special attention should be given to the specifications for quotations, reference citations in the text, and reference lists or bibliographies. Papers not adhering to these specifications will not be considered for publication.

Lecturettes

Lecturettes are brief, simply worded statements of theoretical positions. They are intended for the use of the facilitator who wishes to introduce theory or background information to a group. Because these papers specifically are intended to be delivered orally as well as to be used as handouts, the topic of a lecturette should be presented clearly, simply, and directly, with emphasis on ease of presentation. They should be written from an objective point of view.

The length of a lecturette generally is from four to twenty typed pages (double-spaced), which will appear as one to seven printed pages.

The use of frequent headings and subheadings in the text is helpful to indicate organization, divisions, and emphasis of the content. The author also is encouraged to supplement the lecturette by suggesting activities that would extend the usefulness of the lecture material. Specifications for quotations, reference citations in the text, and reference listings or bibliographies are the same as those delineated in the "General Specifications for Typing Manuscripts" section at the end of these guidelines.

GENERAL SPECIFICATIONS FOR TYPING MANUSCRIPTS

All copy must be *typed or printed double-spaced on white 8 1/2" x 11" paper.* Computer-printed manuscripts are acceptable if printed double-spaced with a fresh, *black* ribbon (not gray) and with fully formed, *letter-quality* characters. Manuscripts that are not double-spaced or legible will not be considered for publication. No draft quality or low-resolution dot-matrix printouts will be accepted. Nonjustified text is preferred. Two copies of the manuscript should be submitted.

IBM PC-compatible disks will be accepted if accompanied by two printed copies of the entire text (see guidelines above for computer-printed copy).

The title and the author's name should be typed alone on the first page. (If there is more than one author, the names should appear in the order of the significance of their contributions, with the senior author or contributor listed first.)

The author's last name should be typed in the upper-right corner of each page.

Pages should be numbered consecutively in the upper-right corner of each page.

Ideal margins are (approximately) as follows: left margin, 2 inches; right margin, 2 inches; top margin, 1.5 inches; bottom margin, 1 inch.

All heads and subheads should be typed flush with the left margin. Major heads dividing sections of the manuscript should be typed in all caps. Secondary or subheads should be typed in caps and lower case. Heads should *not* be underlined. Each heading should be preceded and followed by an extra double-space.

The *first* paragraph following a heading should not be indented (i.e., the first word of a lead paragraph should be typed flush left). All other paragraphs should be indented five spaces.

Where possible, words should not be broken (hyphenated) at the end of a line.

Each figure, chart, table, graph, or other illustration should be typed or drawn on a separate page, double-spaced, and should be inserted at the appropriate point in the text (on the page following the first mention of the figure, chart, table, etc.). If possible, any graphic work other than type (such as grids, maps, and drawings) should be done in India ink on heavy white paper, suitable for reproduction. Tables (numerical grids, columns and rows, etc.) should be numbered consecutively and distinguished from figures. Figures (illustrations, depictions of processes, etc.) also should be numbered consecutively.

Footnotes should be either typed at the bottom of the page on which the footnote number appears or listed consecutively on a subsequent page.

Please note that a reference citation should be included *in the text* for every quotation and to indicate any work on which the current text is based or any work that is referred to in the text.

Reference citations in the text must include the names of all authors and the date of publication, following the APA format (as given in the *Publication Manual of the American Psychological Association,* third edition, 1983). This may be purchased from the Order Department, American Psychological Association, Inc., 1200 Seventeenth Street, N.W., Washington, DC 20036.

A complete reference listing must be supplied for each reference noted in the text. The reference list or bibliography must be in alphabetical order and typed on a separate sheet or sheets at the end of the manuscript. Each reference or bibliographical listing must be *accurate and complete* and should follow the format prescribed by the APA *Publication Manual.*

CONTRIBUTORS

Mark Alexander
Vice President, Human Resources
Shirmax Fashions, Ltd.
472 Montpellier
St. Laurent, Quebec
Canada H4N 2G7
(514) 748-7831

Will Anderson
Anderson & Associates
P.O. Box 126
St. David's Church, Virginia 22652
(703) 984-4947

W. Warner Burke, Ph.D.
President
W. Warner Burke Associates, Inc.
87 Wolf's Lane
Pelham, New York 10803
(914) 738-0080

Michael W. Cooney
Assistant Superintendent
of Manufacturing
Delco Remy Division G.M.C.
(Department 8560)
2401 Columbus Avenue
Anderson, Indiana 46011
(317) 646-7882

Celeste A. Coruzzi, Ph.D.
Organization Development Consultant
W. Warner Burke Associates, Inc.
87 Wolf's Lane
Pelham, New York 10803
(914) 738-0080

Charles A. Cotton, Ph.D.
Chairman, Queen's Programs
for Management
School of Business
Queen's University
Kingston, Ontario
Canada K7M 4P8
(613) 545-2370

Mary Kirkpatrick Craig
Training Manager
Foodmaker, Inc.
9330 Balboa Avenue
San Diego, California 92123
(619) 571-2564

Bob Crosby
Consultant
Management Analysis Company (MAC)
P.O. Box 85404
San Diego, California 92138
(619) 481-3100

Russell J. Denz
Director of Human Resources
Compton Forge, Inc.
1721 N. Alameda
P.O. Box 4819
Compton, California 90224
(213) 774-9700

Hedley G. Dimock, Ed.D.
Director, Centre for Human
Resource Development
Puslinch, Ontario
Canada N0B 2J0
(519) 822-2749

Patrick Doyle
Principal
High Impact Training Services
RR2 Perth Road Village
Ontario, Canada K0H 2L0
(613) 353-6517

Daniel C. Feldman, Ph.D.
Professor of Management
Graduate School of Business
University of Florida
219 Business Building
Gainesville, Florida 32611
(904) 392-5835/0163

Gary D. Geroy, Ed.D.
Training & Development
Program Coordinator
Department of Education
113 Rackley Building
The Pennsylvania State University
University Park, Pennsylvania 16802
(814) 863-0275

Leonard D. Goodstein, Ph.D.
Executive Officer
American Psychological Association
1200 Seventeenth St., N.W.
Washington, D.C. 20036
(202) 955-7660

John E. Hebden, Ph.D.
Senior Lecturer, Business
  and Management Studies
University of Salford
The Crescent
Salford M5 4Wt
England
(061) 736-5843

Leland W. Howe, Ph.D.
Consultant and Psychotherapist
Howe Associates
10779 Bismark Highway
Vermontville, Michigan 49096
(517) 566-8255

Hank Karp, Ph.D.
Personal Growth Systems
1441 Magnolia Avenue
Norfolk, Virginia 23508
(804) 489-2586

Roger Kaufman, Ph.D.
Director, Center for Needs
  Assessment and Planning
Learning Systems Institute
The Florida State University
Tallahassee, Florida 32306
(904) 644-6435

Carol Rocklin Kay, Ed.D.
Assistant to the Vice President
  for Student Affairs and
Assistant Professor,
  Adult Education
Iowa State University
311 Beardshear Hall
Ames, Iowa 50011
(515) 294-8914

Diane McKinney Kellogg, Ed.D.
Associate Professor of Management
Bentley College
Waltham, Massachusetts 02254
(617) 891-2000

Chuck Kormanski, Ed.D.
Career Development and
  Placement Center
The Pennsylvania State University
Altoona Campus
Altoona, Pennsylvania 16603
(814) 946-4321, ext. 38

Charles A. LaJeunesse, Ph.D.
Assistant Professor of Psychology
Division of Professional Studies
College Misericordia
Dallas, Pennsylvania 18612
(717) 675-2181, ext. 364

Charles E. List, Ph.D.
Consultant and Educator
Management & Organization
  Development
4940 Winterset Drive
Minnetonka, Minnesota 55343
(612) 935-3923

Andrew Mozenter
Acting Director
Office of Student Organizations
  and Program Development
The Pennsylvania State University
218 Hetzel Union Building
University Park, Pennsylvania 16802
(814) 238-3726

Kenneth L. Murrell, D.B.A.
Associate Professor
Management Department
University of West Florida
Pensacola, Florida 32514
(904) 474-2308

John E. Oliver, Ph.D.
Associate Professor
Department of Management
Valdosta State College
Valdosta, Georgia 31698
(912) 333-5963

Udai Pareek, Ph.D.
President
Indian Society for
  Applied Behavioural Science
S7 Vivekanand Marg
Jaipur 302001
India
(0141) 76870

Sue Kruse Peyton, Ph.D.
Leader, Staff Development
  and Training
Iowa State University Extension
108 Curtiss Hall
Ames, Iowa 50011
(515) 294-4512

Robert W. Pike
President
Resources for Organizations, Inc.
6440 Flying Cloud Drive, Suite 130
Eden Prairie, Minnesota 55344
(612) 829-1954

Marshall Sashkin
Senior Associate
Office of Educational
  Research and Improvement
U.S. Dept. of Education
Washington, D.C. 20208
(202) 357-6116

Eva Schindler-Rainman, Ph.D.
Adjunct Professor
School of Public Administration
University of Southern California
4267 San Rafael Avenue
Los Angeles, California 90042
(213) 257-8962

Allen J. Schuh, Ph.D.
Professor, Management Sciences
School of Business and Economics
California State University
Hayward, California 94542
(415) 881-3322/3329

Joseph Seltzer, Ph.D.
Associate Professor and Chair
Management Department
LaSalle University
Philadelphia, Pennsylvania 19141
(215) 951-1037

Richard A. Swanson, Ed.D.
Professor and Director
Training and Development
  Research Center
Department of Vocational
  and Technical Education
University of Minnesota
1954 Buford Avenue
St. Paul, Minnesota 55108
(612)624-9727

Susan Hoefflinger Taft
Consultant
2989 Washington Boulevard
Cleveland Heights, Ohio 44118
(216) 321-0083

Gilles L. Talbot
Professor of Psychology
Champlain Regional College
St. Lawrence Campus
790 Neree Tremblay Street
Ste-Foy, Quebec
Canada G1V 4K2
(418) 656-6921

C.R. Tindal, Ph.D.
President
Tindal Consulting Limited
RR 1
Inverary, Ontario
Canada K0H 1X0
(613) 353-6083